Empty Cradle,
Broken Heart

Empty Cradle, Broken Heart

Surviving the Death of Your Baby

REVISED AND EXPANDED EDITION

Deborah L. Davis, Ph.D.

FULCRUM
GOLDEN, COLORADO

Cover and Book Design by Bill Spahr
Cover Photograph: Copyright ©judywhite/GardenPhotos.com

Parts of chapter 8 were adapted from the author's book *Loving and Letting Go: For Parents Who Decided to Turn Away from Aggressive Medical Intervention for Their Critically Ill Newborns.* Omaha, Neb.: Centering Corporation, 1993.

The information contained in this book, although based on sound medical judgment, is not intended as a substitute for medical advice or attention. Please consult your doctor or health care provider for individual professional care.

Library of Congress Cataloging-in-Publication Data

Davis, Deborah L.
    Empty cradle, broken heart: surviving the death of your baby/ Deborah L. Davis. — rev. and expanded ed.
        p. cm.
    Includes bibliographical references and index.
    ISBN 1-55591-302-4 (pbk.)
    1. Perinated death—Psychological aspects. 2. Bereavement—Psychological aspects. 3. Adjustment (Psychology). 4. Parent and child. I. Title.
    RG631.D38   1996
    155.9'37—dc20   95-53333
                                                                          CIP

Printed in the United States of America

20 19

Fulcrum Publishing
4690 Table Mountain Drive, Suite 100
Golden, CO 80403
(800) 992-2908 • (303) 277-1623
www.fulcrumbooks.com

To all of your babies, loved and remembered still

A Mother's Love Song

Last night, I awakened to sounds of laughter outside my window
But the nearer noise of my fast-beating heart enveloped me
With memories of soft, sweet baby cries when you were born
Before the ones in white tore you from my arms
And bore you to your first and last crib, a small white casket.

An old, old wound, a long time closed, the pain now dull,
Unhealed and bled afresh and red from my mourning heart
Absorbed by earth, your eternal bed, my second born
In unfair death, in wretched, selfish death
That cheated me of a lifetime of loving you.

Part of me, deep and secret, lies with you in a maternal embrace
Wrapped in infant arms I never touched or kissed
Near a tiny face I saw but one too brief moment
Just long enough to engrave forever in my heart a question—
What would you have given this world if not your life?

—Carol J. Curtis
For Tom Eric Wilcox
Born 12/7/68, Died 12/7/68

Contents

Contents

Preface

One purpose of this book is to let bereaved parents know that they are not alone in their grief. Many mothers and fathers are quoted in this book, and although everyone's grief is unique, the sentiments expressed are common among bereaved parents.

Many parents have experienced the death of a baby—at any time during pregnancy, during delivery, shortly after birth or during infancy. In spite of medical advances, more than one-fourth of all women will at some time experience miscarriage, stillbirth or infant death. Each year in the United States, out of an estimated 4.4 million *confirmed* pregnancies, there are more than half a million miscarriages, twenty-nine thousand stillbirths and thirty-nine thousand infant deaths under 1 year of age. (Some fertility specialists estimate that another one million unconfirmed pregnancies end in miscarriage shortly after embryo implantation, but before the pregnancy is acknowledged.) Thousands more *wanted* pregnancies are interrupted after problems are detected. However, many parents keep their losses and feelings about them a secret, partly because of society's hushed attitudes toward death and partly because many people do not recognize the depth of such losses.

This book strives to cover many different kinds of loss. In ectopic pregnancy, the fertilized ovum becomes lodged outside the uterus, most commonly in the fallopian tube. Surgery is necessary to remove the embryo to save the mother's life. Moreover, if scarring occurs or if a fallopian tube or ovary is removed, the woman's fertility can decrease.

First trimester miscarriages often occur for undetectable reasons. Even though this does not necessarily preclude later successful pregnancies, many mothers feel betrayed by their bodies. It is also common for mothers to feel solely responsible. Although she is not to blame, the woman's role—adverse conditions in her uterus, ova, hormones or immune system—has been considered paramount. Now fathers are coming under scrutiny, as new research shows sperm to be particularly (and often invisibly) susceptible to damage from chemicals, pollutants, smoking, alcohol and drugs, making a significant contribution to the genetic problems that account for many losses.

Early miscarriage is often discounted, "It wasn't even a baby yet," or treated as a blessing, " It's nature's way of weeding out the weak." However, with home or lab testing, parents can confirm pregnancy very early on, and this affords them more time to bond with the baby. The depth of the loss depends on what meaning the pregnancy held for the parents, but for many, miscarriage is a baby who died. Usually, when a baby is born too early for any chance of survival, the mother is not allowed to see the body, for fear that it will upset her. But for the mother to see her baby is to validate that the child existed and lived inside her.

Some mothers must consent to a therapeutic abortion due to illness, infection, toxemia or other conditions in which pregnancy endangers the mother's life. Other mothers consent because the baby has birth defects. In a pregnancy with multiple babies, selective reduction may be employed to give some of the babies a better chance of survival. For these mothers, the heartache of making such decisions often goes unrecognized.

During the last trimester, a baby's chances for survival increase with each additional week—up to full term—spent in the womb. However, many premature babies die during delivery or shortly after birth due to immaturity or illness. Sometimes labor is induced when ultrasound tests confirm there is no fetal heartbeat. The mother is then faced with enduring labor and delivery, knowing her baby is already dead. For many stillborn babies, death is caused by umbilical cord constriction, placental abruption, infection or birth defects, but for one-third of stillbirths, the cause of death remains a mystery.

By thirty-eight weeks a fetus is considered to be full term, yet these babies may still die before or during delivery. Even after a baby is born and seems fine, infection may set in, or birth defects incompatible with life outside the womb may be discovered. For some of these babies death comes quickly, while for others death may come only after months of struggle. Some parents face the agonizing decision of whether to attempt treatment or whether to stop it.

According to the SIDS Alliance, sudden infant death syndrome (the unexpected death of an otherwise healthy baby) is the leading cause of death of babies between 1 week and 1 year of age. The cause or prevention remains a mystery. Thousands more babies succumb to other diseases, infections and accidents every year. For SIDS babies and many babies who contract bacterial or viral infections, death is so swift that the joy of a healthy baby can turn to tragedy in a matter of hours. For babies with lingering illnesses, parents feel the additional devastation of watching their suffering or debilitation. For babies who die from accidents such as drowning or automobile collisions, parents may be especially wracked with "what if's" and "if only's."

As treatment for infertility is becoming more common and accessible, there are more families who face high-risk pregnancies with multiple babies. When parents face the death of some or all of the babies from a multiple gestation, their grief can have many facets. To grieve for more than one baby can compound their sorrow. It can be a challenge to simultaneously grieve and nurture surviving babies. Parents may also grieve for the lost chance to raise twins, triplets or more, a special event in itself.

Across the board, if conception occurred after infertility, parents may fear that this was their last chance to bear a child. For them, the future can seem especially bereft and uncertain.

Although the circumstances can vary widely, and babies die from many different causes, parents share in common a shattering grief. This book is for them.

About This Book

This book doesn't try to tell you how you should feel or what you must do. Rather, it strives to show you the wide range of experiences that can follow the death of a baby and to offer strategies for coping with this loss. With factual information and the words and insights of other bereaved parents, you can establish realistic expectations for your grief. You can also gain reassurance that you are not crazy, you are not the only one who has felt betrayed or angry, you are not the only one to cradle pillows in your empty arms. This book is meant to help you through your grief by giving you things to think about, providing suggestions for coping and encouraging you to do what *you* need to survive your baby's death. Whether your baby died recently or long ago, this information can be useful to you.

It is not necessary to read this book from start to finish. Some sections may feel more appropriate than others at different times, depending on your unique situation, your personality and where you are in your grief. Take in whatever seems helpful, and pass by whatever isn't. Come back to the passages that are particularly comforting, and try reading other parts later.

If reading this book moves you to cry, try to accept this reaction. These are healing tears—of grief and empathy, even joy. They are also tears of courage, health and strength that merge with those of other grieving parents. You are not alone.

Acknowledgments

This book is based on more than ten years of research and clinical work with bereaved parents. The original research for my Ph.D. dissertation was funded in part by the March of Dimes Greater Colorado Chapter and supervised by Robert J. Harmon, M.D., and Marguerite Stewart, R.N., Psy. D., at the University of Colorado Health Sciences Center in Denver. I am indebted to them for guiding me to this important issue: to Bob for taking me on as a graduate student researcher and widening my horizons, and to Margy for opening doors and teaching me so much. I am indebted to Marvin Daehler, Ph.D., and Edward Tronick, Ph.D., my advisers at the University of Massachusetts, for being flexible and having faith in my ability to pull off this daring idea of going to Colorado to finish my graduate work.

Special gratitude also goes to the following women for their support—my co-facilitators at the Boulder County Hospice Pregnancy/Infant Loss Support Group: Jane Karyl, Dee Paddock and Lynn Kimball, R.N., who also helped me compile medical information on physical recovery; my dear friend, Terri Macey, Ph.D., for introducing me to the Pregnancy/Infant Loss Support Group and mostly for all her encouragement and confidence that this book could happen; my editor, Karen Groves, who knew that this book was important and should be published. All five of these women also know firsthand what it is like to have a baby die, and their special sensitivity has influenced my writing.

I am indebted to the mothers who participated in my dissertation research study, for sharing a very personal and painful part of their lives with me. I also want to thank the many parents of the Boulder County Hospice Pregnancy/Infant Loss Support Group, for sharing their stories, struggles and acquired wisdom. Although many names have been changed to ensure anonymity, I hope these mothers and fathers will know how vitally their experiences and insights have contributed to this book.

Bereaved parents are special. They are survivors, and I am always inspired by the courage with which they face their pain, and the strength by which they cope with their devastating loss.

Finally, I am grateful to my husband Ken Kirkpatrick, who has supported and encouraged my desire to write.

For this revised edition, I'd like to thank the following people: Jean Kollantai of CLIMB for her comments and suggestions on including more about multiple birth and loss; Claudia Putnam for reviewing the chapter on agonizing decisions, plus Karen Hatch and Mark Yaw for their special contribution to that chapter; Angela Pfaffenberger, Dipl. Ac., for reviewing the section on alternative medicine; John Hicks, M.Div., for reviewing the chapter on fathers; Barbara Guyton, and in memory of Jaye Bronson Litchard, fellow members of the Grief Education Project, for their inspiration; Helen Harrison, Sherokee Ilse, Joy Johnson, Elizabeth Mehren and Judith Murray for their enthusiastic support of my work; and Maribeth Wilder Doerr of Pen-Parents for inviting me to be a columnist for the PAILS newsletter, a satisfying outlet and a place for me to hone some of my ideas for this edition. I am also grateful to the parents who contributed new quotes, poetry and ideas to this edition and to all the parents who have shared their stories with me.

A Parent's Lonely Grief

The "D" Word

In our society, unfortunately, death is not talked about freely. Rather than being seen as an inevitable and natural part of the cycle of life, death has become something we try to avoid. We want to prevent it from happening to us or loved ones. With the discovery of antibiotics and vaccines, we expect our children to survive into adulthood and to outlive us, and most of us expect to live until we are very, very old. With new advances in medical science and technology, many previously fatal conditions are now curable, and it is possible to prolong life almost indefinitely, sometimes without regard to quality of life.

We also avoid contact with the dying and the dead. Up until the middle part of this century, most people died at home. Family members bathed and dressed the body, and friends and relations gathered to view the body and grieve together. Now, most people die in hospitals or nursing homes, and the body is shipped off to be cremated or embalmed according to community health standards. Death has been taken away from the home and family and placed in modern, sterile institutions. Additionally, with increased mobility of families and friends, being present at the death of a loved one, or even attending the funeral, is less likely. These trends make death less familiar to us, and having little experience with dying or death we feel uncomfortable or afraid. Death has been separated from the continuity of life and the living.

We also avoid talking about death. We have all kinds of euphemisms in our language for referring to death, such as: the delicate "passed away," the vague "is no more" or "has been taken," the spiritual "met her maker" or "departed this life," the technical "expired" or "deceased," or the crude "croaked" or "kicked the bucket." Many parents have difficulty talking about death with their children, not wanting to scare them or tarnish their innocence. These attitudes toward death isolate the bereaved, as it is considered almost impolite to talk about the death of a loved one, except at a funeral.

The death of a baby is even more hidden because it violates our expectations. In addition, when we hear about the death of a baby, many of us do not recognize the depth of the loss to the parents. The fact that the baby was in the womb or in the parents' arms for such a brief time adds to their pain and isolation.

A Violation of Expectations

I was so excited. This was going to be the neatest thing in my whole life. I figured everything was going to go great because you always assume that with your first child. I had a beautiful pregnancy. You couldn't have asked for a nicer one. No morning sickness, I stayed active, it was great.

—Lena

Nowadays, with the development of modern medical procedures and technology, many infertile couples can conceive. Hormonal treatments enable some mothers to maintain a pregnancy through the first trimester. Progress in pregnancy management can increase the chances that a mother will carry a healthy baby to term. Babies born prematurely, who several decades ago would have perished at birth, can now survive infancy. Babies with life-threatening illnesses or birth defects can undergo treatments and surgery, allowing more of them to lead normal lives. Babies can be protected from disease with vaccines, and health can be restored with antibiotics and other medicines.

Expectant parents, having faith in modern medicine and little exposure to infant death, are not likely to seriously consider the possibility that their baby may die, particularly after the first trimester of pregnancy. They naturally assume that a healthy baby will be born, and if sick, that the baby will survive. This assumption accompanies the belief that by "doing all the right things" during pregnancy, even in preparation for pregnancy and certainly after delivery, a healthy baby will be guaranteed.

Medicine isn't what it's cracked up to be. It makes me realize that medicine and doctors don't hold special powers. They're as human as the rest of us, and they're only as good as the job they do. There's just no magic in medicine, and I think at one time I thought that.

—Kara

I went off the pill for a year and a half in anticipation because I knew that was something to think about. I did not drink any caffeine, I did not drink any alcohol, I did not smoke, I did not do anything. I led my life so perfectly as far as going by the rules. ... I really wasn't aware that babies could die. I remember feeling so serene the week before the baby's birth. I didn't have any worries. I thought when you made it past a certain point ... .

—Bryn

Everybody thinks of pregnancy as a positive outcome ... and then to have two miscarriages on top of a stillbirth. After the second miscarriage, it was, like, this is just ridiculous, and what am I doing to deserve this? ... I remember meeting the mother of a test-tube baby and thinking, "They can do this but they can't take my seven-and-a-half-pound healthy girl and get her out safely"—now come on! There's something not right here!

—Holly

Now, when I hear people talk about statistics with different situations I get a little upset because, you know, statistics are fine until you become one of them, and then they take on a different meaning!

—Sarah

With the availability of effective methods of birth control and the movement of women beyond the realm of homemaking and child rearing, parents are increasingly likely to plan when and how many children to have. In addition to the assumption that they will have a healthy baby, they have an enormous emotional investment in conceiving within a few months, each pregnancy having a positive outcome and each child surviving infancy.

When a baby dies, the parents' expectations are cruelly violated, their emotional commitment dashed. Unfortunately, even when they "do all the right things," bad things can happen.

The Depth of Your Loss

Whenever and however it occurs, your baby's death is a profound loss because your attachment can begin even before conception. Even if the pregnancy is unplanned, a special bond materializes as you think about the reality of parenthood.

Throughout this bonding process, you fantasize about the future. You may wonder about your baby's familial characteristics and envision summertimes, wintertimes, holidays, birthdays, graduations, weddings, grandchildren. You look forward to the special "firsts" of childhood, such as baby's first smile, first wobbly steps, first words, first day of school, first school dance. You imagine sharing all kinds of special experiences with your child. In such heartfelt and intimate ways, you become bonded to your baby long before the birth.

When your baby dies, you never get the chance to know the baby in the way that we normally think of knowing someone. But your hopes and dreams for this child have already become a part of your life. You have not only lost a child, you have lost the chance to see your baby grow, become a vital part of the family and realize his or her potential. Your baby's death represents a deeply felt loss of a wished-for child, as well as a loss of your fantasies, hopes and dreams. Indeed, it represents a denial of part of your future, part of yourself.

Special Difficulties

Grieving for a baby is very different from grieving for a spouse, parent, sibling, older child or other loved one. There are many factors that can affect the course of a person's grief, but for a number of reasons, a baby's death is especially difficult to endure.

A baby's death upsets the natural order of life. Many parents are struck with the realization that their children are not supposed to die before they do. It feels so unfair that children, especially babies, can die before they have a chance to grow old and live a full life.

Other parents feel that this experience challenges the way they view life, nature or the universe. Their beliefs are shaken to the core and it can take years to come to terms with the senselessness of their baby's death. Moreover, parents are faced with the difficulty of feeling intensely angry and having no one to hold accountable.

Coping with a baby's death is particularly difficult because the length of time spent with the infant is so brief. When you never or barely get to know your baby outside the womb, you may feel cheated of the chance to learn about this child's special qualities and how he or she would have graced your life.

Feelings of Responsibility

When a baby dies, parents may feel especially responsible for what happened. These intense feelings arise from the natural and biological urge to protect your children. Because babies are so vulnerable and helpless, your guardian instincts can be at their peak. Even though your baby's problems were beyond your control, you may also feel a sense of failure, self-doubt and guilt. These feelings can be particularly acute if there were difficulties during conception, pregnancy or delivery, birth defects, a chance of recurring problems or if you have not already borne a healthy child. Feelings of responsibility can be magnified if you had to make decisions about continuing the pregnancy or enlisting aggressive medical intervention.

Mothers tend to feel principally responsible. You may feel like a failure as a woman, angry at your body's betrayal or tremendously guilty about things you did or did not do that might have contributed to your baby's plight. You may feel angry toward women who seem to renounce the rules of good health and good habits during pregnancy, yet have the satisfaction of healthy babies. All of these normal feelings originate from the belief that you should have been able to protect your baby.

Loss of the Idealized Baby

Particularly if you had very little time to get to know your baby, you may have difficulty separating the typical idealized fantasies about this baby from the probable realities. We all fantasize about giving birth to a baby who will grow to attain intelligence, creativity, social skills, beauty, grace, honesty and courage. The reality is that we will probably give birth to a normal child, capable of keeping us up all night, being a picky eater and refusing piano lessons. However, if you did not have the opportunity to know your baby and his or her unique personality, charms and annoyances, it is more difficult to let go of this "perfect" child who never moderated your dreams.

> Some of the fantasies you have are not true. You picture yourself in the spring out there and the baby toddling around and you're digging in the garden. But that doesn't happen because you've got to watch that kid every second. After I had another baby, it helped to see that reality, and I could finally let go of a lot of those fantasies.
>
> —Bryn

Loss of a Part of Yourself and Your Future

Because fantasies about your baby often reflect personal attributes or desires, a baby's death may magnify a sense that you have lost a part of your inner self. Likewise, if you and your baby shared similar qualities, you may feel like a part of you is missing. Claudia had a strong kinship with her baby and feels this loss keenly. She says, "Jacob was such a strong, independent little guy. I felt like I could have really understood him because he would have been so much like me, like I would've been able to understand his rebelliousness, especially as a teenager." This loss of self is often particularly acute for mothers, as the life growing inside was physically and psychologically a part of her.

While the death of a parent or friend represents a loss of your past, when your baby dies you lose a part of your future. You grieve not only for your baby, but for your parenthood. Times you had looked forward to—maternity leave, family gatherings and holidays—can seem worthless or trivial without your baby. If you preferred to have all your children by a specific age or spaced a certain number of years apart, the death of your baby means that your family will not be what you planned. If you were anticipating the birth of twins, you will grieve for the lost chance to raise those babies together. Indirectly, any death represents a missing branch of the family tree as you consider the prospective generations that might have been. All of these deficits in your future make it particularly painful to get on with your life.

> I didn't get to take him fishing, and he didn't get to take swimming lessons, he didn't get to throw rocks in the pond and make snowballs or have a frog collection. I would've let him have one too. I was made to be the mother of a little boy.
>
> —Lena

> I had never experienced anything so deadening. You know the commercial about "celebrate the moments of your life." I was

picturing that—all the family being there for holidays and other occasions. I pictured us as a family with the baby sitting around watching the World Series. All those experiences were so hard to bear. They were losses each time.

—Bryn

Lack of Memories and Rituals of Mourning

Memories are important for the bereaved. Dwelling on memories is a way to experience a more gradual goodbye. Unfortunately, when your baby dies before or shortly after birth, you have only a few memories and it is unclear how this baby fit into your life. Your baby is gone, and you have little tangible evidence that he or she really existed.

Grieving is made more painful and complex when the "hello-goodbye" is so abrupt. Many mothers speak of the shock of experiencing a glowing pregnancy, an uncomplicated delivery or even the return home of a healthy baby, only to have something go wrong with no warning. Suddenly their baby is gone. To them, the brief hours or few months with the baby are not enough time to gather precious memories.

Spending time with the body, arranging a funeral, attending the burial and recognizing a mourning period are rituals designed to support the bereaved, but these rituals are often denied, overlooked or minimized when a baby dies. Rose remembers the limousine driver on the way to the grave site making little jokes and chatting about local and national news events. To her, it summed up the feeling that her life had frozen and the whole world was going on without her; that her baby's death was but a droplet of mist that made no ripples when it hit the water.

Lack of Social Support

Unfortunately, many friends and relatives do not recognize the depth of your loss. It is difficult for them to imagine your grief over a baby you never saw or perhaps held only briefly. Even if your baby died later in infancy, you may feel as though you are expected to grieve minimally and be "back to normal" after the first few weeks or months have passed. Add to this the fact that death is an uncomfortable topic to discuss, and you may begin to feel isolated, unwelcome to talk and share your feelings. Because your grief is ignored or considered unnatural, you may wonder if your baby and the events surrounding his or her life and death are insignificant. Moreover, friends and relatives may have never seen the baby, so you have even fewer memories to share with others. These feelings of isolation, being the only one who knew the baby or the only one who cares, can make grieving very painful.

If my mom died, or my sister, or anybody that had lived for years and years, I would talk about them every now and then. But because my baby wasn't born alive, people think I'm harping on it if I talk about it, which isn't true, not to me.

—Cindy

It's been four years and I haven't closed the book on it. She was still a part of my life. She was a daughter just like my other daughters are now. I don't think anybody would expect me to forget if Lori or Anna were to die now. I don't think they would force me to get over it, because they're not a newborn, like newborns are something less.

—Rose

I think it's hard because I think I'm the only one that's thinking about her, and maybe my husband and I wonder if anyone else is thinking about her.

—Kitty

Lack of Professional Support

For parents who have experienced the death of a baby, grieving is necessary and healthy. However, it has only been in the last decade or so that health professionals have begun to recognize that these parents *need* to grieve. In the past, it was assumed that parents would not grieve the loss because, after all, "They never really had a chance to know their baby." Parents were admonished for feeling upset or sad, because these feelings were considered destructive and unhealthy, evidence that the parents were "dwelling on the baby" or "crying over spilt milk." Parents were pressured to forget about the baby and to think about having another one. They were dissuaded from cradling their dying baby, for fear that they might have to endure more painful memories. After death, the baby was whisked away to spare the parents the sight of their child and the grief they might have experienced if they had been allowed to hold the baby.

As a result of these attitudes, parents were deprived of expressing love to their baby in physical ways, and they buried their feelings or felt crazy for having them. When friends and family echoed these attitudes, bereaved parents were left with little or no support for coping with their baby's death.

I never saw him or held him. Before the delivery the nurse asked me if I wanted a service, but I was in a state of panic. I couldn't relate to such finality, so I said, "No." They never asked me again. Now I wish they had. I regret not seeing him.

—Karen

Gradually, as research has been done on the effects of miscarriage, pregnancy interruption, stillbirth and infant death, health professionals have learned what parents have known all along: The death of a baby is a profound loss, and parents need to grieve this loss. To hold their baby before, during or after death is now seen as an opportunity to love and gather memories of the baby. Feeling sad, angry, helpless or lonely is now viewed as a healthy reaction associated with grief. Talking about the baby to someone who can listen is now considered therapeutic. At best, grieving parents are finally beginning to receive the respect and attention they deserve.

> All the work to create this baby,
> summoning his soul from who knows where,
> all to end as ashes in a little box.
> I can't stand the endless goneness of him.
>
> —Claudia Putnam

Points to Remember

- Many people find death difficult to talk about.
- People do not expect babies to die; for you, the death of your baby is a cruel violation of these expectations.
- Many people do not recognize the depth of your loss. In fact, you may be surprised by the intensity of your grief.
- Your baby's death is untimely, unfair and senseless.
- When your baby dies, you not only lose a child, but also your dreams, a part of yourself, a part of your future.
- The brevity of your baby's life can make grieving complex and painful. You can't get fully acquainted with this special child, and the lack of memories makes it harder to experience a *gradual* goodbye.
- A lack of mourning rituals and a lack of support from friends, family or health care professionals can make you feel desperately alone with your grief.
- In spite of all these barriers and difficulties, you *can* grieve and survive the death of your baby.
- You are not alone.

2

Grieving and Emotional Recovery

A baby's death is a devastating loss. It represents an end to all the fantasies, hopes and dreams of what might have been. Whether or not the pregnancy was planned, whether it ended in miscarriage, interruption or stillbirth, whether the baby lived one minute or one year, parents need to grieve.

Grieving: A Bewildering Process

Grief encompasses a multitude of thoughts and emotions. Many people have little experience with grief, and most have never felt the emotional impact of losing a child. As a bereaved parent, you may experience a range of feelings. It can be impossible to predict how you will feel from day to day, or hour to hour. Your life seems hopelessly altered and uncertain. You may wonder if you are going crazy. Because grieving the death of a baby is a bewildering experience, it can help to learn about what to expect, what other bereaved parents have experienced. By knowing about the grieving process, you can be reassured that your emotions are valid and normal. By knowing that others have mourned similarly, you may feel less isolated and better able to cope with your grief.

> It would have helped if somebody had educated us and told us what it was going to be like and said, "You're going to feel these things. Don't think you're going crazy, because it's normal." I didn't know what was going on. So I thought I was going crazy and I didn't want to tell anybody about the feelings.
>
> —Desi

Perhaps one of the most important things to remember is that there is no right or wrong way to grieve, and there is no established length of time for the process. The bereaved parent who expects to feel a certain way after a certain amount of time will only be distressed to discover that grief is not so predictable.

Moreover, no two people grieve in the same way or with the same intensity. Different feelings surface at different times. During this stressful period, you need to remember that it is normal for you and your partner to grieve in unique, personal ways. Counseling and support groups can help you communicate more openly with each other about the baby and your sadness. Open communication will help you understand, support and comfort each other.

The Grief Reaction

Grief is a definite syndrome involving intense feelings of distress. There are a number of psychological symptoms:

- preoccupation with thoughts of the deceased
- irritability
- restlessness
- anxiety
- fear
- yearning
- hopelessness
- confusion

There are also a number of physical symptoms:

- shortness of breath
- tightness in the throat
- fatigue
- sighing
- crying spells
- empty feeling in the abdomen
- sleeplessness
- change in appetite
- heart palpitations and other manifestations of anxiety

These symptoms of intense distress can occur in waves lasting from several minutes to more than an hour. During these acute attacks, it's important to take time out to deal with the grief until activities can be resumed safely or attentively.

There may also be changes in personality brought out by emotional stress, anxiety and despair. A fastidious person may become careless; an outgoing person may become withdrawn; an even-tempered person may become quick to anger.

In addition to the above symptoms, many bereaved parents report empty, aching arms and illusions of seeing, hearing or feeling the presence of the baby. These intense symptoms may peak after several months, with variable peaks continuing for many months thereafter. Although many people expect grieving parents to recover and "get back to normal" within a few weeks or months, grief appears to be an open-ended process of recovery with no tangible ending. Parents gradually regain steady functioning, but many report that "back to normal" can take several years. Some parents feel that "back to normal" is an unrealistic goal, that this experience has changed them forever.

Understanding the Grieving Process

A common way to think about grief is in terms of stages to progress through after a loved one's death. These stages include (1) shock and numbness, (2) denial and searching-yearning, (3) anger, guilt and failure, (4) depression and disorganization and (5) resolution. Thinking about the grieving process in terms of these phases gives some organization to an otherwise bewildering emotional experience.

Unfortunately, this paradigm gives the impression that grieving should be a linear, smooth and timely progression. As a result, parents can become discouraged or concerned when they notice that their emotions don't adhere to a schedule when, in fact, they are only experiencing the true nature of grief. While there *is* a general progression, grief does not march through these distinct emotional stages. Indeed, a phase can take days or months, even years, and at times grieving parents may vacillate from one to another. It is not at all uncommon for parents to feel numb one minute and angry the next, or to feel both denial and depression at the same time.

Therefore, it may be more helpful for parents to think of the grieving process as a more fluid experience of a variety of emotions with one underlying theme: coming to terms with the loss.

Throughout our lives, we form durable emotional attachments to others. When a loved one dies, we feel deprived, reduced and resistant to the changes and adjustments that must be made. Grief is the painful price we pay for our heartfelt connections with others.

Because these relationships are so durable, we cannot immediately and fully confront the reality of a loved one's death. To do so would be emotionally overwhelming. Instead, we require a gradual goodbye in order to work through all the painful emotions and try to make sense of our loss. Many of the emotions of grief, including numbness, denial and anger, are forms of avoidance or protest. These allow us to adjust slowly to the death and the impact it has on our lives.

As you, the bereaved parent, work through these feelings, you may feel a growing realization that the baby is gone and what might have been cannot be recovered. As you confront reality, eventually you may feel a sense of resignation about your baby's death, and with that, a deep sadness and disorganization. Even so, you may still feel anger and even occasional denial as you fluctuate between yearning for the baby and saying goodbye. Eventually, as you adjust to the changes that your baby's death has wrought, you can reinvest your time and energy in regular activities and relationships. In this way you begin to reorganize your life and perhaps experience a renewing sense of acceptance and resolution.

Many parents have compared their grieving process to riding a roller coaster. Grieving is rarely a predictable or smooth progression toward resolution. As you weave through avoidance, protest, confrontation, resignation, adjustment and reestablishment, you will experience many ups and downs. At first the bad days will outnumber the good days. But as time goes on, the bad days will become less frequent and the good days will occur more often. After several years the downs may become less intense, but for many parents, the downs can remain as painful and intense as ever. This can be discouraging, but eventually you *will* have more prolonged ups and you *will* survive the downs.

> After a year, a surge of grief can be as hard as ever, but it only lasts a couple hours instead of days on end. ... It becomes slivers of pain. As time goes on it is still very painful but less consuming and less overwhelming, like you find a small place for it instead of it being your whole existence.
>
> —Claudia

Multiple Birth and Multiple Realities

If you have gone through a pregnancy with multiple babies and one, some or all of your babies died, you may face special challenges to your grieving. Not only must you grieve for the death of one or more babies, you must also grieve for the lost chance to raise twins, triplets, quads, quints or more. If more than one baby died, you have more than one bereavement to bear. In addition, unless all your babies died similarly and simultaneously, multiple babies usually mean multiple realities. These might include still-birth, illness, neonatal intensive care, emergency hospitalization, surgery, treatment decisions, death and—with survivors—homecoming. If you used selective reduction, you have not only the agony of that decision and the risks, but at best, you are excited and bereft at the same time.

If you are dealing with multi-realities, you will react and respond to any one differently than a parent for whom a particular event is the only reality. You need to find people who can understand and listen to all of your experiences with each baby. This will help you celebrate each life and mourn each death. Remember that the realities you have endured would be considered overwhelming for any family to deal with over a number of pregnancies and several years. You've experienced them *simultaneously*.

> As we cried tears for Brian, we got another phone call saying Marc was close to death. Again we went down that long hallway to NICU [Neonatal Intensive Care Unit]. We held Marc and watched as his heart rate and respiration slowed. Rick was crying and saying "Come on, Marc, you're a fighter—you can make it!" It was breaking my heart. As I was holding Marc, his vital signs picked up—did he know I was his mother? Was he going to make it? The nurse grabbed him from me and said, "We have to keep him warm." As soon as he left my arms, his heart rate began to drop and we watched our son die ... . We felt the crushing weight of our

children's deaths—not once, but twice within two hours. I can still feel my heart breaking, a piece of me lost with each of my boys.

—Sheila

Common Grieving Emotions

Numbness and Shock

There will be times, especially right after the baby's death, when you may feel as though you are in shock. Even the fact of your baby's death may not register for several days, almost as if your mind tries to protect you from the awful reality. You may appear to be unaffected by this tragedy or taking it in stride, largely because it hasn't hit you yet. Throughout the months following the baby's death, you may still endure occasional periods when the baby's death seems unreal, but the pervasive numbness normally occurs during the weeks immediately following the death.

The day James died I was very numb. It was very undramatic. I didn't start really feeling anything for a long time, for a couple of weeks, before I started to really hurt. It was like I was watching somebody else go through the whole thing. My husband fell apart and I watched myself go over and comfort him and I watched myself go for the next two weeks, feeling guilty as hell that I wasn't hysterical or that I was actually laughing. I watched myself do these things, but I wasn't a part of what was happening.

—Sarah

At first you're in shock and when you come out of it, then it hits you what happened and then you're back in shock again. I'd say the first two months were like that, and then it started easing up a little bit at a time.

—Martina

Because feeling nothing at all is preferable to the pain of grief, numbness is a common way to avoid distress. However, in the long run, grief and pain cannot be avoided, only disguised. If you habitually avoid or repress grief, it will appear indirectly, in ways that may severely compromise your health and happiness. Avoidance or repression of grief may result in the following symptoms:

- physical illness, such as recurring viral or bacterial infections, fatigue, allergy sensitivity, aching muscles or joints
- overactivity, such as working overtime, keeping busy all the time, filling up the calendar with commitments, feeling restless
- anxiety, a vague, uncomfortable feeling of fear or dread, which may be accompanied by rapid breathing and heartbeat, nausea,

diarrhea, headaches, sweating, irritability, insomnia, trembling, nightmares
- depression, including vague feelings of dissatisfaction, unhappiness, boredom, loss of interest in life, excessive sleeping or insomnia, difficulty concentrating or making decisions, intense guilt, irritability, crying spells
- disrupted relationships, such as troubled marriage, broken friendships, conflict in family relationships, isolation
- substance abuse, including alcohol, food, cigarettes, tranquilizers, other drugs
- other compulsive or addictive behaviors, such as engaging excessively in exercise, religion, shopping, gambling, cleaning, sleeping, television watching, sexual activity, romantic infidelities
- violence, such as getting into verbal or physical fights with anyone, including family members; car accidents
- other self-destructive behaviors, such as lack of good judgment, accidents that might have been avoided if you had been normally cautious or alert

While occasional avoidance can help you cope by alleviating the intense pain of grief, a prevailing or continuing feeling of detachment may indicate that you are repressing grief to your detriment. If this is the case, you may benefit from counseling with a therapist who recognizes the importance of grieving and the significance of your baby's death. You may need to talk to someone who can help you gradually say goodbye, work through the pain and cope with your loss. (See "Reclaiming Your Emotions" in chapter 9 and "Counseling" in chapter 12.)

Denial and Yearning

As the reality of your baby's death registers, shock and numbness subside. Periodically, however, you may find yourself believing that the baby is still alive. This is normal. For a while, you may wonder if this is all a bad dream and you'll wake up soon to find a healthy baby in your arms. If your doctor diagnosed miscarriage, you may wonder if the ultrasound simply failed to detect the fetal heartbeat within you. If the baby's death was diagnosed just before delivery, you may believe that you detected fetal movement and that the baby was indeed fine. You may feel a strong desire to retrieve your dead baby, wanting to resuscitate the lifeless body or wondering if the dead infant really belongs to someone else and that your baby is somewhere, alive and well.

I did a lot of denial. I kept trying to believe all this really didn't happen and I kept hoping that I'd wake up tomorrow morning and everything would be all right. I felt like I was living in a nightmare. That lasted quite awhile.

—Lena

Even after she was stillborn, it was kind of a relief to finally have her in my arms. But then again, I wanted her to be awake and I wanted her to cry and I wanted her to act like a normal ... I wanted her to be alive. I really didn't realize she was dead until I held her. I mean, I kept thinking during labor, "maybe, maybe." Even after seeing that monitor and that line where her heartbeat should've been was just a solid line, I still didn't believe it. ... But my subconscious or me not wanting to believe the truth kept saying, "maybe she'll cry and everybody will be shocked." A few days later in the funeral home I kept thinking, "Why don't you just wake up. Just wake up and cry. CRY and then we'll be all right, and I'll take you home!"

—Cindy

I think everybody must have little fantasies that are a part of denial that help you. Sometimes I feel like he didn't die, that somehow someone else had become attached to him and they realized it was going to be hard to separate them. I know that this isn't true, but it's a little fantasy that keeps me going. So every once in a while I have that feeling that this is *so* unreal that that's what really happened, that someone else took him.

—Liza

In yearning for your baby, you may feel totally preoccupied with thoughts of him or her. You may be able to feel the sensation of your baby kicking inside you. At times you may believe you hear the baby crying. When you peek into the nursery you may, for a split second, believe you see the baby lying in the bassinet. You may dream vividly about your baby. These illusions and dreams occur as part of a normal protest, but also enable you to gradually face the fact that your baby is gone.

Blaming Yourself, Resenting Others

As you squarely face your baby's death, you may experience feelings of failure, anger and guilt. These emotions are part of protesting and confronting the death. Feelings of failure tug at you as you wonder if you are able to produce a healthy baby. Diagnostic terms such as *genetic mutation, habitual aborter, irritable uterus, incompetent cervix* and *blighted ovum* can add to your discouragement. A sense of inadequacy, particularly for mothers, may arise from the idea that your body betrayed you, or that you are less of a woman or less of a mother because your baby died. Like many mothers, Kelly recalls, "I didn't feel I was a good mother, a good person, because I couldn't do this one thing right."

Bereaved mothers usually feel jealous toward pregnant women or mothers with infants. You may resent mothers who seem to effortlessly produce healthy babies despite abominable habits during pregnancy. You may bristle when you hear about abusive or neglecting parents. It's so unfair. You may also feel angry at fate, God, doctors or your partner as you search for reasons to explain your baby's death.

> All these women who don't even want their babies or the ones who don't take care of their bodies can pop them out with no problem and practically no medical care. How come I couldn't do it?
>
> —Desi

> I suppose I should say, "It's so unfair, but I don't wish other moms and babies harm." But oh, I do. I know it's not right and I don't want children to die, but I want those mothers to feel what I feel so I'm less isolated, so I'm not the only one. I am slightly disappointed when a healthy baby is born—they don't know how lucky they are.
>
> —Stephanie

> My first feelings were like I'd been singled out or something. Why did God do this to me?
>
> —Liza

Guilt is anger directed at the self. It is most apparent when you wonder whether there was something you did or did not do that caused your baby's problems. Was it genetic or environmental? Did your body betray you and contribute to your baby's death? Could you have somehow prevented this? Did you do something to deserve this awful tragedy? Bess remarks, "I thought maybe I was getting paid back for something I did that was wrong."

> It was the guilt that I have a baby inside of me. I'm the only person that could hurt or help that baby. What I consume in my body is what goes to that kid, and I couldn't even know when something's wrong and I couldn't even act and get her out and take care of her. I mean, this is the inside of my body. That was the guilt. I just felt like people thought, "Well, gosh, she was inside of you; didn't you know something was wrong? Couldn't you tell?"
>
> —Cindy

Unfortunately, this self-directed anger can lead to self-destructive behavior and chronic depression. It is natural and valid to feel anger, but it is healthier to direct your rage at your doctor, nurses, fate, God, insensitive people or even pregnant women, rather than yourself. After all, you would never have done anything knowingly to hurt your baby. No matter what, you do not deserve this tragedy. If you feel responsible for death because you interrupted the pregnancy or turned away from aggressive medical intervention, remember, you did so to protect your precious little one from suffering. If you used selective reduction, you did so in an attempt to save some lives. You did the best you could.

> At first I thought, "You're not a woman anymore if you can't have a baby that lives. It's your fault." But it's not your fault. You go through guilt and then you realize finally that it wasn't you that did it. And then you try to blame it on everybody else. But I can remember blaming it on myself more than anything.
>
> —Martina

Failure, anger and guilt are very common but difficult feelings to cope with. See chapter 6 for a more detailed examination of these feelings.

Depression, Disorganization and Despair

As you grasp the fact that your baby is gone forever, you begin to adjust to the changes in your life. Naturally, you feel depressed and disorganized and extremely sad. You may feel apathetic and unable to enjoy your friends, hobbies or other pleasurable activities. You may feel pessimistic, hopeless, victimized, deprived, vulnerable and powerless.

> I got real depressed, which I'd never experienced. ... You know, everybody has days when they're down in the dumps, but I was why-even-get-out-of-bed depressed, where all I wanted to do was sleep. ... I just couldn't think of any reasons why I wanted to continue, that's how depressed I was.
>
> —Sarah

> Just any routine thing was like a major ordeal. It just seemed like your whole world had been totally turned upside down, and then to just go back to the mundane stuff like going to the grocery store when your baby had died, it was, like, what difference does it make?
>
> —Hannah

If you feel like your everyday functioning is impaired—that you lack energy, don't care anymore, can't concentrate or feel so disorganized that it is impossible to get much accomplished—realize that this is normal. Set aside time for yourself. Do things that don't require much energy or concentration. Make lists to help your memory and organization. If you can't handle much responsibility, have someone else take up the slack for a while.

> There are days where you wonder if you'll make it to the next day, and days where you don't even care if you do.
>
> —Claudia

I went through a stage where I just didn't care. When it was time to pay a bill I thought, "Well, big deal, if it gets paid, fine, if it doesn't, fine." I mean, I didn't care about anything. Now I'm back to caring about certain things. But I went through that feeling that nothing is important anymore; I've lost what's important to me, so why should anything else be important?

—Martina

If you become concerned about your depression, you may find it helpful to talk to someone. If your depression is due to an attempt to submerge your grief, a counselor can help you get back in touch with your feelings so you can cope with them more constructively. A counselor can encourage you to express your sadness, anger and disappointment, and help you adjust to a different relationship with your baby.

The Bittersweet Path to Resolution

You will never forget your baby. Many people mistakenly believe that resolution means you stop grieving, forget about the baby and meekly abandon your baby to death. To the contrary, grief does not end. You will always feel some sadness and wish things could have turned out better. But with time, the denial, failure, guilt and anger fade; the sadness becomes manageable. You haven't surrendered your baby. Instead, your relationship to the baby has changed. You learn to accept it and integrate the experience into your life. Your memories of the baby are not idealized and can evoke pleasant emotions. As you remember your baby fondly, thoughts become bittersweet: sadness merges with your happier memories, and you acquire a sense of peace.

Her life and death feel like a very integrated part of my life right now and not something that I could or would change, just something that happened and I'm going to cope with it. I don't feel as though it's limiting anymore, it's just part of my life.

—Jessie

When I think about it, it's always going to be sad. I can look back on the time we had with him, and although it was the only time we'll ever have with him, I can smile. I didn't think I'd ever smile. Every time I thought about that, it would make me cry. It doesn't make me cry anymore. Now it makes me real grateful that I had that time. I feel really, really grateful that I had him for three days. And I didn't think I'd ever feel that way.

—Sarah

Resolution takes time. Of the mothers in this book, most needed more than four years to feel resolved. Some mothers needed less time, some mothers needed more. Some mothers still do not consider themselves resolved. They continue to feel intense sadness many years after their baby's death.

It will always be there, I'm sure. Even in fifty years I'll still remember. I'm not grieving like you do right afterwards. But I still have sadness and pain. It still bothers me, but not every day.
—Rayleen

How do I feel now, seven years later? That there is a missing part in our life, that the family is incomplete. ... I still miss him and I don't know that that ever goes away. It's less now—it used to be every minute of every day and then it was just a few days a week and then a few weeks in the month. Sometimes I'll be like this only once in a year. Sometimes it's worse and sometimes it's not. I just wish it had never happened, never, ever, ever.
—Bess

The peaceful feelings that come with resolution are a blessed change from the ravages of grief, and most parents hope to find some resolution. Chapter 7 looks at resolution in more detail and describes how some mothers have integrated their babies' deaths into their lives.

Surviving Grief

It's important to remember that people grieve in different ways. Not everyone will feel guilt, failure, loneliness or deep depression. No one will feel like that all the time. Your grief may be intense or gentle, overwhelming or manageable, somewhere in between or vacillating between extremes.

It's also important to remember that the only way to work your way through grief is to acknowledge all of your feelings. However painful this may be, it's the only way, and in the long run, acknowledging is actually less harmful than repressing or avoiding grief. In fact, experts in bereavement agree that *the quality of your grief work can determine the quality of your life*. By experiencing and dealing with your emotions, you increase your chances of healing and of finding peace and happiness again. Suppressing feelings increases distress.

Many parents benefit from attending bereaved parent support groups, as well as individual counseling. Both resources offer a place where you can express your feelings. If you feel stuck, overwhelmed, at the end of your rope, that your life and relationships are unraveling, or if you feel nothing at all for longer than you think you should, you may benefit from talking to a counselor. Doing so may help you work through your grief toward resolution. Seeking help is a sign of strength. You deserve to feel better. Your doctor, local community mental health clinic, support group leaders, hospital social worker or psychologist, hospice organization, grief institute or other bereaved parents may be able to refer you to someone to talk with. (See chapter 12 and appendix C, "Resources for Bereaved Parents.")

Points to Remember

- Grieving is a process of coming to terms with your loss—trying to make sense of it and gradually saying goodbye.
- Grief includes a broad range of emotions.
- Many other parents have felt these same powerful feelings, but all people grieve in their own personal way, with their own intensity, on their own timetable.
- Grief cannot be avoided, only delayed or disguised.
- You are entitled to your feelings; give yourself permission to feel them. The quality of your grief work will determine your chances for healing and finding peace.
- Grieving is a process that takes time.
- Be kind to yourself as you make this journey through grief.
- You will survive.

3

Physical Recovery

I felt a real physical loss because she was attached to me for her whole life—then she was gone. And then I had all this milk and there was no baby. I felt as though a part of me had just been cut out, a real overwhelming, intense sadness.

—Jessie

When your baby dies, not only do you feel emotionally devastated, you may also feel physically devastated. Many mothers report fatigue, insomnia, and empty, aching arms. If your baby died in the womb or shortly after birth, you have all the signs of pregnancy and giving birth, but no baby. Your emotional load can be further increased by postpartum depression, caused by the natural readjustment of your hormones to nonpregnant levels. This period may last several weeks and accounts for some of your mood swings and mothering urges. If your baby died while you were still breast-feeding (or getting ready to breast-feed), you must also cope with your breasts as they continue to produce milk.

These cruel twists of nature can make your physical recovery very painful. You may feel angry at your body or impatient for the signs of pregnancy, childbirth or breast-feeding to disappear. It seems so unfair. But with time and by taking care of your body, you will soon recover physically. Good nutrition, rest and emotional support can lessen the fatigue, anxiety and depression normally associated with postpartum recovery. After you feel better physically, you may find that you are better able to cope with your grief and focus on your emotional recovery.

This postpartum information is adapted for bereaved mothers. All parents may find useful information in the sections on sex, contraception, fatigue, sleep, employment, diet, exercise and relaxation. Although based on sound medical judgment, this information should be used in conjunction with advice given by your doctor or midwife, as well as your own common sense. You may need more specific recommendations based on your special condition and requirements. Always consult your doctor or midwife if you have worrisome or complicating problems.

Breast Care

In addition to physical discomfort, engorged breasts can make you feel emotionally distressed. If you planned on breast-feeding your baby, your sadness or anger is only heightened—here you are, beautifully equipped by nature to feed and nurture your baby, but there is no baby. Many mothers report that this is a very difficult part of postpartum physical recovery. If you have been breast-feeding, you may deeply miss this nurturing, loving act with your baby.

Your body produces milk because of the hormones in your bloodstream after delivery. Your breasts feel full and uncomfortable when you stop breast-feeding or when your milk comes in the second or third day after delivery. This engorgement period lasts up to forty-eight hours. Engorgement is caused by the pressure of fluid, which prevents further milk production. If you pump just enough to relieve painful pressure, you can gradually taper off your milk supply. Be sure not to pump any more than necessary or your body will step up milk production.

Some mothers prefer to gut it out as pumping baby's milk is too distressing. If you wait it out while the milk is absorbed by your body, your breasts will soften gradually. Binding your breasts tightly or wearing a snug bra at all times should reduce discomfort. Ice packs on your breasts may also help, as the cold reduces swelling. A five-day regimen of vitamin B_6 in two-hundred-milligram doses has been shown to reduce engorgement. Relief can occur in about twelve hours. When your breasts are most swollen, you can also try kneeling in a hot bath with your breasts suspended in the water. The heat allows the milk to flow out without providing the stimulation that increases milk production.

> It was the third day after my baby was stillborn. My milk had just come in and I had forgotten that was going to happen and I thought, "Oh, is this another torture thing here?" My sister had a baby and she couldn't breast-feed, and here I was with all this milk.
> —Elaine

> I've never been so empty in my life. I pictured breast-feeding him, I pictured him just laying in bed with us. I woke up in the middle of the night, wanting to get up to nurse him.
> —Meryl

Call your doctor or midwife if you notice any signs of breast infection:

- any red, warm, hard or tender areas in your breasts
- fever above 100 degrees
- general ill feeling
- tender lymph glands in the underarm area

Dilation and Curettage
(D & C)

If you had a D & C, you may feel a sense of violation. After the doctor determined that miscarriage was imminent, you may have wished that you had been able to go home and let nature take its course. If an incomplete miscarriage was diagnosed, you may have needed more time to adjust to your loss before this stark and final action. If you had a therapeutic abortion (by D & C or another procedure), you may feel especially violated by this intrusion into your body. If a curettage was performed to remove placental fragments and stop you from hemorrhaging, you may have feared for your life or your fertility.

You need to allow four to six weeks for physical recovery. During this period you can expect to tire easily. Your hormones may also be out of balance, which can make you feel extra moody or depressed. Check with your doctor about restrictions on driving and other activity. To reduce chances of infection and to promote healing of your cervix, avoid intercourse or using douches, tampons or menstrual sponges and cups. For additional information, consult "Uterine Healing" later in this chapter.

Call your doctor or midwife if you notice any signs of infection or complications:

- pain that is not alleviated by nonprescription pain relievers such as aspirin, ibuprofen or acetaminophen
- vaginal discharge that increases or smells unpleasant
- unusual vaginal swelling or heavy bleeding
- headache or muscle aches
- dizziness or general ill feeling
- fever above 100 degrees

Cesarean Delivery

If you had a Cesarean birth, you may feel additional grief over the disappointment that you could not deliver your baby vaginally. Or you may wonder why Cesarean delivery was not carried out sooner to save your baby's life. You may feel that a very invasive procedure was done to your body, all for naught. In any case, your body must recover without benefit of a baby in your arms.

It is important to remember that you are recovering from major surgery. Your body needs about six weeks to heal completely. You may tire easily for several months after delivery. Walking or standing for long periods of time can be exhausting. Give yourself time to heal before you resume your normal activities. Check with your doctor about specific activity restrictions. Restrictions often include lifting anything heavier than twenty pounds, mopping and vacuuming. Do not drive during the first one or two weeks, since your reaction time is slower.

You need to examine your incision every day to make sure it is healing properly. If your doctor used steri-strips, you should leave them on your incision until they start peeling off on their own. Check with your doctor about bathing. For additional information, consult the next section, "Uterine Healing."

Call your doctor or midwife if you notice the edges of the incision coming apart, or any signs of infection:

- increased pain or tenderness
- increased swelling or reddened skin around the incision
- fluid or discharge from the incision
- fever above 100 degrees
- continuing urge to urinate frequently

Uterine Healing

Vaginal bleeding is normal for up to ten days after miscarriage and eight weeks after delivery. The flow is called "lochia" and consists of the lining of your uterus and blood from where the placenta was attached to your uterine wall. Over time the color changes from red to pink or brown to whitish-yellow. Occasionally you may notice clots, up to the size of a quarter. You may also notice an increase in flow when you stand up or engage in vigorous physical activity. Within seven to twenty-one days after delivery, the clotted area at the placental site loosens, and you may notice more bleeding for a few days. In general, increased bleeding is a signal that you need to slow your activity, get more rest and drink lots of fluids. To reduce chances of infection, avoid vaginal penetration, including intercourse, tampons or douches, for at least four weeks. Your uterus will need four to six weeks to heal and return to its normal size and position and for the cervix to close.

Watch for symptoms that may indicate infection or abnormal bleeding. Call your doctor or midwife if you have any concerns or if you notice any of the following:

- bleeding that saturates one or more sanitary pads in an hour
- dizziness or lightheadedness, particularly with heavier bleeding
- vaginal flow or discharge that smells unpleasant
- fever above 100 degrees
- pain or burning with urination
- red, warm or tender areas in your breasts or legs
- general ill feeling or any new symptoms of discomfort

Episiotomy Care

An episiotomy heals and the stitches dissolve in about three to six weeks. To prevent infection, keep the area clean by rinsing with warm water after going to the bathroom and by always wiping from front to back. Change your pad at least every two hours. To relieve soreness and promote healing, sit in a shallow amount of clean water two to four times a day for about fifteen minutes. Use warm or cold water, whichever relieves your discomfort. You might also try sitting on a donut-shaped pillow, or squeezing your buttocks together before sitting and using ice packs, anesthetic sprays, ointments, witch hazel pads (Tucks) or prescription pain medication.

Call your doctor or midwife if you notice any signs of complications or infection:

- any increase in pain, swelling, redness, drainage or bleeding around the incision
- headache, muscle aches, dizziness or general ill feeling
- nausea, vomiting, constipation or abdominal swelling
- fever above 100 degrees

Postpartum Visits

About six weeks after delivery, your doctor or midwife will want to give you a pelvic exam and check your general physical condition, your urine, your breasts and your abdominal wall. These exams can reassure you that your body is healing properly. You may want to make another appointment prior to the six-week checkup, to ask questions and learn more about what happened. Because doctors' offices are generally full of pregnant women and mothers with infants, you may want to ask for the first or last appointment of the day. Many bereaved mothers find it too painful to be around pregnant women and babies. If sitting in the waiting room would make you feel uncomfortable, explain your situation when you arrive, and ask the receptionist to seat you in an exam room.

Sex and Contraception

Parents vary on their interest in sex after their baby dies. For some parents, sex provides the intimacy they want; for other parents, it seems like a worthless or painful activity, especially when associated with conception. When you are intensely grieving or if your relationship is stressed, you may feel too emotionally drained.

Fatigue, soreness and hormonal changes may also affect your interest in sex. You may be advised to avoid any vaginal penetration until your healing is checked at the six-week postpartum exam. Physically, you are able to resume intercourse when your bleeding stops and when you feel comfortable with penetration. It is important to be gentle during intercourse the first few times. A water-soluble lubricant (such as K-Y Jelly or even better, Astroglide) may be helpful in reducing discomfort. Try different positions to minimize discomfort caused by pressure on your episiotomy or other tender areas. You can also try other ways to express sexual intimacy and physical affection. (See chapter 10 for more information on couples and sex.)

Many mothers long to be pregnant again immediately, but if you are still recovering from pregnancy, you need time to heal physically. To avoid conception, you need to use birth control as soon as you resume intercourse. Pregnancy can occur before your menstrual period reappears, as the first ovulation can happen anytime. The refitting of a diaphragm is necessary after each pregnancy due to changes in the size of the cervix. In addition, a diaphragm needs to be fitted after the six-week period during which the uterus and cervix return to their normal size and position. Other birth control methods can be adopted immediately, including condoms and foam. Discuss birth control with your doctor or midwife to find the method that is right for you.

> At first, birth control was just out of the question. I just couldn't use anything, I just *couldn't*! Then, after a couple months, I decided I was feeling a little bit better, and I wasn't going to risk any more pain. But at about the time we decided we weren't going to have any more children, I discovered I was pregnant.
>
> —Sarah

Whether you are still recovering from pregnancy or not, you need time to think about this important decision. (See chapter 13 for more information on timing another pregnancy.)

Fatigue and Sleep

After pregnancy, including one cut short by miscarriage, a bereaved mother's fatigue is different from that of other postpartum mothers. Any comparisons are unfair because grief contributes immeasurably to the fatigue of recovering from pregnancy. If your baby died after your postpartum period, fatigue is still a common symptom of grief.

> A lot of times I would just sit and either write or just close my eyes for hours. There were a few times I couldn't even get up. I would try to make dinner and my arms would be so heavy—there would be no energy. I couldn't even push the spatula in the pan. I just was like, "I don't care, I'm not hungry." I felt real sick in my stomach. I couldn't even breathe right. It was just like big sighs.
>
> —Rose

The biggest thing I remember was empty arms. My arms just ached. I've read about this and it's hard to believe, but to me there was actually a physical emptiness. I could almost feel my arms cradling, but there wasn't anything there.

—Meryl

Trying to take on too much too soon can exhaust you and prevent your physical or emotional healing. This is a time to take it easy and do what's best for you. The following suggestions may help reduce fatigue and thereby increase your ability to cope with your grief as well as manage the activities of everyday life.

- Let others help, or hire someone to do the household chores, the cooking and the child care for any other children you may have.
- Do essential housework and errands during the part of the day when you feel most energetic.
- Keep meals simple; limit housekeeping to a minimum.
- Sleep or rest whenever you find the opportunity; don't limit your relaxing hours to nighttime. You may find that you don't always get enough rest in those hours you set aside.

It is very common for grieving parents to experience sleep disturbances. You may fall into bed exhausted, only to be consumed with thoughts, regrets and grief about your baby. Or you may waken in the middle of the night, unable to get back to sleep. Especially if you are very busy during the day, nighttime may be when your mind demands the time to grieve.

An *occasional* sedative prescribed by your doctor can help you get much-needed sleep, but beware of using medication (or alcohol or other drugs) to avoid the pain of grief. Anesthetizing yourself does not get rid of the feelings—it only increases their pressure and power inside you, making them more volatile and painful to deal with in the long run.

Some bereaved parents notice that they sleep more, not less. Additional sleep may give you the energy you need for the hard work of grieving. However, excessive sleep can be a way of avoiding grief by providing the same escape as anesthetizing yourself with drugs or alcohol. Both insomnia and excessive sleep are also common symptoms of depression. If either problem is prolonged or concerns you, seek out counseling or support groups to help you cope with your grief.

I had trouble sleeping for a while. I'd wake up in the night after I had her—I'd try to listen for something, and that lasted for months.

—Erin

For many parents, sleep irregularities are temporary or occasional. You can try inducing healthful sleep with the following ideas.

- Give yourself opportunities during the day to grieve and think about your baby.
- Keep a journal. Write down your thoughts and feelings—putting them on paper releases them from circulating in your mind. Try doing this during the day; it can also help during a restless night. (See appendix B for suggestions on journal writing.)
- Exercise during the day. This can help you to feel more relaxed at bedtime and to sleep more soundly.
- Remind yourself that you deserve the respite of sleep and tranquility.
- Set aside time in the evening for winding down with a warm bath or other passive activity. Avoid caffeine (including soft drinks and chocolate), nicotine and other stimulants. Alcohol can also interfere with normal sleep patterns.
- If you fall asleep to music, have an automatic timer turn it off. Research indicates you can sleep more deeply in silence.
- Practice relaxation techniques at bedtime and when you wake up in the night. For instance, close your eyes and think of gentle, downward movement. Picture yourself floating down like a feather from the sky or gliding down stairs or descending in the elevator of a skyscraper. (For more techniques, see "Relaxation" later in this chapter.)

Employment

If you were employed outside the home before the baby died, you may feel pressure to give up maternity leave and return to work. Instead, consider taking a leave of absence—as much as you can afford—for emotional and physical recovery. For some mothers, returning to work gives them a sense of worth, something to do, a way to be with people. Other mothers prefer not to resume their jobs. They may worry that they would be unable to concentrate on their work or lack the energy to put in the necessary effort. They may prefer to be alone with their thoughts and their grief. The thought of having more things to do may feel overwhelming. Your decision may depend on whether your job is normally a stressful one and whether you find balancing job and family difficult, as many mothers do. Remember, adjusting to the death of your baby has already put you under a tremendous amount of stress. To make a decision about returning to work, consider your physical and emotional needs and how you can best fulfill them.

Diet and Exercise

Ask your doctor if you have any special dietary needs. You may have little interest in food, or you may feel like eating foods that are not particularly nutritious. Because you are under stress, be sure to eat enough protein, vitamins and minerals, especially the B and C vitamins, iron and zinc. Drink plenty of water to keep your body functioning smoothly.

Many mothers are concerned about regaining their normal figures after pregnancy. You may feel impatient about losing weight, but find it difficult to diet. Restricting your eating will make you feel deprived, adding to the feelings of deprivation you already have over the death of your baby. You may discover that it is more helpful to avoid dieting than to lose weight. In our culture, especially for women, a dieting mind-set includes preoccupation with shape and weight, and dysfunctional beliefs about food. Whether it leads to weight loss or gain, dieting often becomes an eating disorder.

People who are concerned about weight are better off working on other areas of their lives and abandoning the "When I get thin, my life will begin" philosophy. When you work on your life, then food and weight issues become relatively unimportant. Instead, go after what you are really seeking—a sense of well-being and wellness.

With regard to food, replace dieting with natural eating patterns. Get away from thinking in terms of "good" and "bad" foods—all foods are good, some are just more healthful than others. Consider "forbidden foods" to be those you find distasteful. When foods you like are no longer forbidden, they won't hold such power over you. Give yourself permission to "eat whatever I want, anytime I want" and you'll be able to let go of "this is my last chance to indulge" mentality. Before long, you'll find yourself reaching for more healthful foods, as those are the ones that make you feel well nourished. Besides feeding yourself kindly, discover what other things you can do to nurture yourself. For more support, books by Geneen Roth are an excellent resource (see "Books on Infertility, Pregnancy and Health" in the bibliography). With time and good nutrition, you will feel better emotionally and physically, and eventually your body will return to normal.

Ask your doctor or midwife if you should follow any exercise restrictions. You may feel as though you don't have the energy to exercise, but even a walk around the block can help clear your mind and get your body back in shape. Many mothers notice that physical activity helps reduce the stress of grieving. A bicycle ride can lift some depression; hitting a tennis ball against a backboard can be a good outlet for anger. To release tension or anxiety, try swimming, walking, jogging, aerobics, yoga, dancing, even gardening or housework. For recovering your prepregnancy body, exercise is more effective than cutting calories because it keeps your body's metabolism humming along. Once you discover that exercise adds to your sense of well-being, you will find it more appealing.

Relaxation

Along with nutrition and exercise, relaxation can help you reduce fatigue, anxiety or insomnia. Relaxation also enables your body to put its resources into healing. There are a number of good books and audiotapes on progressive relaxation techniques, including yoga and meditation. The basic idea is to make your body relax by consciously releasing muscle tension or by using meditation or imagery to put you in a relaxed state of mind. To release muscle tension, lie down so you are comfortable and all your body weight is supported. Relax your facial muscles, your jaw, your eyes, your brow. Starting with your toes, slowly work your way up to your scalp, relaxing each body part. Make your toes limp, then your ankles, calves, knees, thighs and so on. Concentrate on breathing slowly. Letting tears flow will deepen your ability to relax.

To add imagery, close your eyes and imagine a place that makes you feel peaceful. A sandy beach, a mountain lake, a flowery meadow, a grassy prairie, an evergreen forest. Picture a soft breeze, puffy clouds, brilliant colors, cool water, whispering pines, whatever pleases you. This is a place you can always go to if you want to feel relaxed and at peace. You can also try turning on some calming music. Gregorian chant, a cappella, New Age and Native American flute music have very soothing qualities. You deserve to take time out to relax.

To meditate, breathe deeply while focusing on a silent mantra—a simple word or phrase that works for you. This can help lower blood pressure and muscle tension. Regular meditation can reduce your anxiety and enhance your resistance to stress.

You can also try making a list of the friends and activities you find relaxing. Refer to the list when you are looking for a break. Plan to do something pleasurable every day. Socializing, recreation and hobbies are as important as good food, exercise and sleep. Keep a list of short- and long-term goals. Include everything from washing the kitchen floor to reading the complete works of Laura Ingalls Wilder. This can help you define priorities and give you a sense of self-control. Checking them off can give you a sense of accomplishment *and* permission to relax.

Alternative Medicine

If you have physical or emotional complaints that have not been adequately addressed, treated or cured by western medicine, you may want to look into alternatives. While western medicine tends to have success treating acute infections and traumatic injuries, there are many problems, such as migraines, asthma, sinusitis, depression, infertility, arthritis, back pain and allergies that can be more responsive to other therapies. Alternatives can offer fewer side effects and better treatment of underlying causes, rather than just alleviating symptoms. Sometimes alternative therapies complement western medicine and your physicians may already recommend them.

There are "lifestyle" programs that focus on healthful eating—macrobiotics, vegetarian/natural foods, food supplements—and managing stress with yoga, meditation and other relaxation techniques (see the preceding sections). Others focus on the mind-body connection, including biofeedback, visualization, art or music therapy, even prayer. There are "touch" therapies, such as chiropractic and massage. Finally, there are therapies traditional to other cultures, including acupuncture from China; Ayur Veda, an ancient healing system from India; homeopathy, a microdose pharmacology from Europe; and Native American healing practices, such as the sweat lodge. It might be worthwhile to explore the alternatives that appeal to you.

To guard yourself against quackery, use the following guidelines.

- Get referrals from people you trust who've had experience with alternatives.
- Be skeptical of unrealistic claims of cures with little effort, especially on the practitioner's part.
- Have realistic expectations—no therapy is a cure-all for everyone, all of the time. Otherwise, everyone would be flocking to it.
- Avoid practitioners who tell you that the medical establishment wants their remedies kept secret. They are trying to ensure that you won't get outside opinions.
- Work with someone who is willing and able to explain the rationale behind the treatments. Good medicine arises from a coherent and consistent system of ideas and observations. If it's "magic" or "miraculous" or if they can't explain it to you in a way that makes sense, take this as an indication that either they are deceiving you or they don't know what they're doing.
- Look for credentials such as rigorous education from accredited schools and certification from accrediting bodies.

Points to Remember

- Establish your own timetable for postpartum recovery.
- Take care of your body as a way to help you cope with your grief.
- Give yourself a few months to decide about another pregnancy.
- Practice relaxation techniques to help you cope with fatigue, insomnia and anxiety.
- Give yourself opportunities to grieve and think about your baby, especially during the day.
- Be sensitive to your own special needs for sleep, nutrition, exercise, relaxation and sexual intimacy.

4

The Early Months

When your baby died, you may have been awestruck by the power of your feelings. Your parental instincts and urges seem to come out of nowhere. You may be engaging in behaviors that previously you would have considered unfit for a civilized person. And yet, the depth of your feelings is somehow proof that you are experiencing the essence of what it is to be human.

Parental bereavement is a social and emotional experience, to be sure. But it is also a biological experience. Whether you subscribe to the Book of Genesis or Darwin, it is a fact that we have urges to be fruitful and multiply. Another fact is that human babies need devoted and protective parents who are willing and able to supervise them for many years. Their very survival requires a strong, resilient bond between child and parent. This bond can begin forming before conception and is very powerful even before the child's birth.

When the bond is broken by death, parents are still left with irresistible biological urges to nurture the baby. If you are a mother, the biochemical changes that occur as a result of pregnancy and delivery can make the rest of you feel like you're in parental overdrive. You may feel like you should be able to recover this baby, if only you could figure out how. You may be obsessed with your baby's body, wanting to be with it, to know where it is, or to make the *perfect* plans for burial or cremation. Your preoccupation can lead to hallucinations and mothering behaviors that make you question your sanity. But you are not insane. You are bereft of the very thing that would give these natural feelings and behaviors meaning: a baby.

As time goes on, these emotions and urges will fade. Without a baby to reinforce this devotion, your instincts will move on. In the meantime, accept yourself for where you are. The resilience of your mothering urges is evidence of your biological inheritance as well as the depth of your maternal love.

Decisions after Your Baby's Death

After a baby dies, most parents must make the difficult decisions of whether to give consent for autopsy, whether to cremate or bury the baby's body or whether to let the hospital handle it. Although painful, these decisions can give you a sense of control and the chance to make arrangements that hold meaning for you.

Depending on how your baby died, you may not always be given choices. If you suffered a miscarriage in the hospital, they may dispose of the remains unless you insist on your right to keep them. If your baby died of SIDS or other accidental death, an autopsy may be required by law. Unfortunately, decisions made without your consent can enhance your feelings of powerlessness.

If your baby died *in utero*, you may have had to decide whether to remove the baby from your womb, or to wait until your body took care of this. Early in pregnancy, many mothers are encouraged to have a D & C. Later in pregnancy, mothers are sometimes encouraged to induce labor rather than to go home and wait for labor to begin. For you, a D & C or induction may have been the most reasonable option. Emotionally, you may have dreaded the anticipation or the idea of carrying your dead baby. Perhaps it was recommended for health reasons. In any case, it is normal to have regrets, to wish that you'd given yourself more time to either go into labor or prepare for the invasive procedures. Or maybe you waited for labor because of medical reasons, but were horrified by the experience. Either way, recognize that your regrets may also arise from the feeling that this was a catastrophic moment, when your baby was taken from your body's embrace. It is natural to go over and over the events surrounding the delivery. It is normal to grieve for the fact that there really is no "good" way to give birth to a dead child.

If you have regrets about any decisions made around the time of your baby's death, remember, you made the best choices you could at the time, given the facts and your emotional duress. If you feel you were not given a choice or enough information on any matter, and wish you had been, tell your caregivers. Doing so may help you regain some feelings of control. And other bereaved parents might benefit from your insights.

Autopsy

You may be encouraged or required to give consent for an autopsy to determine the cause of your baby's death. Because of your natural, protective urges, giving permission for an autopsy can be very painful, especially if you don't like the idea of this invasion on your baby's body. If your baby was bombarded with wires and tubes and needles, the idea of the baby suffering any more may be unbearable, even though you know he or she cannot feel any more pain.

If the baby died of a specific known cause such as a heart defect, your doctor may suggest that only that specific part of the baby's body needs to be examined. In the case of stillbirth or newborn death, examination of the placenta and umbilical cord may yield important information. You may be comforted by the idea that an autopsy may add to medical knowledge that will help other babies, or that an autopsy will give you information that will increase your chances of having a healthy baby in the future. Or you may decide to refuse consent, in which case your doctor should respect this decision.

If you give consent for an autopsy, you may anxiously await the results. If you need results sooner to ease your mind, ask your doctor about this. After the autopsy is completed, you will probably want to discuss the results with your doctor, have your questions answered and even have a copy of the autopsy report. For many parents, the autopsy report is another memento, tangible evidence that the baby existed. For others, it's just an impersonal scientific report.

Unfortunately, autopsies don't always yield the exact cause of death. Especially in miscarried and stillborn babies, the cause of death is often unknown. If your baby died of SIDS, you will receive no answers about causes or prevention.

In any case, try to remember that the baby's death was not your fault. People like to think they have control over their bodies and their lives, but the scary truth is, they don't always. Sometimes bad things happen in random ways. It may take awhile to believe this, but anger at yourself for what happened to your baby is anger better directed at fate, God, genes, medical science or Mother Nature.

> I think the autopsy helped a lot because if you don't have a reason, it makes it harder to go on, and you never know whether the next baby is going to have the same problem. But if you have an autopsy, you know what was wrong.
>
> —Martina

> I really needed answers, but the autopsy couldn't tell why she stopped breathing inside of me. At first I really felt it was my fault because I carried that baby for nine months. So I thought I'd done something wrong, but I couldn't figure out what. I have no answers.
>
> —Erin

> They lost the autopsy results! That was a problem in that there was no completion as far as that goes. I never had an answer that I could completely rely on, but I know that that's the case a lot of times anyway. It took awhile to work through those feelings.
>
> —Anya

Burial or Cremation

You may find it difficult to choose between the options of burial or cremation, as neither is a comforting thought. Some parents feel badly about their baby being in the cold ground, and others can't imagine reducing their baby's body to ashes. It may be comforting to view cremation as returning your baby to the air; burial returns your baby to the earth. Even though the baby is dead, your desire that he or she be comfortable is quite normal, and these feelings should be respected.

Some parents feel that the hospital or family pressured them to make decisions before they were ready. Martina remembers that she and her husband were expected to make these decisions right after their baby was stillborn. She points out, "They ask you those questions so soon and they don't realize you're not all there. When they asked me what I wanted to do with his body, I looked at my husband and he looked at me and we were stunned. 'What are you asking us this for right now? We don't want to talk about his *body*. He's our *son*!' " Winnie agrees, "I decided I wanted ashes. Actually, I was SICK about ashes. I wanted a plump, soft-skinned, healthy baby."

Whenever possible, parents should be given as much time as they need to make this difficult decision. Anya remembers, "I wasn't ready to make a decision for more than a week. I wanted to check out funeral homes and visit cemeteries and I was very grateful that the hospital didn't pressure me. I could wait until I was ready. I felt like this was a decision I had to live with for the rest of my life and I didn't want to be forced to make a snap judgment."

Money is often an issue. Some parents don't have the money to spend and others are outraged at the principle of having to pay a lot of money for a tiny casket or the injustice of paying all this money and not having a healthy baby in their arms. There are funeral homes that provide free services for infants, but unless your hospital refers you, you may not have the knowledge or energy to track down this information. Some parents elect to use free hospital services—the hospital arranges cremation at a local mortuary, but then there is no way to obtain the ashes. Unfortunately, many parents later discover that they would feel comfort in knowing where the baby is. Erin observes, "We've always wondered if we did the right thing because we've driven out to the cemetery and the hospital babies, stillborns, are all together. We put flowers out there, not knowing where she was. ..."

It is normal to wonder what you might have done differently or how it might have eased the pain. Remember, your decisions were based on your circumstances, needs and options given at the time; if you suffered a miscarriage, interruption or stillbirth, you may not have been offered any options.

If you feel you were denied adequate choices, time or information to make some of these difficult decisions, you may consider talking to your doctor or midwife about this. (See chapter 5 for more information about decisions concerning cremation/burial and funeral/memorial services.)

Bewildering Feelings

Grieving poses many questions, especially in the beginning.

- Will I survive this tragedy?
- What is this grieving process? How do I get through it?

- What will I feel tomorrow, next week, next month, next year?
- Are my feelings and behaviors normal?
- Will I feel better, ever?

In time, you will find some answers to these questions. For instance, yes, you will survive this, and in doing so, you may feel you can survive anything life presents.

What will you feel tomorrow, next week, next month, next year? Grief is unpredictable. You will know what you feel when you get there. Since no two people grieve exactly alike, you must find your own path through grief.

One thing is certain: you can disguise grief, but you cannot avoid it. If you try to avoid your feelings of sadness, anger and hurt, you will compromise other areas of your life. For instance, you may find yourself having difficulties at work or in your relationships. You may feel embittered, angry, that others are "out to get you." You may shut off all your feelings so you can honestly say you feel nothing at all—about anything. You may engage in compulsive behaviors, such as overeating, overspending money or extramarital affairs. You may rely on alcohol, tobacco or drugs. You may work all the time, dive into volunteer activities or keep the house immaculately clean. While you may feel that you are successfully distracting yourself from grief, you are actually a prisoner of your grief. To free yourself, you can't go over it, you can't go under it, you can't go around it, you just have to go through it.

Going through grief is painful, but you will gradually feel better as the months and years go by. If you take the time to grieve and avoid placing expectations on yourself to feel better at a certain time, you will work through your grief more easily than if you try to forget about it or pressure yourself to get over it quickly. Remember that grief is not a sign of weakness, rather, it takes strength and courage to acknowledge your emotions. This is a time to listen to your feelings, to nurture yourself, to value yourself, to get the emotional support you need.

Grief is also bewildering, and at times you may not know whether you are coming or going. You may worry about whether your feelings and behaviors are normal. You may wonder if you or your partner are doing OK. The following questions are shared by many grieving parents. (For more on the grieving process, see chapter 2.)

Is It Normal to Feel Crazy?

Because grieving can be such a powerful experience, full of bewildering and unpredictable emotions, many parents wonder if they are going crazy. However, since most parents experience these overwhelming feelings, they must be a normal part of grieving.

Some of the common disturbances parents experience include insomnia, lack of concentration, forgetfulness, confusion, illusions of hearing or seeing the baby, feeling short-tempered and feeling suicidal.

Talking to someone about these feelings can help you handle them. While these reactions are normal, they do range from benign to serious. It may help just to be able to talk to a supportive friend, family member or another bereaved parent, someone who can really listen and let you express your thoughts and feelings. If you have some concerns about your feelings or your behavior, or if you are feeling overwhelmed or "stuck," it may be helpful for you to talk to a professional. Contact your doctor, local community mental health clinic, hospital social worker, support group leader or hospice organization. These professionals can refer you to a counselor who understands bereavement. Talking can help you to work through your powerful emotions and to gain reassurance that your feelings are quite normal and reasonable. Remember, grieving is hard work and takes a lot of energy.

> It was hard going on with the daily living, all the little stuff. There wasn't a lot of sense to it for a while. I remember distinctly feeling like I was losing my mind.
>
> —Bess

> I tried to leave the hospital by way of jumping out the window. I can remember doing things like that, just trying to get away from it, thinking, "Now if I leave the hospital, everything will be OK." It just seems like your mind ... you can really be a sane person, but when something like that happens, you just lose it.
>
> —Martina

> I knew that it wasn't crazy to feel crazy, but even though I had that understanding, it was helpful to have people around me who would say, "That's normal, it's OK to feel that way, let yourself feel that way."
>
> —Sophie

Is It Normal to Feel Some Relief Upon My Baby's Death?

When parents know ahead of time that death is possible or inevitable, they can begin to grieve even before the baby dies. This "anticipatory grief" can begin during early signs of miscarriage, premature labor or emergency Cesarean, or when the baby is diagnosed as having a severe illness or abnormalities. Even as you hope for the best and maybe even deny the possibility of death, some anticipatory grieving allows you to prepare yourself. It can also give you the opportunity to say special goodbyes. When the baby dies, you may feel relieved that the uncertainty is over. You may also feel relieved that your baby's ordeal has ended. If the death is sudden and unexpected but due to a disabling condition, you may feel relief that your baby did not suffer any longer.

Although you may feel relief, you can still expect to feel angry and sad. Even with anticipatory grieving, your emotions may intensify after your baby dies.

> It wasn't until after she was stillborn that the doctors discovered she had a fatal heart defect. Although I'm really angry that something was wrong with her heart, and that they couldn't know it or do anything about it, I'm so thankful that she didn't have to suffer.
>
> —Stephanie

You may also experience feelings of relief if the pregnancy was unplanned or if the baby had disabilities and you weren't sure how you were going to manage. Margaret felt guilty about this until she realized, "I wasn't relieved that my baby died, but I was relieved that I didn't have the financial and logistical worries this child would bring."

Is It Normal to Find Comfort in Nurturing Behaviors?

Some parents become concerned when they find themselves or their partner cradling a pillow as if it were a baby or cuddling their baby's clothes. While these behaviors may seem strange to outsiders, you may find great comfort in these nurturing gestures. You may want to consider keeping your baby's nursery intact for a while so you can spend time holding and caressing your baby's things. You may be comforted by:

- smelling your baby's clothing
- putting your baby's photograph under your pillow
- sleeping with your baby's pajamas or a teddy bear meant for the baby
- dressing a doll in infant's clothing
- sitting in a rocking chair, cuddling a baby-sized stuffed animal
- cradling your baby's ashes
- writing your baby a loving note in your journal before starting the day or going to sleep at night
- talking to your baby

Even though your baby is dead, the nurturing instinct can be very strong. By engaging in these behaviors, you can gradually adjust to your baby's absence. It is normal to find comfort in anything that helps you feel close to your baby as you slowly let go. Do what you need to do to cope with your loss.

> The first time we went away for a weekend, I felt like I was abandoning Jamie. So I held the urn that holds her ashes and I wrote a little note to her, telling her how much I loved her and that we'd be back, and I put it on the dresser with her urn.
>
> —Stephanie

I got out my favorite baby doll from my childhood and dressed her in a newborn sleeper. I slept with that doll for a couple of months around the due date. I just *needed* to have a "baby" nearby.

—Winnie

Is It Normal to Also Grieve Past Losses?

Besides the secondary losses associated with the death of your baby—the dreams, fantasies, plans for the future—you may be reminded of other losses you've experienced. If other loved ones have died, you may resume any unfinished mourning. If you've lost other children, you may feel that the death of this baby pushes you to the limits of your endurance. The death of your baby can act as a catalyst for you to deal with old, buried emotions and incomplete goodbyes.

In dealing with these old emotions, it helps to pinpoint other losses—and not just those involving death. Human experience contains many different kinds of loss, all warranting some degree of grief. We lose relationships through misunderstandings, shifting interests, moving to distant towns, divorces (particularly our own or our parents'), graduations, changing jobs. Even after we marry and start a family, some friendships fade. These life changes can also involve loss of trust, status, opportunities, goals, familiar places or favorite activities.

Symbolic losses deserve recognition too. For instance, if we lose our great-grandmother's jewelry in a fire, in a burglary or by accident, we may feel as though we've also lost a part of our heritage or the last tangible part of her. Even losses we experienced long ago can be dredged up, such as being dethroned as the only or youngest child when a new sibling arrived or losing confidence or dignity when we had to wear eyeglasses and braces in sixth grade. We may never have acknowledged these previous losses, nor taken the time to deal with our grief over them.

When an overwhelming loss occurs, such as the death of a baby, it is normal for these earlier traumas to rear up and cause despair. Rather than trying to focus solely on your grief over your baby, give yourself permission to acknowledge your feelings about other losses as well. By working through these unfinished mournings, you enhance your ability to cope with your baby's death.

Is It Normal to Feel So Irritable?

Irritability arises from the fact that you are under a tremendous amount of stress. It isn't easy to cope with the minor inconveniences, delays and aggravations that occur every day. You may notice that you have less patience for things that never bothered you before. Careless drivers or delays in the grocery store checkout line may bring you to the brink of violence. Your partner or other children may drive you to distraction. If something unplanned happens or if you cannot find something you need, you may feel very frustrated. It isn't so easy anymore to shrug off these common inconveniences.

Your intense reactions may be coming from your anger about your baby's death as well as from the stress of grieving. You react with anger because that's the emotion seething under your skin. As time goes on and you work through your grief, you will feel less stressed and less angry, and your patience will return. In the meantime, reduce stress by not making many commitments. For now, grieving over your baby's death and adjusting to your loss are your priorities. Do things that relax you—take a bubble bath, listen to music, take a brisk walk. Find constructive ways to express your anger. (See chapter 6 for ways to cope with anger.) It may help to remind yourself (and others!) that you are having a hard time because your baby died. Sometimes, just knowing where strong reactions are coming from can help you express and work through those feelings.

> My reactions were so strong that it was the closest thing to being insane. I'm a pretty emotional person anyway, but I don't think I've ever felt that intensely.
>
> —Liza

> About four months after Casey died I found myself turning around once—and I don't even know what it was, or why—and slapping my youngest child. Then I just fell to pieces, and I thought, "Oh my gosh, you can't even control yourself."
>
> —Meryl

Is It Normal to Feel Happy Sometimes?

At first many bereaved parents feel awkward if they laugh at something funny or enjoy a pleasurable activity. After all, the baby is dead. How can anything seem funny or enjoyable in the midst of such tragedy? If you aren't sad all the time, you may feel disloyal to the baby, as though you are desecrating the baby's life and death.

To the contrary, it is normal, even healthy, to experience positive as well as negative emotions while you are in mourning. You deserve to have respite from the pain and still enjoy the good things life has to offer.

> One time I found myself whistling at work and I couldn't believe it, you know, that I'd forget for just a little while and I'd be happy. And then I'd feel guilty that I actually forgot about the baby.
>
> —Kent

> I remember the first time I laughed at something. It really hit me that I shouldn't be happy about anything, that it was wrong or disrespectful or something. But then again it was such a relief to know that I wasn't going to be this totally somber person for the rest of my life.
>
> —Courtney

Is It Normal to Feel So Isolated?

Many people are unacquainted with miscarriage, interruption, stillbirth or infant death until it happens to them. It is easy to feel alone and isolated when you are unaware of how often other families are struck by these losses. Unfortunately, this isolation can add to feelings of self-blame and doubt.

When you feel that you're the only one, your mind can really convince you that it is directly related to your behavior, and you become paranoid. It took me so long to drop the intense guilt and questioning—"What did I do? Was I so sinful? Was this a punishment?"—on and on. When you see that it does happen to all kinds of people—through reading, seeing it on TV, joining a support group—it lessens the questioning and paranoia and helps you do the job of grieving for your child.

—Rose

After the first weeks or months following your baby's death, you may feel isolated from friends and family. You may notice that the initial rush of support from others subsides. People seem to expect you to be back to normal and may even say things like "Aren't you over this yet?" or "Buck up—no use crying over spilt milk!" Because you are still grieving so intensely, these remarks can make you wonder if your feelings are silly or unjustified.

Ironically, as the first few months pass, your numbness wears off and you really start grappling with difficult feelings, such as anger and despair. Many mothers report that the third or fourth month is most difficult, and yet people aren't as supportive when they need it most. You may feel that you are grieving alone, that no one else misses your baby the way you do, that no one cares but you.

Try to surround yourself with people who can listen and care. Learn to avoid the insensitive ones. A bereaved parents support group can be a good place to meet people who will help you through your grief, as you in turn help them. Befriending other parents who have experienced this tragic loss can reduce your feelings of isolation. (See chapter 12 for more on support.)

Unfortunately, you will find yourself in situations where people just don't understand what you are going through. This can feel intolerably lonely.

I went right back to work and got involved in that. I thought I had to put on this big front that everything was fine. So I was functioning and everybody expected things of me and people were real sweet, but they didn't know that inside I was going crazy. I just remember not caring and being frustrated and just feeling like I was one big act and that inside I was dying. During the holidays, Thanksgiving was unbearable, Christmas was unbearable, everything was unbearable.

—Holly

Is It Normal to Feel So Impatient about Grieving?

Grieving can be a long, often discouraging process. During the first several months you may feel that your baby's death will always be the center of your attention, that nothing positive will ever be realized, that you will never accept it or integrate it into your life, that you will never adjust or get back to normal. Other bereaved parents will try to reassure you that in time you will feel better, but when you are in such agony, that's hard to believe. Especially after a few months, when the shock has worn off and you are facing the stark, painful reality of your baby's death, you may feel more despondent than ever.

Even as you start feeling better, you may experience times when you feel worse. These setbacks are a normal part of the roller coaster of grief, but you may feel very frustrated and discouraged that you can still feel so terrible. Courtney observes, "Time seems to be dragging, taking forever! The bad days are as bad as ever, less frequent but just as bad—like it happened yesterday, so fresh! I just try to get through one day at a time, although some days I feel like I'm just trying to get through one minute at a time."

As time goes on, these setbacks happen less frequently and, eventually, are less overwhelming. In hindsight, many parents can see that the passage of time is a healing thing.

> I remember feeling impatient because I wanted my emotions and my heart to heal as quickly as my abdomen. I knew that wasn't going to happen, but the feeling was "I want to be done crying, I want to be done being sad, I want to be done being angry, I just want to wrap this up and get on with my life."
>
> —Sophie

> It's a very sad thing, but you don't feel like such a victim after you get to a certain point. You just go on, and time will finally just do something that does kind of help.
>
> —Bryn

> Time is a very good healer. I think for everything that happens to me, if I can just take a breath and think, "Someday I'm going to see this from a different perspective," I think it helps me get through.
>
> —Jane

Is It Normal to Feel Suicidal?

At some point, many mothers feel it would be easier to end it all than to cope with their baby's death and the turmoil of grief. Some thoughts of suicide are harmless, while others can be quite serious, leading to an actual suicide attempt. Basically, there are two kinds of suicidal feelings: passive and active. Passive feelings occur when you think about suicide as an option but don't make plans to actually do it. These passive thoughts of suicide are like fantasies—you comfort yourself by imagining death as an escape from despair or as a way to be reunited with your baby.

Active feelings are evident when you make concrete plans for committing suicide. You may buy an overdose of sleeping pills or devise plans to drive over a cliff. Rose recalls, "I knew exactly where the gun was and I was wondering how I could do it where I would be sure that I would die and not be a vegetable. Then I would think, 'No, I can't do that. I would really hurt a lot of people.' And then I'd think, 'No, I wouldn't, they would just go on with their lives just like after Jessica died.' "

If you are concerned about your suicidal feelings, talk to a friend, your partner or one of the following resources:

- your doctor
- a suicide hotline (look under Emergency Numbers often listed inside the front cover of the phone book)
- a community mental health agency (look for a 24-hour or "crisis" number under Hospitals or Mental Health Services in the Yellow Pages)

Talking about your feelings with someone who cares can help you see other ways to function, other options for coping. With or without help, it can be a struggle to keep a perspective on things. Mira remembers: "I had a really bad night and I thought about overdosing on Valium, but then I thought about my husband and my 2-year-old, and I couldn't do that to them."

> I remember that first week, waking up one night shaking and losing control. I told my husband, "I want to die, I just want to die, and I want to be with my baby and if that's what it takes, then I want to die, God just take me, please!" I couldn't take my own life, but if it happened, it would have been welcomed because I would have been with Nicole. I kept thinking, "Why didn't I die too, why didn't we both die together? And then we'd be together." At that time, Nicole was the only important thing in my life. I couldn't see ahead, I couldn't think ahead. All I thought was, "I want my baby and if that's what it takes, let it be."
>
> —Cindy

Is It Normal to Think about My Baby So Often?

There may be times when your thoughts are consumed by your baby: you hear cries, you see something that makes you think he or she is alive and well, or you vividly dream about your baby. You may have trouble concentrating or remembering things because you feel so preoccupied.

These illusions and thoughts are not abnormal or morbid. Going over your memories, hopes and dreams is a central part of the grieving process. You can also benefit by telling your story over and over to friends and acquaintances. This is your mind's way of gradually adjusting to the fact that your baby is dead and your plans have changed. For instance, you may have envisioned sharing certain times of the year with your new baby—taking your baby to the beach during the summer or visiting your parents at Thanksgiving, baby in tow. Maybe you resent going back to work sooner than you had originally planned because you thought you would be staying home with the baby. Part of grieving over your baby's death is recognizing that you lost more than just your baby—you lost all your plans for parenthood and your dreams for this baby. Repeatedly thinking about all these losses and changes is the way you gradually adjust to them.

Parents vary in how often they think about their baby. At first you may feel preoccupied with the circumstances surrounding your baby's life and death—whether your baby died early in your pregnancy or many months after birth. As time passes and you adjust to your loss, you will gradually feel less preoccupied with your baby and you'll regain interest in your regular activities. Even years later, however, some mothers report thinking about their babies every day or several times a week.

More important than how often you think about your baby is whether thinking about your baby prevents you from getting things accomplished. At first, this will be the case, but eventually you'll discover that you can think about the baby without dissolving into tears. If you stumble into the baby food aisle in the grocery store, you may think wistfully about what might have been, but you can still finish the shopping. If a colleague brings baby pictures to work, you can be reminded of your own baby and still finish the task at hand.

As the years pass, mothers who think daily about their baby point out that it can become a ritual rather than an obsession. Some mothers include their baby in nightly prayers or have a picture or other memento displayed in a special place.

> It's kind of hard to describe, but I just thought about Laura all the time, just constantly. In the first few weeks I could probably think of maybe half an hour where I didn't think of her, when I was distracted. But it was just a real constant dwelling on her and talking about her and what had happened. Then it lessened and I was aware of thinking about her several times a day. But I thought about her an awful lot for an awfully long time—for at least a year, intensely for at least six months.
>
> —Hannah

Is It Normal to Feel My Baby's Presence?

Particularly early on, you may experience mild hallucinations where you hear, feel or see your baby. While you know these sensations are mirages, for a moment, they can be very convincing. As you are still struggling with shock and denial, and while your yearning is at its peak, the realness of these sensations may be quite disturbing.

> At night when I try to sleep I hear Allex cry. His was the only baby's voice I heard. For a couple of weeks after the triplets were born, I could still feel them kicking inside me. A couple of weeks before that, it was comfort; now it's a nightmare because I know the kicks aren't real.
>
> —Georgia

Many mothers report feeling the presence of their baby's spirit. You may hold religious or spiritual beliefs that your baby exists in heaven or on another plane and that perhaps you will be reunited upon your own death. These beliefs can give you great comfort.

> One evening I heard three slow knocks on the front door. I had a feeling no one would be there, but I opened the door anyway and I felt a rush of warm air. Was that Matthew?
>
> —Kea

> I believe in an afterlife, so I don't believe Jessica is completely out of my life. I don't believe she's hovering around or anything, but I believe she is somewhere, in a place, and eventually, someday, when I die that I'll be in the same place.
>
> —Rose

Is It Normal to Feel like a Changed Person?

> I don't particularly think everything's going to go uphill all the time anymore. I don't count on things. I can't be quite as trusting as I maybe was before.
>
> —Hannah

Bereaved parents often remark that they feel changed. At first, while you grieve intensely, you may feel more temperamental, more pessimistic and more sensitive than usual. But as you work through your grief, you will notice that it is more your perspective than your personality that changes. You may feel older, wiser, more vulnerable to tragedy, more a part of the cycle of life and death. Like many mothers, Anya observes, "I've learned more about myself, that I'm stronger than I thought I was." You may feel that certain things such as work, money, status and expensive possessions have lost some of their value. You may find a heightened appreciation for other things, including children, fertility, health, life, supportive relationships and yourself.

When Jessica died, everything lost meaning. I just don't care about anything except spiritual things, eternal things, things that last. Relationships are much more important to me, deep relationships. My only long-term goal is raising my kids. Since Jessica died, being a mother means everything.

—Rose

I feel like my values are different. A big nice house isn't important to me anymore. It's more simple things, like spending time with my husband.

—Kelly

Should I Feel Better after a Certain Period of Time?

Throw deadlines out the window. Don't place expectations on yourself to feel better after a certain amount of time. Give yourself permission to feel your feelings, to feel bad when you feel bad and to start to feel better whenever that occurs. Remember that grief has its ups and downs, and you may feel discouraged when you have setbacks. You deserve all the time you need. Do what is best for you, what you need to do to cope with your baby's death.

It's been nearly two years since Kevin died, and I'm having a hard time these days. I think I should be feeling better than this! Kevin would have been 2 years old this month. My baby daughter is now the age Kevin was when he died. It's the holiday season, and I should have three children, not just two. After my new baby was born, I grieved very hard. But after a few weeks I thought, "That's enough, I'm done," and I put Kevin's photo album away. But I guess I need to give myself permission to grieve some more ... .

—Cathryn

Points to Remember

- It is normal to feel protective of your baby's body.
- Although painful, decisions concerning your baby's body can give you a chance to make arrangements that hold meaning for you. If you have regrets, acknowledge them and your sorrow.
- It is normal to feel crazy; grief is a bewildering experience.
- It is normal to feel relief; anticipatory grieving can give you the opportunity to prepare yourself for your baby's death.
- It is normal to find comfort in nurturing behaviors; do things that let you remember and feel close to your baby.
- It is normal to grieve for past losses; acknowledging these bereavements can enhance your ability to cope with your baby's death.
- It is normal to be irritable; try to reduce your stress by finding constructive outlets for your anger as well as engaging in relaxing activities.
- It is normal to be happy sometimes; enjoy any respite from your grief.
- It is normal to feel isolated; surround yourself with people who care.
- It is normal to feel impatient with grief; let yourself have bad days.
- It is normal to feel suicidal; fantasizing about reunion with your baby can help you cope, but get help if you are concerned or make concrete suicide plans.
- It is normal to think about the baby often; going over memories of your baby and what might have been can help you gradually adjust to your loss.
- It is normal to feel the baby's presence; find comfort in the belief that your baby exists somewhere else.
- It is normal to feel like a changed person; many parents grow emotionally as a result of experience with loss and grief.
- It is normal to expect to feel better after a certain deadline, but allow yourself the time to grieve without regard to how many months or years have passed.

5

Affirming Your Baby

Memories and Grief

Memories can help you cope with your grief. Although it can be painful, dwelling on memories is a way for you to slowly adjust to your baby's absence. Memories allow you to reminisce about your pregnancy or the baby's special qualities and happier times. Memories make it possible for you to say goodbye to your baby at a gradual pace. If friends and relatives also had a chance to know this baby, their memories enable them to recognize the significance of your loss and to share your grief more easily.

When the time you spent with your baby was cut short, there are few memories to hold on to or share with others. This makes grieving difficult, whether you are able to recall a little person or simply a person who might have been. You may have difficulty acknowledging your grief because it is not so clear how this baby fit into your life, nor did you have much opportunity to become acquainted. The baby is gone, leaving little tangible evidence of his or her existence. Even if your baby lived for many months, you may feel an intense emptiness as you grieve the loss of the hopes, wishes and fantasies associated with this child and the future. You may idealize the baby and resist letting go. ("Maybe this was just the child we wanted.") You may feel isolated in your grief, having no one to share memories and swap stories with. Some friends and family members may fail to recognize this baby's special significance, making you feel as though your grief is invalid. Most notably, grieving can be painfully difficult because the lack of memories makes your adjustment seem overwhelming and goodbyes too abrupt.

In the past, mothers were encouraged to forget their dead babies. Because there was so little to remember, it was assumed to be an easy task. However, it is not so easy, because to forget is to abandon a part of yourself. You need help in remembering and affirming your baby so you will be better able to grieve and adjust to a different future. When your baby dies, you benefit from getting to know the baby and gathering as many memories as possible.

A lot of people say, "It would've been worse if she had lived." But I think if I had even one hour with my child alive, thank God for that hour. I feel cheated. ... I didn't have any time with her outside of my body. I thought, "If you just give me fifteen minutes, just a little bit of time—just to tell her that I love her and to know that she heard me and to know that she knew, that she was alive and breathing when I told her that." So I don't like people to tell me that it would've been worse.

—Cindy

A friend of mine lost a baby when he was 6 months old, and she was saying, "You just don't know how lucky you are that your baby was taken at birth." I said, "At least you have some memories!" I really *wanted* to have some memories.

—Bryn

Every Baby Is Important

When your baby dies, you need to affirm your baby's life however possible—by gathering mementos such as ultrasound pictures or photographs, sorting through your baby's things or having opportunities to hold the baby. Visiting the grave site or the place where you keep the ashes also commemorates your baby's existence.

After your baby dies, you also need to affirm your baby's importance and the significance of your loss. To do this you may want to arrange rituals and create memorials that acknowledge your baby's life. By arranging funeral or memorial services or by sending out announcements, you are inviting family and friends to recognize this devastating loss, giving them a chance to realize your baby's importance and to grieve along with you. These rituals also provide you with more memories of your baby. Creating memorials can help you honor your baby's place in your life.

Sadly, some opportunities for making memories and collecting mementos may have already passed. It may be too late to take photographs, clip a wisp of hair or dress the baby. In retrospect you may wish you had decided on burial instead of hospital cremation. With a multiple birth, you may not have been given the opportunity to know whether your babies were identical or fraternal. How could you have known at the time that these would be comforting things to do? These circumstances must be grieved also. Expressing anger, disappointment and sorrow at these losses can help you cope with them.

At this hospital they didn't take pictures, they didn't save anything, they didn't do anything. I didn't realize at the time that you need all these things. I didn't know that the mementos would be important, that the picture would be all-important and that holding the baby is real important for the grieving process. ... That's probably, above all, the thing that makes me the angriest or the saddest. It's like, if she *had* to die, they could've *at least* handled it right!

—Holly

Kevin was our second child, and you know how it is with the second one. In the three months he was with us, I only took enough pictures to fill three pages in the photo album. I never clipped a wisp of his hair. I feel so bad about that. I wish I had more things to remember him by.

—Cathryn

If you lost more than one baby from a multiple pregnancy, it is important to mourn for each baby as an individual. Although you may not be encouraged to do so, you can acknowledge all your babies, no matter how many have died and how many have lived, or the timing of the death, even if months before. It can be particularly helpful for you to assign names, collect mementos for each baby, and label your keepsakes. If you wish, you can ask people to refer to the babies separately by name, instead of lumping them all together as "the twins," "triplets," "quads," "quints" or more. You may also find it meaningful to collect or notice artwork and other objects that contain two, three, four or five of anything. Whether you are raising survivors or all the babies died, this can help you to recognize each baby as a separate identity, and at the same time the specialness of their twin, triplet, quad or quint connection.

Even though you may have some regrets about decisions made or circumstances that may have been out of your control, there are still some things you can do. It's never too late to remember and memorialize your baby(s) in special ways.

Remembering Your Baby

Memories of Your Pregnancy

Your pregnancy holds a major chunk of memories of this baby. These memories can be especially important if you suffered a miscarriage or interruption. You may recollect the day you discovered you were pregnant, the excitement of hearing the heartbeat or the first time you saw your baby's image on an ultrasound screen. If you carried your baby well into the second trimester, you may be able to remember the first time you felt your baby move inside you. Was this a quiet or a rambunctious baby? Did he get the hiccups often? Did she like to stretch out? You may want to set aside a few maternity outfits that you especially associate with this time, instead of giving them away. Your "positive" pregnancy test slip or any ultrasound pictures may also be cherished as mementos.

If you delivered in the hospital, medical clinic or office, you may find it helpful to go over the events of labor and delivery with your doctor, midwife and nurses, especially if you were medicated. Details about the baby's birth, illness and condition are additional memories to recall during your grieving process.

If you have unanswered questions about your baby, even if it is years later, you can request medical records from your doctor, your midwife or the hospital. The more you know, the more you can resolve your grief.

I went back later to the hospital and met my primary nurse because I wanted to know everything that had happened. She answered all my questions and told me everything my mind couldn't fill in. She told me what the baby looked like, which was really sweet because that's really all I have, is what she told me.

—Holly

When my second baby died at 18 weeks, they didn't let me see it. They wouldn't even tell me if it was a boy or a girl. The doctor just said, "You don't need to know that." So now, seven years later, after my baby girl Susan was stillborn, it brought back a lot of questions about my other baby. With the encouragement of my support group, I went back to that hospital and requested the medical records to get some answers. The baby was a little boy—I named him David—and now I feel like I have a better idea about what I lost, who I grieve for.

—Janet

Memories of Being with Your Baby

As you grieve, you can reflect on memories of being with your baby. During your pregnancy, your baby was cradled inside you. If you were able to hold your baby after delivery, you can try to remember how he or she looked and felt. If your baby lived many days or months after birth, you had more opportunities to get to know your baby. Although it may never seem like enough, these memories can be cherished.

I remember when they brought David in. My husband was standing there at the bed and I was laying in the bed and the nurse walked in the door with the baby all wrapped up as a newborn, and I remember thinking in that short distance from the door to me, "What was she going to do? Was she going to put him in my arms? Was she going to lay him on the bed? What was she going to do?" And very naturally she walked in, didn't say a word and handed me the baby and left. We immediately started to cry very, very hard, and I took his little hand and held it around my finger the way you do any baby and I just held him like that and kept looking at him ... and then my husband leaned down and kissed him on the forehead.

—Bess

I spent most of the afternoon holding her, and then they withdrew life-support systems, disconnected everything, and we held her again. It was so sad, but I'm really glad we were able to hold her as much as we did. I think maybe it helped her a little bit, at least she had us there to hold her.

—Hannah

Right before they took Stephanie off the machines, we each had hold of one of her hands. ... Then she opened her eyes and she was gripping each of our hands, which was amazing because she was so sick. It was like she was acknowledging we were there. It was as though she was saying, "It's OK, I love you and I know you love me and I'm leaving." It was amazing we both had that same sense, that message from her.

—Sophie

Memories of being with your baby are important because they confirm the fact that a baby really existed. If you were able to see your baby, this experience helps you view the baby as an individual and gives you someone tangible to mourn. Holding and touching your baby also gave you an opportunity to express your love in a physical way. Being with your baby before and after death gave you an opportunity to say hello *and* goodbye.

He was *so little.* ... I knew there was no way he could live, he was just too little. As they were wheeling him by they let me hug him, and I told him his name and I told him how much I loved him ... because I knew I wouldn't have much chance to do that.

—Lena

I was only twelve weeks along, and being able to see the tiny baby helped. She fit right in the palm of my hand. ... I wasn't sure what to wrap her in for the trip to the hospital, and then I thought of my grandmother's lace handkerchiefs. So I picked one out and wrapped her up very carefully.

—Clara

I think when I was going through nursing school, the attitude was more "Just don't let the mother see the baby." And that's the opposite of what you really need. Holding her was good because we knew her from during the pregnancy, and now here she was and she was a real baby and a real person. That helped, rather than just "She's gone, there's nothing to it, just like it didn't happen, you didn't have that baby inside you for nine months and just forget about it ... ." There really was a baby there.

—Hannah

Seeing the baby after delivery also alleviates fears about the baby being horribly deformed. Fantasies are usually much worse than reality, and parents are often relieved at how normal and beautiful the baby looks. Even if the baby is malformed, health care professionals have noticed that parents focus on and find comfort in positive body features. Seeing the baby also satisfies curiosity about what the baby looks like and can help parents register and verify the fact that the baby is dead.

If your baby died before or shortly after birth, some people will wonder if holding your baby makes grief more painful because you risk becoming too attached. You can remind them that you've already held the baby in your womb and felt a bond long before your baby died.

I thought the doctor was awful when he asked me if I wanted to hold Caleb after he died. I thought about it though, and agreed to. ... When I first saw him, he was grey and pale and I just screamed with devastation. It hurt so badly ... but I did hold *my son* for the first and last time with no tubes or hoses in the way. It was the most fulfilling thing I could have done outside of taking him home with me. I now have a wonderful memory to carry me through the hard times.

—Ginger

I was glad I held the baby. It helped a lot to be able to see him and hold him and know that they didn't take our baby and give it to someone else and give us a dead baby. It helped to know that he was ours.

—Martina

If I hadn't seen her, definitely her—with the hospital band that said Jessica—dead, I don't think I could've settled it in my mind that she was really dead.

—Rose

After he was born they brought him up to the bed, and my husband and I sat and looked at him and touched him. I was glad. That was really the best thing that could've happened. I think I thought he was probably a monster, that he was deformed, that there was something wrong with him. He was a beautiful baby. I think it also helped to ease the sorrow and filled in all those empty areas where I could have wondered what he looked like or what he would have been. Just seeing him gave him a personality, a real concrete substance.

—Meryl

Two nurses took time to go down and get my babies because I could not stop crying. How I needed to see them again—to undress them and look at them and create the only memories we will have.

... They put Kayla and Regina on the overbed table and watched as I unwrapped them. One nurse silently cried while the other one stood by me telling me how beautiful they were. That made me feel so good—knowing they understood. Then they left us alone and closed the door so Mel and I could be alone with our babies. For an hour and a half, we were a family.

—Deidre

If you were not encouraged or allowed to see your baby, you may feel angry or cheated or desperately curious about your baby's appearance. You may feel an added sense of loss that not only is your baby dead, but you were denied the only chance you had to hold him or her. If you had a miscarriage, you may not have known what to look for. If you had a D & C or D & E, your doctor may not have allowed you to see the baby or the remains. Being able to see whatever there was might have been helpful.

If you had some babies survive from a multiple birth, you may not have been encouraged to see the baby(s) who died. This misguided effort to have you focus on the living robs you of memories and mementos. This also discounts the individuality and specialness of each baby you carried in your womb. Even if you were encouraged to see all your babies, you might not have had the opportunity to hold or see them all together, to validate the experience of "my twins," "my triplets" or "my quads." If you missed this chance, you may feel preoccupied with somehow getting them all together or being recognized as a parent of multiples. An artist's rendering of all your babies together can be quite healing.

Although researchers have found that most parents regret not seeing their baby, there are some parents who fear that seeing the baby would be too upsetting. They want to remember the baby as they imagined during pregnancy. Fortunately, hospital policies are changing. Most health care providers recognize how important it is to encourage parents to hold their baby, but realize the choice is a personal one.

With miscarriage and interruption, changes are coming about more slowly. If you wish you could have seen and held your baby, inform your doctor. This opportunity may then be offered to others.

The doctor wouldn't tell me anything about Matthew. He just said, "The baby was normal. That's all you need to know." But I've had nightmares about him, what he is like in the grave, digging him up, things like that. I still wonder what he looked like. Every once in a while I think about what's happening in the grave, and I don't know why I do that. I guess I just wonder what it would be like to look at him now. I think I'm just obsessed. I needed to see him.

—Desi

Never Enough Time

Parents who are able to see their baby are generally glad to have that experience. However, they also report regrets, such as not having more time with the baby or not doing nurturing things such as cuddling or dressing their baby's body. Although it can be painful, it is necessary to grieve for these missed opportunities. You can cope more easily if you pinpoint these moments and talk or write about your thoughts and feelings instead of burying them and letting them fester. (See chapter 6 on coping with anger and guilt.)

It is also helpful to know that you are not alone. Many parents express regret that they were unable to spend more time with their baby before death. If the baby was placed in intensive care or transported to another hospital for treatment, this sense is heightened. Rose's baby was transported to a children's hospital after delivery, but they didn't run any tests for two days. She says, "I'm really angry about that. ... If she was just laying there, she could've been laying there with me. I just remember there was no concern about me being with the baby. Of course, at the time I thought I'd have a lifetime with her so I wasn't that concerned."

Stephanie wishes she could have seen the color of her daughter's eyes or felt the grip of her tiny hand. This is a common regret of mothers whose babies die before birth or are born very prematurely. Many parents felt confused, rushed or morbid, so they gave up the baby before they were ready. Kelly points out, "I really resent not being awake for Scott's delivery. I can accept his death a lot better than I can accept not being with him for the few hours he was alive." Many, like Kara and Liza, didn't realize or couldn't grasp how seriously ill their baby was.

> When Matthew was born they handed him to me and said, "Oh, this looks like a healthy little baby boy." He was beautiful. But the nurse picked him up right away because he was having trouble. So that was the only time that I got to hold him while he was alive and it just seemed like it was only a second. Looking back on it now, I wish I could've held him a little longer, but I just didn't see the tragedy that was going to occur. When he was in intensive care, we kept vigil as much as we could. I was right on top of him, as close as I could be to him. Then, after he died, I demanded that we see him. It was like, "You're not taking my baby. I want to see him RIGHT NOW." Nowadays, I wish I could have held him much, much more before and after he died.
>
> —Kara

> I've always wished it were longer. But it felt like I was supposed to give him to the doctor, like he was going to take Daniel back over and put him on the oxygen. It was like he's not really dying, this is

some kind of game or something. But I always wonder why I didn't hold him longer—there was so much confusion.

—Liza

Looking back, many mothers wish that the nurses had offered the baby again, more than once or twice. Mothers need time to recover from shock or from anesthesia so they can spend a more meaningful time with the baby. Seeing the baby again also helps parents remember more. Bryn and Holly talk about their disappointing experiences:

I still feel kind of cheated because I was in such a state of shock. I remember looking at the baby, but I cannot remember what he looked like. I remember asking the doctor to go ahead and take him away because I was afraid I was going to get crazy and say, "No, you can't have my baby." I don't think I would have, but you just don't know what you're doing. I wish they had offered him to us again later.

—Bryn

After I came out of the anesthesia I was really out of it, but the doctor brought her into the recovery room. ... I held her and touched her but I couldn't really move or anything because I was in such pain. One of the things that's real frustrating to me is I can't remember her because I was so out of it.

—Holly

If a baby dies before or shortly after birth, it may not occur to the parents to unwrap their baby and caress the little body or dress the baby in special clothing. As Erin says, "It would've helped me to be able to dress her, so she could've felt my touch somehow ... ." Some parents wish they'd had more privacy so that they could have felt free to explore their baby's body or express emotions without feeling self-conscious. Kara recalls, "There were people there and it was great having their support, but I just kept feeling interrupted."

Parents who are able to see their baby later may be dismayed when the baby is cold. Cindy wishes the nurses had warmed her baby so that holding and touching her would have been more comforting. She remembers, "I held her again the next morning and she was like a block of ice. I almost could not hold her. I kissed her forehead and it was so cold."

Later, many parents wish that others in their family and circle of friends could have seen the baby, so that these people could have gotten to know the baby too. The parents' other children might have also benefited from seeing the baby.

Some parents regret giving in to pressure from a partner or other relatives to not see the baby or to cut the visit short. Lena, Rose and Kara had husbands or other relatives who were trying to protect them from their sadness instead of letting them face it.

> Life support was taken off him, and we let him go for it. Looking back on it, I wish I had held him as he died. But at the time, I think my husband was trying to protect me because he knew how much I wanted that baby. So when he approached me about it, he said, "You don't want to hold him now do you?" and I went, "No." ... I deferred to his judgment. I was a little mouse. Looking back on it, I wish that I had cuddled Stephen close. If I had to do it over again, I would pick him up and hold him, hug him, rock him, talk to him and sing to him. Hugging him in his incubator isn't quite the same.
>
> —Lena

> My husband felt like I needed to rest, so I remember he took me home. I was fighting and screaming all the way. I didn't want to go. I just wanted to spend the time with the baby. This was the first day I'd had with her and he was just *so* insistent and at the time I just wasn't as confident. I wasn't the kind of person who would say, "I'm staying. You can go home if you want to." I wasn't that person then. I was a lot younger, dumber, less confident. So now I have all these things I should have done, to spend any second that I had with her.
>
> —Rose

> My mother-in-law was saying, "Well, you know, you need to let go. The longer you hold on to him, the harder it is to give him up." And I was kind of, "Well, maybe she's right." But I could've held on to him longer. I *wanted* to hold on to him longer.
>
> —Kara

In hindsight, you may wonder why you didn't demand more time with the baby or do more things like kissing and cuddling. But you did the best you could at the time. Even mothers who feel like they spent plenty of time with the baby will always wish they could have had more time, a lifetime with the baby.

Photographs

Photographs can be some of your most treasured mementos. Particularly if you experienced an early miscarriage, any pictures of you during that pregnancy can be special. If your baby never left the hospital, photographs may have been taken by a health care provider and offered to you. Or you may have been able to use your own camera. (Polaroid photos fade over time, but you can take them to a custom film developing lab and ask for a copy negative, which will last.) If your baby was at home, you may have many photographs to keep. Having at least one good quality photograph can help you remember your baby. Along with other mementos, it helps acknowledge the baby's existence and your loss in a tangible way.

> I'm really glad we have pictures. I look at them a lot. Some people think that they're kind of gruesome, but they're real important to me.
>
> —Jessie

> I'm glad we've got a picture because you never forget the baby but you can forget how they look, and later on if you want to look at it, you can.
>
> —Martina

> When they asked if we wanted them to take some pictures of him, at the time I thought, "You've got to be kidding me. That's disgusting!" And a week or so later someone from the hospital called and said, "I've got these photographs of Matthew and I'd really like to send them to you." I said, "Send them! I want them!" Now we treasure them. The pictures are something that really helps me go through the grieving process.
>
> —Kara

If you don't have a picture of your baby, you may feel bereft over this lack of tangible evidence that your baby existed. Bryn wishes she had a picture to refresh her memory because she can't remember her baby's face. This is difficult for her "because he was a part of me." For others, like Dara, a photograph would have been their only chance to see what the baby looked like. Dara remembers that the pathology department at her hospital took photographs for research purposes, but they've never been able to get copies. She says, "That's something I go through in phases every once in a while, wanting to try again and get them." Desi was never able to see her baby, nor were photographs taken, but she believes her curiosity could be somewhat satisfied by seeing someone else's picture: "I want mothers in my support group to bring a picture of their dead baby so I can see what they look like. But I never have the nerve to ask anybody."

Parents who do have photographs may be dissatisfied with the quality or wish they had one of the baby before death or of a close-up of the face, the undressed body or them holding their baby. After a multiple birth, many parents want a photograph of all the babies together. Anya has most of these regrets, but it still helps her to have photographs of twin daughter Rachel. She notes, "The pictures are blurry and fuzzy and don't look like much, but I know they're there. It's real important. It's something tangible."

If you don't have a photograph or if your photographs are disappointing, you can have a portrait drawn or painted of your baby. One mother took her single blurry photograph to a portrait artist who did a wonderful job of capturing what her baby looked like. Another mother, whose baby died thirteen weeks into the pregnancy, took a collection of family baby pictures to an artist who drew a portrait of what the baby might have looked like as an infant. With the right props, an artist could even render a touching portrait of mother embracing her baby.

Some custom photo labs or restoration artists can remove bruising and sharpen edges in fuzzy or blurred photographs. With digital computer programs, they can also combine separately photographed images into one picture. You could try this for babies from a multiple birth, or find other creative ways to have them all in the same picture frame. You can also collect other pictures that hold meaning—of places, things or people you associate with the baby.

Photographs and portraits are one way of preserving a memory, but not the only way. If you don't have a portrait of your baby, you can still imagine what he or she looked like and hold that picture in your mind's eye.

Keepsakes

Mementos of the baby that you may treasure include footprints, record of the baby's length and weight, lock of hair, hospital ID bracelet, autopsy report, sympathy cards and flowers, any clothing or toys or stuffed animals you acquired, and baptismal, birth and death certificates. You may collect recordings of special songs you associate with your baby or your pregnancy. Even if you were pregnant for a short time, you can save anything you associate with this time period. And it's never too late to make a baby blanket, buy a teddy bear, light a candle or display an ornament for your baby.

Some parents keep their mementos in a special box, baby book or envelope and look through them as a way to spend time with and affirm their baby. Even if these keepsakes are tucked away in a drawer, it helps to know you have them.

I kept all the flowers. I have them dried in a little glass vase with a cork in it. It means a lot to me. I still have the ribbons from the graveside service. That really helps to keep things like that.

—Rayleen

I love my mementos. It's good for me, another thing that makes it real. I have a picture of my baby; I have her hair. She was alive at one time and she was my daughter, and you just can't pretend she isn't real. So it does, it makes it real.

—Cindy

When I first found out I was pregnant, a good friend gave me a tiny pair of socks. When I miscarried at 12 weeks, those socks were such a comfort. It was something that had *belonged* to this baby, something I could hold on to.

—Winnie

If your baby died before birth, you will not receive an official birth certificate. This can feel disappointing because it somehow denies the fact that your baby was alive inside you! As an alternative, some hospitals and organizations provide a "baby certificate," which lists the baby's name, date of birth and other life-affirming information (see appendix C). You can also design your own or find a print shop to make one for you.

Often when a baby dies, people assume that baby gifts would be meaningless or painful to the parents. To the contrary, these gifts can be viewed as acknowledgments of your baby and can serve as treasured mementos. If someone mentions it or if you know a gift was being made for your baby, don't hesitate to tell them how meaningful it would be.

If you feel pressure to go through your baby's things and put away the nursery, wait until you are ready. Putting baby things away is a big step in saying goodbye, and you may need more time. Meanwhile, it may help just to spend time in your baby's room, among your baby's things.

I remember I would take Matthew's little cap he wore in the incubator and smell it after he died because I can remember that it smelled like him. ... I saved everything I could. He was real important to us.

—Kara

Rituals

A Name for Your Baby

Naming the baby is another way to acknowledge the baby's existence and individuality. A name is personal and lasting. If you suffered a miscarriage, interruption or stillbirth, you may wonder if a name is appropriate. Do whatever feels right to you. Some parents may want to save a favorite name for a future baby. Others feel that the name originally chosen rightfully belongs to this baby.

Giving the baby a nickname or other term of endearment may be most meaningful to you. Some mothers use the Native American custom of choosing a name associated with nature, Mother Earth or celestial bodies to encompass their intuitions about the baby's spiritual essence. Many mothers have remarked how naming their baby, even years later, assigns a specific identity to the baby and gives them someone tangible to mourn.

You may name your baby informally or formally, recording the baby's name on all documents. Later, if you want to officially change or add to the baby's name, you can contact the state agency that handles birth and death certificates.

My family decided that we weren't going to name him, and I can remember coming up out of that hospital bed and saying, "OH YES WE ARE!"

—Desi

We all talked so much about her and we called her by name— Melanie. I was happy that people could say her name so easily.

—Kitty

Respect for Your Baby's Body

It is natural for you to have protective urges toward your baby, even after the baby dies. The thought of the baby being cold and alone somewhere in the hospital may seem unbearable. You need your baby's body to be treated with respect—it is a gesture that confirms your baby's importance and worth. If hospital staff are providing you with emotional support, it is also likely that they are treating your baby's body respectfully. For your sake, the baby should be kept comfortable, even after death.

I remember going back to the hospital, and my nurse friend took me to the room where they had put the baby and then left him there for a little while. That upset me so much, not that they'd done anything wrong, but that he'd been alone. I just kept thinking he was alone in there, the poor thing, and he was cold, and that upset me.

—Bess

Baptism

For some parents, baptism is a meaningful way to have the baby recognized as a valued and real person. For these parents, the baptism holds special memories and a baptismal certificate is another treasured memento. Meryl asked her priest to come to the hospital and bless her baby because she wanted acknowledgment that this baby was a person, that he had lived. She remembers, "Even though he wasn't born alive, he needed that blessing—*I* needed the blessing."

Burial or Cremation

If you buried your baby, the grave site can be a place where you can go to be with the baby and express your sadness. If you cremated your baby's body, you may decide to scatter the ashes in a special place that you can visit. Or you may decide to keep the ashes. Many parents find comfort in knowing where the baby's body or ashes lie. If you decide you don't want to keep the ashes forever, it still may take you a long time to feel ready to scatter them or place them in a cemetery. No matter when you are ready, it may help you feel a sense of closure.

It was important to me for quite some time to have a grave I could visit and to pick out a special bronze plaque that's in granite.

—Anya

I think it helps us to know we have a place to visit and we can see where it says David, Son of ... and I think that's real helpful somehow.

—Bess

Three months after Daniel died, we finally walked to the top of a mountain and let his ashes go. There was a real sense of ... that his spirit was already free and that it was trying to let go.

—Liza

In hindsight you may wonder if you should have done some things differently. Holly wishes they had scattered her baby's ashes in a more accessible spot. Deidre wishes her triplets could've been buried together. Erin wishes she hadn't let the hospital handle her daughter's cremation and burial. She says, "I think if I could do it over again, I would take Barbie's little remains and say something, rites over her, and place her remains in a little tiny coffin box. I just think it would have helped me know that she's OK, she's all in one piece, she's all together. ... Sometimes I just wonder why we didn't do that. When we drive by the cemetery I always think of her. I think she's in there somewhere. I hope she's there."

Particularly if you were not encouraged or given the option to take your baby's remains, you may wonder what the hospital or clinic did with them. Many places handle babies' remains sensitively, cremating and either scattering or burying the ashes with other babies in a meaningful place. Because of the tiny mass and lack of hard bones, if your baby died early in the pregnancy, cremation leaves no remains. The body simply evaporates and goes into the air.

If you want to know what happened to your baby's remains, call your clinic or hospital's pathology department. You won't be the first or last parent to call for such information. Especially with miscarriage or early interruption, if you wish you had been given the choice to take your baby's remains with you, tell or write to your caregivers and this choice may then be offered to others. If you are upset with the way your baby's remains were handled, you can register your complaint and suggestions with your caregivers, chief of pathology and laboratory supervisors.

If you have regrets, express your anger and sorrow about them and then figure out ways to memorialize your baby—ways that hold meaning for you now. Even if you don't know where your baby's remains are, you can have a headstone or plaque made for your baby and put it in a special place. You can put flowers in a peaceful part of a cemetery. Any of these gestures can confirm your love and help you grieve.

Funeral or Memorial Service

Although it can seem sorrowful, a funeral or memorial service for your baby can be helpful in a number of ways. A service creates an opportunity to say a special goodbye. It acknowledges your loss and need for comfort and support. Friends and family can share your sorrow and, in turn, lessen the isolation you may feel. Any ritualized gestures—naming, baptism, burial, scattering ashes, funeral or memorial service—whether simple or elaborate, can heighten your friends' and relatives' ability to recognize your loss as significant and enable them to give support. With this support, you may feel better able to cope.

Because most parents have not had experience arranging a burial, cremation or memorial service, the process itself may pose too many obstacles. Bess wishes they could have done more than just arrange a private graveside service. Dara feels that it wasn't enough to just dedicate a mass to their baby. Rose had feared that no one cared, but after so many people attended the graveside service, she wished they had arranged a "full-blown funeral in a church." Holly also remembers thinking no one would come and now wonders if it is too late to have some kind of memorial service, just to "add to making it a more real thing, that she had been a *child*."

It is important to remember that memorial services are appropriate any time you feel ready or decide it's something that you want to do. Any rituals that allow you to say goodbye can help. You can arrange a formal memorial service and invite a lot of people, or you can keep it small and private by inviting only a few people or even just your clergyperson. You can read something that has a special meaning as you spread the ashes. Any memorializing gesture like this can be a release—a way of letting go. What's important is that you make arrangements that suit your special needs.

> To do nothing would be to act like she'd never existed. I had a need to acknowledge that she was here ... to make a statement about her being here and what she meant to us. What we didn't anticipate was the response that we got from other people. As a result of both the announcement and the service, people were a terrific support for us. Also, I didn't account for the fact that a lot of those people and some of our close friends had a need to grieve. The service helped them do that as well. It was a good decision.
>
> —Sophie

> In ways I think it would've been good to have a service in order to have closure. But I got that closure when I went up to visit his grave. I realize talking to a stone on the ground is kind of absurd, but I managed to get out a lot of the things I would've said to him if he had lived and I'd had the time to say them. To me that was important.
>
> —Lena

We decided not to have a funeral because Nick and I knew him and I just couldn't see people coming because they didn't know him and maybe they wanted to express their sadness for us, but we didn't feel right about it. ... To scatter his ashes was a release; it was our letting go.

—Kara

Memorializing Your Baby

Most parents find it helpful to have the baby memorialized in a tangible way. There are many ways to publicly acknowledge your baby's existence. You can have your baby's name engraved in stone or brass and mounted somewhere meaningful. You can write a poem or a story about your baby and publish it in a newsletter, magazine or newspaper. On anniversary dates or holidays you may want to sponsor flowers at a religious service or make a donation in your baby's name to a charity or research foundation associated with the cause of death. During the holiday season, some philanthropic organizations give out names of needy children. If it makes you feel good, buy something for a child that is the age your child would have been. Donate some helium balloons to a children's hospital or the intensive care unit where your baby stayed. Jessie and Kent donated a tree to a botanic garden in Meghan's memory. After Clara's second miscarriage, she sent announcements to family and friends. This enabled her to acknowledge her baby and share her grief. The announcement read, "It is with great sorrow that we inform you of the passing of our child Emily Rose. We know that you understand the importance of this child in our life and will share in our grief." You may think of other meaningful, public ways to honor the memory of your baby.

There are also many private ways to memorialize your baby. You may find it comforting to plant a tree or a flowering shrub in your garden or keep a houseplant as a living memorial to your baby. You can display the baby's portrait in a special frame somewhere in your house. During the holiday season—or any time of year—you may want to display an ornament or burn a candle in memory of your baby. You could buy a piece of jewelry or another object of some value that symbolizes your baby; for instance, Courtney wears a necklace with a gold, heart-shaped locket containing a wisp of her baby's hair.

You may want to make your own memorials—patchwork, quilting, needlework, knitting, sewing, doll making, drawing, painting, silkscreening, journaling, engraving, sculpting, gardening, flower arranging, stained glass working, pottery, poetry or music. Build a piece of furniture, hang things on a wall, display things under glass or frame anything that reminds you of your baby. Janet made her own memento by designing a card with her baby's name and date of birth and death. She included a poem and Susan's footprints and had it professionally printed and framed. John made a pine chest to hold mementos of Jacob. Eva received a potted plant upon William's death, giving her "something meaningful to nurture."

Many parents find that the creativity involved in these projects gives them a sense of accomplishment and worth—that they are still capable of making beauty after their baby's death.

> Some friends gave us a houseplant and I thought, "Oh, no, something else that will surely die." I put it in the extra bedroom and whenever I thought about it, which wasn't often, I'd toss some water on it. Then, by some miracle, a couple months later the flowers started to bloom. It was so meaningful. I felt like Micah's life was acknowledged by that plant.
>
> —Amy

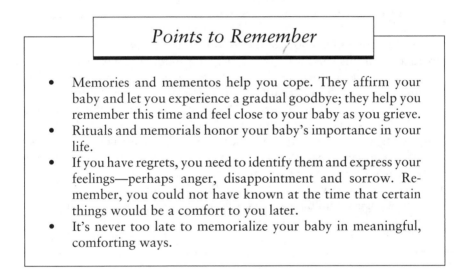

Points to Remember

- Memories and mementos help you cope. They affirm your baby and let you experience a gradual goodbye; they help you remember this time and feel close to your baby as you grieve.
- Rituals and memorials honor your baby's importance in your life.
- If you have regrets, you need to identify them and express your feelings—perhaps anger, disappointment and sorrow. Remember, you could not have known at the time that certain things would be a comfort to you later.
- It's never too late to memorialize your baby in meaningful, comforting ways.

6

Painful Feelings

Grief encompasses many painful feelings and some are especially difficult to express, cope with and work through. Feelings of failure, anger, guilt and vulnerability to tragedy are common among parents whose baby has died. If you are prone to these feelings in other areas of your life, they may arise more intensely when your baby dies.

Your own tendencies and personality can intensify these feelings, as well as factors associated with fertility, pregnancy, delivery, birth defects, cause of death and supportive relationships. If it took a long time to get pregnant or if this baby was your only living child, you may feel an added sense of failure and vulnerability. If you have been told that future pregnancy is unlikely or a recurrence of genetic defects is probable, you may feel especially angry and wonder, "Why me?" If, on the other hand, the pregnancy was unplanned or if you had a particularly difficult day before tragedy struck, you may feel intensely guilty that your negative feelings somehow caused the baby to die. The particular circumstances surrounding your baby's demise may point to someone or something to blame—or perhaps you blame yourself. This search for answers sharpens the usual feelings of anger or guilt. Lack of a stable intimate relationship or supportive friends and family tends to deepen feelings of anger and failure.

Three of these feelings—anger, guilt and failure—arise from the belief that you are in charge of your destiny. Until a tragedy strikes, you may have thought you had control over what happens to you. You make plans; you follow them. You have goals; you attain them. You place a lot of faith in doctors and other caregivers who have always come through in the past. You may have put your faith in God, fate, Mother Nature or universal justice. Many people do this with their health, their finances, their careers, their relationships, their children.

This sense of control is the source of many of your painful feelings. You may be angry that your baby died in spite of happier plans; you may feel guilty you could not prevent it; you may feel there must be something wrong with you that such a terrible thing could happen. If you interrupted the pregnancy or refused medical heroics, you may feel an additional sense of responsibility that can heighten these feelings. You may agonize over the questions "Why me? Why my baby?" You want answers to ensure more control in the future.

Another approach is to realize that you don't always have the power to prevent bad things from happening to you and that misfortune can strike even when you least expect it. This vulnerability to tragedy can be a terrifying feeling to face.

To avoid the fear and helplessness that come with vulnerability, you may want to hold on to anger, guilt or failure for a while. These emotions protect that comfortable illusion of being in total control. Later, as you begin adjusting to your baby's death, you will come to the painful realization that you don't have control over everything that happens in your life.

You may also hold on to anger or guilt as a way to avoid sadness and despair. If grieving is like a roller coaster, profound sadness and despair are at the bottom of the deepest dips. These emotions are so painful that you may try to build bridges so you don't have to plummet so far down. Feelings like anger and guilt can serve as bridges.

You may wonder, "Why shouldn't I use these bridges to avoid feeling the depths of despair?" Unfortunately, holding on to these feelings forever can be incapacitating. Guilt and failure can eat away at your feelings of self-worth. Anger can interfere with your enjoyment of life. You are entitled to say, "How can I ever feel good about myself and enjoy life—MY BABY IS DEAD!" But as time goes on, you may become weary of being angry or guilty and want to move on. This can be a sign that you are ready to tackle your sadness and despair over your baby's death.

Sadness and despair can be excruciatingly painful. These feelings can make you feel broken, discouraged and overwhelmed. You may be afraid that if you start crying, you may never stop. But, in fact, you may notice that if you really take the time and energy to cry, to think about your baby and your loss, to really feel the pain, then you can also feel relief from holding these powerful emotions inside.

One way that you might try to get in touch with your sadness and despair is to drop the defenses of failure, guilt and anger. First, try to replace the failure or guilt with anger, and then replace the anger with sadness. For example, if you feel failure or guilt about not being with your baby when he or she died, you might try saying, "I feel angry that I wasn't with my baby when he (or she) died." After you say that a while, you might be able to let yourself feel angry. Then, after you are comfortable feeling angry, replace "angry" with "sad" or "hurt": "I feel sad (or hurt) that I wasn't with my baby when he (or she) died." Then let yourself express those painful feelings of sadness.

Parents have found other ways to get in touch with the deep feelings of grief. For several months after her daughter died, Stephanie made sure that every morning before doing anything else, she would look at Jamie's pictures, talk to her, cry and write about her feelings in a journal. She discovered that by doing this she felt better and was able to get through the day more easily. Likewise, Kitty knew that when she was feeling stress, she needed to take the time to go through her "memory box" where she kept pictures and mementos of her baby. Tearfully she would examine the keepsakes. Afterward she would feel better, relieved of the tension. You may discover your own rituals to help you release your deepest feelings of grief.

There were times when I made it hurt. I'd look at the pictures and I'd want to hurt and I couldn't figure out why, but I guess I knew I needed to grieve. I'd get out the pictures and I'd read stories and I'd go to her grave and I'd cry and I'd hurt. I'd feel the pain like it had just happened. And now I can't feel that pain anymore. I can look at the pictures, I can do everything I would have done a year ago, and it doesn't hurt like it did. It's just, I've dealt with it. If I hadn't done that, the pain would still be in there and I wouldn't even be able to talk about it. And then it would be harder to deal with. I believe that as the years go on, if you don't let it out, it's going to be harder.

—Cindy

I made myself do what I had to do to get through it. I think the reason I feel as good as I do now is because I made myself grieve for my son, by forcing myself to confront how I was feeling. As your grieving goes on, when you first cry, you cry all the time. After a while you can stop your tears and put them away, but I *always* took them back out again and I made myself look at my picture of Jamie and I made myself read all the literature and I *made* myself grieve for him. Grieving is not fun. It's very easy not to, it's very easy to go on, go to the movies or change the subject. It's something that you have to force yourself to do, and I think because I did, that is the reason I feel so much better now.

—Sarah

While some parents immerse themselves in grief, others bury themselves in work or extra activities. But the outcomes can be different: Parents who give themselves time and permission to grieve are more likely to feel they are on the road to recovery. Those who hold back may eventually recognize that their lives are still compromised by the grief they have tried to avoid. (For more ideas and support, see "Reclaiming Your Emotions" in chapter 9.)

Holly, Lena and Anya provide testimony to the fact that grief is hard work and takes time, but the more it is expressed, the easier it may be in the long run.

I think I've been in a fog for two entire years. I have functioned beautifully to the outside world and pulled an incredible workload and accomplished an incredible amount of things, but personally I've just been in a fog. It's amazing to me that I've pulled it off, but I think by avoiding grief, I've caused myself more agony.

—Holly

I immediately immersed myself in volunteer work as an escape mechanism. I kept myself so busy that I didn't have time to think. At the time I think that's what was needed. I didn't want to wallow in self-pity. I did bury a lot of my feelings and I'm sure there are some feelings I haven't even come to grips with. I still feel a little pit in my stomach when I think about it, so I know there still must be something there. I probably should go back to counseling, but I don't have time.

—Lena

I've learned it's OK to let yourself hurt. You may feel that you're falling apart and going crazy, but it's OK. You'll come back together again.

—Anya

Failure

Feelings of failure arise when you believe there was something you could have done better or more competently. If you have trouble conceiving or if there were problems with your uterus, cervix, hormone levels or placenta, or if things went wrong during labor or delivery, you may feel like your body failed you. If the baby was born with genetic anomalies, you and your partner may feel a great sense of failure that your genes are somehow defective. You may question your ability to bear a healthy child or worry that you don't deserve to be parents. You may wonder if you are a failure as a woman or a man.

I felt really betrayed by my body. I felt like there was something wrong with me physically that I could not complete a pregnancy, and that got to be a goal almost as much as having a baby—to complete a pregnancy successfully. I just really hated my body for a while. I felt like it just wasn't working right.

—Jessie

I don't like the term *incompetent cervix*. It sounds like I got an *F* in the class. Incompetent. I've never been incompetent at anything in my life!

—Lena

Some mothers feel an intensified sense of failure because they have experienced prolonged infertility, complicated pregnancies, the death of more than one baby, or the death of one or more babies from a multiple gestation. Or perhaps they are also raising a child with birth defects or problems associated with prematurity. When a survivor from a multiple pregnancy has health problems or developmental delay, this invites a whole new level of questions and regrets.

Everybody was so excited because we were having twins. So when Jeffrey died, I felt so sorry because I was disappointing everyone. Like I was letting people down ... I was worried what people would think, like, "You fool, you can't do anything right."

—Shannon

I had a lot of problems with each pregnancy and for a long time I thought that I was a sinful person or just one who didn't deserve to have these kids.

—Meryl

Sometimes I've really felt a lot of failure because both my other kids have problems. ... So you know, you just feel like you haven't done anything right. I've felt like I couldn't make a baby right!

—Rayleen

About having babies, I feel like I'm not a pro, let me tell you! The thought of having another baby, trying again, scares the hell out of me. Because of not just Nicole, but the miscarriages and premature births. So I guess I do feel like I'm not the best baby producer.

—Cindy

Horrible feelings of failure—that I couldn't carry a pregnancy to term, that I couldn't keep two babies alive, that my body had bailed out on me. I had tried to do all the things you're supposed to do and it hadn't worked. My next pregnancy went fine, but it wasn't twins. It was a one-baby kind of thing.

—Anya

If you are blessed with another baby, this can help to boost feelings of competence and worth. Dara talks about how relieved and reassured she felt: "That we could have a healthy baby was a big thing. With Laurie, the relief was the greatest, being able to have a normal female."

Unfortunately, as some of these mothers discovered, having a healthy baby or another set of twins or triplets isn't easy or even possible. If this is the case, you may feel terribly disheartened. Do remember that whatever happens, you are *a mother* or even, for example, *a mother of a daughter* or *a mother of twins,* and that will never be taken away from you.

Also remember, having another baby or set of babies isn't the only way to ease a sense of defeat and acquire some faith in yourself again. There are a number of ways mothers have found to cope with and work through their uncomfortable feelings of failure.

- Write in a journal. Just putting feelings down on paper can help you feel better, by freeing you of the burden of holding them inside and perhaps giving you the insights you need to feel better about yourself.

- Renew hobbies and other interests. Go back to work. By engaging in activities in which you feel competent, you can regain feelings of self-worth.
- Talk to someone. It helps to talk to someone who is supportive—your partner, a good friend, a clergyperson or a counselor who can accept your feelings and reassure you that you are still a good mother and a good person.
- Accept yourself and your body. Many bereaved mothers learn to accept that they are imperfect. It is healthier to realize you are imperfect than to always strive to be perfect. Perfection is never achieved, whereas imperfection allows you to feel good and worthy for just who you are.

Remember, bad things happen to good people without stripping them of their goodness. Regardless of what has happened to you, you are still a worthwhile person and a good mother who deserves the best life has to offer.

Anger

Anger is a powerful and valid emotion that may consume you at times. You may feel angry at medical technology or the doctors and nurses. "Could they have prevented my baby's death?" "Why did they keep critical information from me?" You may be furious with the injustices of the world, fate, God or Mother Nature. "Why did this have to happen to me and my baby?" You may feel aggravated with pregnant women in general, especially those who seem to produce healthy babies effortlessly despite abominable habits during pregnancy. Sophie remarks, "I'd see or hear about moms that smoke and drink too much when they're pregnant and they have these perfectly healthy babies. I had a perfectly healthy pregnancy and I ate all my proteins and my vegetables and vitamins, and Stephanie wasn't here. It seemed so unfair."

You may also resent mothers with healthy babies if you think they are not being as kind and nurturing as you imagine yourself to be. You may wonder, "Why do other mothers get to keep their babies when I am equally or more deserving than they are?" You may even feel anger at your baby. As Erin admits, "Sometimes I'm a little resentful toward my baby for doing this to me. It wasn't very fair of her." It is unfair to carry a baby—whether for three months or nine or into infancy—only to be cheated, denied from keeping him or her.

Thanksgiving came and I was screaming mad, saying, "What do I have to be thankful for!" because I had lost David, then had a miscarriage and then I wasn't pregnant and was having trouble getting pregnant and I felt there was nothing to be thankful for. I had lost my baby and that was the cruelest thing ever. I felt so cheated that we had wanted that baby so badly and we were going to be such wonderful parents and then to have him taken away. ... I shouldn't have carried a baby full term and then not be able to keep him. The point is, he should be with us right now, we should all be together and he's still not with us, so I think that part is always going to hurt because he'll never be with us.

—Bess

I could not hold a baby. I didn't want to be around babies and anyone that had a baby. I wanted to shoot them. It was a terrible feeling. That's why I think having Robin has helped a lot because now I've got another baby, and now other people can have babies too and it's OK, but back then it wasn't.

—Martina

Being around pregnant women or babies can be intolerable. It arouses the resentment and envy you have, drawing attention to the fact that another person has a baby and you don't. You may try to avoid them, but they appear almost everywhere you go.

If you lost one or more babies from a multiple pregnancy, your anger may focus on the lost chance for the special experience of raising babies together. And since people notice and celebrate twins, triplets, quads and quints, you may feel surrounded by tributes to successful multiple births.

I look at all those people who can have twins and it's maddening. And it seems like it's popular now to have twins. They're everywhere, on TV, all these famous people are having them, like Jane Pauley and Cybill Shepherd. Or that woman who lives nearby, she had 5 babies and they're just fine. Why not me?

—Shannon

If you are raising any survivors from a multiple birth, you may have feelings of anger or envy toward these babies as their strength or luck might have contributed to the others' demise. If sicker babies survived, you may feel resentful that you spent so much time at their bedsides, robbing you of time that you now wish had been spent with a stronger baby or babies who died unexpectedly.

You may also feel angry at the circumstances that surrounded your baby's death: the medical care you received, the lack of information, or the fact that you were not encouraged to hold your baby at all or weren't offered more time with your baby or did not receive a photograph or other mementos. Someone may suggest that you bring a lawsuit against the hospital or the doctors, but most parents agree with Desi: " ... that's not going to bring the baby back."

I was very angry, boy was I mad. I bet I was *nothing* but mad for like a week. I was just furious. I was furious at everything. I was furious at the weather. I was so mad about this particular thing, beta strep. Two years before my son was born they decided to stop testing for it routinely because it was statistically insignificant, the number of babies who got that. That made me so mad I just kept getting madder and madder, and I was just so sad. It was just awful. It was the worst thing I've ever gone through.

—Sarah

It's bad enough when your baby dies, but the care we got afterwards was just horrible. ... They weren't that smart at this particular hospital. My Lamaze teacher dropped off the book *When Hello Means Goodbye* that made me realize that I should do all these things, like having a picture ... I wanted these things, and the next morning I asked for mementos ... they said it was too late.

—Holly

My husband had gone to check on Nicholas in the NICU and the nurse was charting. There was only my daughter and I. She laid peacefully in the incubator and I was comforted knowing we were together. Then the nurse gave me some morphine for pain—I did not want it. I'll never forgive them for giving me that. While I drifted in and out of sleep, the funeral home man came for my sweet Jessica. When I awoke—she was gone! Didn't they know, I could handle the physical pain, it's the emotional pain that is unbearable? Why did I sleep and lose that valuable time with Jessica?

—Sheila

I still feel angry that we didn't go up to visit the baby in the hospital. I wish now we had. ... Nobody encouraged us to. We had planned to go up on the weekend and Elisa died on Friday, and it never occurred to us really to go up after she died. ... Now I think my anger is not that it happened, but now it's the things I wish I'd known to do then that I know I would do now.

—Dara

One of the best ways to cope with anger is to find constructive ways to express it. Many people hold in their anger, for fear that its expression will be too destructive. Indeed, expressing anger in destructive ways only makes things worse because you have to deal with the consequences—feeling pain, apologizing, cleaning up, buying costly replacements, repairing damaged relationships. Unfortunately, holding in anger is not a solution—it can result in prolonged depression, ill health, hurtful outbursts, substance abuse or other compulsive behaviors. Remember, you are entitled to nasty, angry feelings and fantasies. Don't try to control your emotions and thoughts, control your *behavior*. Express your feelings in ways that will not hurt you, other people or valued property. There are a number of nondestructive ways parents have found to express and work through their anger.

- Engage in vigorous exercise. Even a brisk walk can help reduce tension.
- Write an angry letter (you don't have to mail it) to anyone: to your doctor, to God, to fate, to your baby.
- Write in a journal about your angry feelings and thoughts or your fantasies about destructive, vengeful acts.
- Draw a picture that depicts your anger or the revenge you seek.
- Work with clay or Play-Doh; kneading, punching and sculpting can offer release.
- Throw a ball up against a wall.
- Punch pillows.
- Drape a rug over a clothesline and beat it with a broom handle.
- Beat a towel against a hard surface.
- Dig and yank the weeds out of your garden.
- Clean house with a vengeance.
- Throw things, such as plastic containers and other non-breakables.
- Buy old dishes at yard sales and find a safe place to smash them.
- Scream and yell when you are alone.
- Air your grievances and make suggestions to specific people or institutions with whom you are angry.
- Talk to your partner or a friend who can support and validate your anger.
- Talk to other bereaved parents who share your anger.
- Remember that anger is an energy to be mined, not buried in shame.

These methods have helped many parents cope with angry feelings. You may find your own effective, nondestructive ways to express anger. By acknowledging and expressing it, you can perhaps loosen its grip on you and move closer toward forgiveness. Forgiveness comes when you can understand another's frailty, impotence or harshness in the face of your baby's illness and death. Forgiveness comes when you can accept someone's fear, ignorance or inadequacy in the face of your grief. Your anger is valid, but you also deserve the peace that comes when you work through it and let it go.

I practiced expressing anger this week. I threw the adding machine tape, I threw plastic bottles down the stairs, I yelled at a solicitor for baby products on the phone. When I felt angry, I took it out right then on whatever was at hand.

—Janet

Guilt

Along with failure and anger, guilt arises from the belief that you are in total control of your life. When you are pregnant, you take good care of yourself in the belief that if you are healthy, follow your doctor's advice, avoid consuming dangerous substances and monitor your baby's every move, you will deliver a healthy baby. When you do have a healthy baby, you vow to comfort and protect this child for as long as you live.

When fate takes an unexpected, tragic direction, you may wonder if there was something you did or did not do that may have contributed to your baby's problems. It is natural to feel primarily responsible for your baby's well-being. Because that baby was inside your body or under your protective care, you may have fantasies about what you might have done to prevent these problems. When you believe you should have total control, it is easy to feel angry at yourself when things go wrong.

My initial reaction was, of course, "What did I do? I know I must be responsible for this and what could it have been?" So I felt guilty, but I didn't know quite how to focus that guilt because I didn't know what I had done. I had a wonderful pediatrician who actually called me a month and a half later to make sure that I wasn't feeling guilty. And the neonatologist and obstetrician kept laying facts in front of me and saying, "There is *no way* that you were responsible for this. You couldn't be responsible." They helped me through that.

—Sarah

I felt as though either I had done something to deserve this baby dying or I had done something physically to cause her death or that there was something wrong with me that they hadn't noticed. ... I felt the guilt any parent feels when something happens to their child. You're responsible for that child and you're supposed to protect them and take care of them, and I felt like I had fallen down on the job.

—Jessie

Even when your doctor reassures you that there was nothing you could have done differently or even if you *know* that your baby's death is not your fault, you may still have nagging feelings that there was something you should have done differently or that you let your baby down in some way. Especially if you tend to get angry at yourself over things that happen, you are likely to feel some guilt about your baby. Some mothers feel guilty for ever being aggravated with the baby or that they somehow failed to be a good mother. Some mothers think they are getting paid back for "bad" things they've done in the past. Others feel guilty because of difficult decisions, such as interrupting the pregnancy or disconnecting life-support systems (see "Living with the Decision" in chapter 8 for more information on this). Sarah sums up her guilt: "I wasn't there to hold him when he died— I failed him. I had all these hormones that were trying to be mothering and here was my big opportunity and I blew it. And everybody said, 'Well, he didn't know if you were there or not.' But who knows? I felt like I really failed him."

Because guilt is anger toward yourself, it can be self-destructive. It doesn't allow you to feel good about yourself and can be a source of chronic depression. It may even make you wonder if you deserved this tragedy. But, of course, nobody deserves the tragedy of having a baby die. Unfortunately, bad things can happen to anyone, without warning. We cannot always avoid tragedy or know ahead of time the right course of action.

Working through feelings of guilt can be difficult. You need to

- consider that *feeling* guilty is not the same as *being* guilty,
- let yourself off the hook,
- accept that you did the best you could,
- remember that you made the best decisions you could based on information available,
- realize you cannot always prevent bad things from happening, and
- talk to others who can reassure you that you are not to blame.

You want to control things. You feel like you should be able to control things. Did I do something wrong? People would tell me if you lift your arms above your head, that it's supposed to choke your baby or something. And that was a bunch of ... that was so stupid. But all those things went through my mind. Did I ever lift my arms up? Did I ever bend over wrong? You know, *what did I do?* And I didn't do anything. It took a long time and I just realized, she would have died regardless of what I did. And me rolling around on the floor is not going to tie her cord in a knot, that was Nicole's doing. I couldn't have reached my hands in there and untied it or know—how could I know unless I had an ultrasound machine, and even then you can't see the cord. There's no way that anybody could've known.

—Cindy

I think that you feel out of control with almost any death, when you realize that we don't have control. I mean, that we do and we don't. I go back and forth on that. ... Right after Heidi died I'd been confronted about my guilt over her death, and I go back and forth between wanting to take responsibility and saying, "Hey, come on, I did not cause this, this cannot be my responsibility."

—Holly

I wallowed in guilt for a long time. I elicited feedback from other people to the contrary—my therapist, my husband—and I commiserated with other mothers from the support group who understood that feeling. I still feel guilty every once in a while. I think that I've mostly let go of it because even if there was anything I could have done, and I think that right now I feel like there was, but that's past history and right now it's not going to do me any good—or my baby any good—to stay stuck in that place.

—Jessie

Even if you have a strong feeling that you did something wrong, you can still get to a point where you accept the fact that you made a mistake, an error in judgment, and forgive yourself for being imperfect. To do this, you need to find a way to express and let go of your pain. One way is to write down your thoughts and feelings of doubt and recrimination. Write every day, for as many days as you require, until you can forgive yourself. Write until you can look in the mirror and say "My baby was very fortunate to have me for a mother." This may seem like an insurmountable task, but the reward is great. You and your baby deserve a bond full of love and joy, not suffering and regret. While you are entitled to your guilt, by working through it, you can live peacefully with yourself and honorably with your baby.

They were going to disconnect the life support and asked if we wanted to be there, and I said, "No." What a LOUSY decision that was, but I did the best I could. ... But for two years I beat myself up for that a million times over. For probably a good year and a half, I didn't even really deal with my guilt. It was so painful to me that it wasn't until way towards the end of my real grieving time that I was even strong enough to cope with that. It was just admitting to myself that I had done this stupid thing. It was awful. ... I probably worked on it for six weeks in therapy, where I was finally able to let myself off the hook for it. Now I'm able to objectively say I did the best I could in that situation. I would never do it again and a part of me still wishes I hadn't done that.

—Sarah

I felt guilty at first. It took me a long time to work through that. I was very active and at times I've felt like, "Gee, if I had REALLY rested and if I had really stayed in bed, this probably wouldn't have happened." To this day I could probably say to you that I still feel maybe if I had followed the rules a little bit more, I probably wouldn't have lost the baby. But, you know, I feel that that was me at the time, like it was a different person back then and she could have probably done a lot of things to make the pregnancy better but she didn't, and I forgive her.

—Elaine

Some mothers work through their guilt by eventually turning their anger away from themselves and toward someone else, making their anger less destructive to their self-esteem. Many mothers turn their anger toward their obstetrician or pediatrician, fate or God.

I felt guilty. But the only reason I blamed myself was because I was the only person who had contact with the baby, so I must have been the reason why he died. ... I couldn't blame God because I needed Him too much to lean on, so then finally after going to the support group I got to where I blamed the doctor, and that's where I've stayed.

—Desi

It was my first pregnancy and I didn't know, I thought my labor was starting. I called the hospital and said, "I'm getting really weird pains. I think maybe I should be checked. I don't know what's going on." The doctor said, "Don't worry about it." And I still am mad about that because I think, "If I would've gone in, they would have seen the stress and they would have gotten her out."

—Cindy

Remember, whatever reasoning you come up with, YOU DID THE BEST YOU COULD AT THE TIME. Like most mothers, you are incapable of knowingly endangering your baby. Working through feelings of guilt involves realizing that you cannot always prevent tragedy from happening and that you cannot always avoid making mistakes.

Vulnerability

Like many people, you probably thought that with enough foresight and good judgment you could avoid tragedy. Perhaps you believed that living well, being a good person or devoting yourself to religious faith would protect you. Then, when your baby died, you were naturally overcome with questions: "How could this happen?" "What did I do wrong?"

At first, you may be reluctant to accept that the cause of your baby's problems is unknown or that they couldn't be prevented. You can't believe that nothing in particular should have been done differently. You search for the answer to the question "Why me, why my baby?" But as the futility of the situation sinks in, you will discover that you were powerless. This can be quite unsettling and aggravating. As Hannah reports, "It felt like a bolt out of the sky." Even if there are things you would do differently, the fact that hindsight is the only way to see this can be very unnerving. Alas, it is not possible to have 20/20 foresight.

Gradually, as you begin to let yourself off the hook and accept your (and other people's) imperfections and limitations, you will shed the belief that you should have total control over what happens. You will realize that life is unfair and that you are vulnerable to tragedy.

While this vulnerability can be frightening, eventually you will find a balance between feeling powerless and maintaining control over your life. You also will acquire the sense of peace that accompanies "letting go." Letting go is casting off the idea that you have to be on guard, cover all your bases and be in charge of everything around you. Letting go also means you stop regretting the past and you fear less for the future. Instead of adjusting everything to your desires, you learn to take each day as it comes and cherish the time you have. You stop striving for perfection and learn to accept yourself for the very one you are. As you can see, letting go also means you will worry less, not more. (For more on worry see "Overprotectiveness" in chapter 15.)

Many parents simply come to accept the fact that sometimes horrible things happen. Rose notes, "If you think you're protected, it's a real comforting feeling but you're naive. Some people go through their whole lives without anything bad happening to them. It just means they're lucky and when something bad does happen, I guess people try to interpret it a million ways but I think it just happens." Likewise, you will come to understand that death does not mock or thwart you. It is simply a fact of life, unavoidable and not always under our control. Terri reflects, "I know some people consider this callous or too fatalistic, but I really think that everybody picks a number and when your number is up, it's up."

> When I asked, "Why me?" I don't know that I ever got an answer. At first I blamed the doctor because he didn't care. Now I just feel like it was fate. You don't know what to think, but that's kind of where I've left it.
>
> —Erin

> This experience was good for me in the sense that it taught me that you can't think that things go a certain way just necessarily because you do all the right things.
>
> —Anya

> When it first happened, I was terrified of the future. I couldn't stand the thought of bad things happening in my life. Well, now

that it's been four years and nothing bad has happened, I have Leslie now, and everything's been positive. That makes it much easier to deal with it. But I'm still afraid.

—Bryn

You really feel like you don't have any control anymore, and there is a real loss of ego there. For a while I just felt like I shouldn't make any plans because something could happen and it could just wipe everything away. Now I feel more confident. I feel like I might as well make a lot of plans and if they don't work out, at least I had the enjoyment of making them.

—Rose

Points to Remember

- Feelings of anger, guilt and failure arise from the belief that you are always in control of your destiny.
- You can find healthy ways to express and cope with these feelings. If you feel angry, learn to express it in nondestructive ways. If you feel guilty, learn to forgive yourself. Nobody is perfect; nobody can predict the future. If you feel failure, learn to reassure yourself that you are worthwhile.
- For a while, these feelings of anger, guilt or failure can shield you from feelings of deep sadness or vulnerability, but eventually, holding on to them will become incapacitating.
- Getting in touch with your deep sadness and despair is difficult, but it frees you from the destructive clutches of anger, guilt and failure.
- Do whatever helps you to move your grief, and hence your healing, to deeper levels.
- Accept human vulnerability. Tragedies occur, and we don't have control over everything that happens to us.
- Eventually you will find a balance between maintaining control over your life and accepting the limitations.

7

Resolution of Grief

A resolution of grief occurs when you are able to accept the fact that your baby is gone and you begin to integrate this loss appropriately into your life. Resolution does *not* signal an end to grief. You will always feel longing and sadness. Eventually, though, these feelings may mellow to the point that you can feel peaceful when you remember your baby.

As resolution brings some relief from mourning, it enables you to move on with your life in healthy, functional ways. You can find happiness, reinvest your energy in satisfying relationships and pursuits, and feel a renewed sense of hope for the future.

At first, it may seem impossible to accept and integrate your baby's death into your life. In the midst of overwhelming despair, it is difficult to imagine ever being able to think about your baby and the circumstances surrounding the death without suffering. But, as the intensity of the experience fades, acceptance can feel comfortable. Bereaved parents often consider this the hallmark of resolution.

> Just gradually over time it felt for the most part that I could accept it, I could live with it, it was not nearly as painful. It's something I feel sad about and I have regrets that it happened, but it's not anything I feel angry or guilty about anymore. It hurts, but it's OK—an important point to get to and it's not a point I could have understood, I think, before she died, that something can hurt horribly but it's all right.
>
> —Anya

Some parents mistakenly equate a lack of emotional pain with the completion of grief work. Although they say they *feel* resolved, they are hiding from their own feelings, as if there is nothing to be sad about or as though it happened to someone else. This avoidance can create other problems, including substance abuse or failure to maintain nurturing relationships. (See "Numbness and Shock" in chapter 2.)

At the opposite extreme, there are parents who hold on to their grief as a way of giving their life meaning, or as a way to hold on to the baby. Some parents worry that if they stop feeling angry about their baby's death, then somehow they're admitting defeat. Others believe that if they are not despondent, they are being disloyal or desecrating their baby's life. By holding on to these grieving patterns, some parents feel reassured that they will never forget their baby.

It is important to recognize that you can remember, love and miss your baby without grieving continuously. You can go ahead in life without forgetting your past.

> Sometimes I feel happy or proud, and other times just sad. It's all mixed. I can have good thoughts about her, kind of a resolved thing. Even when I feel grief it's not a desperate feeling, it's a comfortable feeling. I know she's dead and I can't get her back. I don't have those Oh–I–can't–stand–it–get–her–back–here! feelings as if I could pull her out of the air if I had enough faith, if I gritted my teeth hard enough or whatever. I can't describe exactly how I feel because it's always up and down, but resolved means I can look at her picture and not burst into tears. ... She's just one of my daughters. The subject is pretty much closed. There's nothing to say. It's all over. I can't bring her back. But it's definitely not like I've put her in a closet and closed the door.
>
> —Rose

> It's a relief. I feel peaceful. I know he's with God and my tormenting is over, but I still love him. He's not forgotten. That's another thing I was afraid of. I thought, "I've got to keep this up, keep grieving so that I don't forget him. I don't want anybody to forget him." But you don't have to be miserable to remember.
>
> —Desi

> I don't think that we ever really get *over* losing a child, but we do somehow get *through* it.
>
> —Ginger

The Journey to Resolution

How Long Will It Take?

Although there is no definite time frame, resolution can take several years. Within the first year or two, many mothers report that the initial hard edges of pain gradually soften. Over time they notice that they don't cry as easily or they are able to look at infants or pregnant women without acute envy. As sad as it is, this experience becomes something to live with on a private, interior level. Martina found that it became less difficult to think or talk about her baby. She remarks, "When I think about him it's not something that is so bold like it was before, that when you start thinking about him you just have to stop everything because you're in a daze for a week." Sarah noticed that instead of focusing on her baby's death, it became a part of her history, a part that will always exist but one that no longer occupies center stage. Peg agrees: "It fades a little bit to the background. I still think about the twins quite a bit and I'm sad and I wish that it hadn't happened, but it just doesn't hurt as much as time goes on."

After your emotional pain fades and your concentration shifts, feelings of acceptance and integration follow. When your grief ceases to tear at you and the longing subsides, you will find that you can have happy thoughts about your baby's short life. Jessie notes, "Now it feels like an unfortunate event that changed me forever. I'll always remember her and be sad that she's not living with us, but happy that we had her for a while." Meryl remarks, "The yearning, the little bit of grief will always be there, but I don't feel it that much anymore. I feel at peace, it's just accepted, it's OK."

Unfortunately, the road to resolution is a bumpy one, and there are no shortcuts. The softening of grief and the acceptance of your tragedy don't always build in a smooth, steady progression. There are ups and downs and heartache along the way, whether it takes several months or several years. Anya remembers the first day she didn't cry for Rachel—seven months after her death. She admits, "I never would have thought it would take that long." Cindy remembers the first year as the worst: " ... the depression, the ups and downs, probably lasted three years. ... Then, as the years go on, it gets easier. People would tell me it gets better with time, but that first year I was sure I would feel that way until I died."

Liza also remembers feeling much better after the first year, but still distrusting the ups because, "as soon as I'd feel really good one day, then almost for sure I'd be right back as bad as ever the next day. It took another year before I felt like there was any plateau." Even so, in the third year, she notes, "I could have a good month and then something would happen, and I'd feel like I was right back again." Bryn remembers it took her a full three years before she could be happy for pregnant friends or see newborn babies. Sarah, five years later, can finally enjoy watching "tearjerker" movies again. She says, "The crying stops when the sad part is over. I can cry again and not be afraid of crying ... just tears for fun." Maya, also five years down the road, describes her experience this way: "Grief is like working on this giant jigsaw puzzle. You work very hard to put it together, and every now and then it feels like it's thrown up in the air and it comes down in pieces. Again, you put it back together, but it's not as bad as starting over, and you may even put it back together a little better."

Is It OK to Feel Unresolved?

If you are unable to find a comfortable place for your baby and the grief you feel, you may simply need more time to work through all the painful emotions. Your grief may be too fresh for you to feel at peace. You may believe you will never be able to accept your baby's death because, as Bess says, " 'Accepted' means you go along with it." Bryn agrees: "I did not want to accept that this bad thing had happened and that I was going to have to live with this terrible thing for the rest of my life."

It may be hard to find anything positive in this experience. You may believe that your baby's death will never make sense. Hannah notes, "I can't say what it means or that it was meant to be—that just doesn't fit for me. I just think it's always going to be sad."

In spite of what people may tell you, there is no hard evidence to support the idea that feeling unresolved is bad or pathological or unhealthy in itself. As you work through the denial, yearning, anger, guilt, sadness, hurt and despair, naturally you feel unresolved. Yet this is a relatively healthy state of affairs, because you are facing grief instead of hiding from it; you are heading toward resolution instead of circumventing it. It may take several years to reach resolution, but in the meantime, life goes on and you learn to live with anger, sadness and the natural protest against this tragedy.

So although your grief may be unresolved and you may even wish you could feel better, if you can face your grief most of the time, if you are able to express a wide range of feelings and if you feel you are making progress as time goes on, then you may be on your way toward resolution.

On the other hand, if you feel as though you are fighting grief, hiding from it or hanging on to it, you may not be making progress toward resolution. Laura and Holly feel this keenly:

I feel like there's a fire-breathing dragon in a box and I'm tossing drops of water on it and trying to force the lid shut. I'm fighting grief, not at peace.

—Laura

It is frustrating to me to think that although I know the pain or the caring never goes away, in a sense I think it should be easier for me now, or I wonder, "Am I hanging on to this and being more negative or sad than is healthy or than I should be?"

—Holly

What If I Have a Surviving Baby?

Typically, mothers who are raising a surviving baby or babies from a multiple pregnancy are distracted from grief. On the one hand, you may feel like you have far too much spare time, considering that you expected to be busy day and night with multiple babies. On the other hand, the time and energy demands of parenting your surviving baby(s) can put grieving on a back burner. Particularly if a survivor is ill, you may put aside your grief completely until the health of that baby is assured.

Perhaps you think and talk about the baby or babies who died, but it doesn't pack the emotional wallop that you think it should. Perhaps you are hounded by feelings of sadness or anger, but are afraid to see their source.

Perhaps you harbor vague but nagging feelings of dissatisfaction with your life. As Shannon reveals, "I feel unsettled. Should I go to school, have a job, get a career, or what? My life has changed so much in the past year and it's not that I'm unhappy, but ... maybe this *is* because of Jeffrey."

You may even wonder whether you are delaying your grief. You probably are, and this is OK. As your surviving baby gets older, your emotional priorities will shift and you'll deal with it when you are ready. In the meantime, as long as you can think and talk about the baby(s) who died, you are dealing with it to an important extent. Do remember that, like any bereaved parent, it is essential for you to set aside time and space to grieve. Having a survivor does not take away your need to do so. Taking the opportunity to grieve promptly and as best you can will benefit you and your parenting. (For more support and ideas, see "Toddlers—Under 3 Years" in chapter 11.)

> I don't really cry anymore but I can't believe I'm over it. I still feel
> bad and I think about Jeffrey, but I don't cry. And normally I'm
> very sentimental and cry very easily. I cried a lot the first month
> while Bradley [the surviving baby] was still in intensive care. But
> once he came home, and for the past year, I've been forced to move
> on. It's so strange because you're so busy and tied up with the other
> one. Having Bradley doesn't give me the opportunity to dwell on
> Jeffrey.
>
> —Shannon

How Do I Resolve My Grief?

To resolve your grief, you must go through the grieving process, that is, work through your denial, anger, guilt, hurt, despair and other painful feelings. By grieving, you can come to terms with your loss and eventually learn to accept that your baby is gone and adjust to a new life without him or her.

It is natural to want to avoid painful feelings, but in order to heal, you must go through the grief, experiencing and expressing all your difficult emotions. In this way, reaching resolution depends on the quality of your grief work. There are a number of ways to ensure that you work through the grieving process.

- Have realistic expectations about yourself and grieving. If you are informed about what to expect and what is normal for a grieving person, you are more apt to have the patience and tolerance for your reactions and emotions. Recognize that your grief is exactly that—*yours*. Do not let others decide how you should feel. Don't measure your grief against anyone else's. You need to find your own path and do what is best for *you*.

- Give yourself permission to experience all of your emotions and thoughts. Some of these may seem unacceptable to you, but if you have them, *you are entitled to them.* By burying or avoiding them, you only give them more power to compromise your life and your happiness. By expressing them constructively, you empower yourself to get through grief and eventually make life meaningful again. Rationalizing or intellectualizing them won't suffice. You must express your emotions from your heart and your gut, not just your mind. (For more ideas and support, see "Reclaiming Your Emotions" in chapter 9.)
- Identify all your different emotions. Separating them makes them more manageable and easier to cope with, instead of burdening you with a huge, confusing mixture of pain. By focusing on individual emotions, you may also figure out their source and get to the bottom of what you are feeling. Label your emotions specifically—anger, guilt, anxiety, despair. Once you do this you can start finding relief from them. You may also need to uncover the anger, hurt and other feelings from previous losses—the unfinished grief from your past. By lessening this emotional confusion, you can express and work through your feelings instead of getting stuck or going around in circles.
- Dwell on your memories and your hopes and dreams of what might have been. By reviewing your experiences and your fantasies, you can identify what you have lost and then gradually let go of your emotional investment. You may need to remember and talk about these memories and expectations over and over as you adjust to the fact that your baby is gone and your life has changed. At first, idealizing your baby is normal. Eventually it will be important for you to remember the good times and the bad and to recognize that no baby is the perfect child. Having a realistic image of your baby can ease the letting go. This eventual letting go is what enables you to focus your emotional energy toward a new future.
- Identify the things you regret not doing with your baby and find appropriate ways to have closure. For instance, if you did not have a chance to hold your baby or show your love in certain ways, you will need to express your sorrow or find ways to express this love. You may want to talk about how you feel with supportive friends or other bereaved parents, write a letter to your baby, or go to the grave or the place where you scattered or keep the ashes and talk to your baby. If you had looked forward to experiencing special occasions or the holiday season with your baby, you can engage in rituals that let you feel close to your baby: Lighting a candle, displaying an ornament,

reading a special poem or making donations in your baby's name are all ways to give meaning to these times when you especially miss your baby.

- Take care of yourself as you grieve. Give yourself opportunities to be alone and cry. Be patient with yourself. Allow for the time and energy it takes and for your uneven progress. Find ways to reduce stress, including good nutrition, exercise, relaxation and giving yourself breaks from grief—allowing yourself to enjoy other aspects of your life. For at least the first year, try to avoid making significant changes in your life. Major changes may only increase your stress and multiply the adjustments you must make.

- Get the social support you need. Grieving in isolation is more painful and makes reaching resolution more difficult. Let others help and nurture you. You deserve their comfort and kindness. At the same time, be assertive and tell people what you need. Don't expect them to read your mind. Find people who can listen and accept your feelings and thoughts. (See "Friends" in chapter 12.)

- Have realistic ideas about what resolution means. Remember that you aren't giving up or forgetting your baby. Resolution doesn't mean you will never feel grief again or that it's OK that this happened, nor does it mean you will return to the way things were before. Continued suffering and misery are not proof of your devotion to your baby. Healthy grief and resolution mean adjusting to a new future while remembering and finding appropriate ways to feel connected to your baby.

How Do I Know If I Am Reaching Resolution?

Bereavement experts such as John Bowlby, Edgar Jackson, Ronald J. Knapp, Colin Murray Parkes, Therese Rando and Simon Rubin have recommended completing the following processes over the months and years after your baby dies, so you can successfully resolve your grief.

- Acknowledge your loss. Have you acknowledged that your baby is dead and will never return to life? Or do you sustain a flicker of hope that there has been a terrible mistake and your baby can be recovered?

- Understand how your baby died. Do you have an explanation for how your baby died that you can accept, whether it can be proven or not? Or are you still mystified about what caused your baby's death?

- Accept all your feelings. Have you found comfortable ways to express your various emotions? Or do you avoid feelings that seem inappropriate or irrational?

- Experience the hurt and sadness. Have you felt your deepest feelings of despair? Or are you still hiding behind anger, guilt, failure or numbness?
- Change your expectations for the future. Have you modified the hopes and dreams that involved this child? Or do you still hold on to what might have been or depend on your baby to give your life meaning?
- Readjust to life without your baby. Have you found other ways to be happy, perhaps other people or activities to enjoy? Or do you still feel empty and unable to find fulfillment or satisfaction in your baby's absence?
- Change your emotional investment in your baby. Are you able to remember or talk about your baby without feeling overwhelmed? Or do thoughts of your baby bring up acute feelings of grief?
- Form a new relationship with your baby. Are you able to think of your baby in terms of what might have been without acting on those fantasies? Or do you act as if your baby is still with you?
- Think of your baby realistically. Can you think about your baby in terms of negative and positive qualities? Or do you idealize your baby, only remembering or superimposing positive qualities?
- Maintain an appropriate connection to your baby. Are you able to recognize your baby's impact on your life and remember and do those things that enhance your life? Or do you continue to retain connections that compromise your happiness or spontaneity or health? Common examples include feeling compelled toward or away from certain activities or things. For instance, you enjoy going on a daily walk, but always have to stop at the playground and touch the swing your baby liked. Or perhaps you avoid preventative gynecological screening exams like PAP smears because they are too reminiscent of the D & C after your miscarriage.
- Reinvest your emotional energy. Can you establish and maintain fulfilling relationships with other people or pursue rewarding activities? Or do you refrain from getting involved in close relationships or satisfying activities?

In the early months after your baby dies, you cannot expect yourself to have worked through any of these processes. You can think of these as goals to strive toward or you can check this list every few months to get an idea of your progress. If you notice that you have made headway through some but not all of these processes, this list may help you focus your energy on those that are keeping you unresolved or unadjusted to your baby's absence.

What Does Resolution Feel Like at First?

For many mothers, resolution appears on the horizon when thinking about the baby is less painful. Eventually, happy feelings are more prevalent than sad ones. Feelings of peace and acceptance creep up, and perhaps silver linings can be appreciated. Sophie feels a glimmer of resolution: "I don't think I'll ever completely accept it, but it has mellowed. Sometimes I feel sad and other times I can feel peaceful about it all and look at the positive effect she had on me." Cindy and Liza recall when they started feeling resolved:

I think I got to a point where I thought, "My baby died, that's the way it is, and I can't change it and I better quit wishing it would change. It can't; it won't. So I have to deal with it, go on."

—Cindy

I began to realize that love isn't limited. The more you give away, the more you have. Instead of being angry at everybody else because they didn't die when he died—that's the way I felt, that the whole world should've stopped—I began to see that other people have pain whether I think it was as great as mine or not. There were a lot of selfish feelings, like "Nobody has ever gone through something like this," but I began to realize that it's a universal thing and to really feel more love for people because of that. Once you have a little resolution you start to see what the rest of the world is going through.

—Liza

Making Sense of Tragedy

Gathering Information about What Went Wrong

After any traumatic event, it is normal to want information—about what happened, why and how to cope. When your baby dies, you may want all kinds of details about what went wrong. You may want to know more about the procedures that were done to you or your baby, and about tests, drugs, surgeries and other therapies. You may want information on the causes, origins and physiology of your or your baby's condition. You may want vivid color photographs.

Since the relevant topics may involve illness and deformity, your obsession may receive less approval than say, an obsession about baseball. Some people, or you yourself, may consider such interests prurient, morbid and a sign of serious maladjustment. However, just as dwelling on memories helps you come to terms with loss, dwelling on details can help you come to terms with what happened.

Having information also can help you feel less vulnerable. If you can have some answers, you can make sense of your experience and feel less victimized by forces beyond your control, or the twists and turns of fate. Having information can also empower you, making you feel that you can try to avoid or surmount these problems in the future.

Finally, poring over this information can give you a sense of mastery over the trials or tragedy you've experienced. Gaining a better understanding of what happened and possible causes can help you heal your sorrow and move on in your life. Even if no one is sure what happened or what the cause was, you can still benefit from learning as much as you can so that in your own mind, you can settle on an explanation, whether it can be proven or not.

It may be a while before you are ready to delve into details, or you may want them right away. Do expect your interest to last a long time, if not a lifetime. Since the limits of medical science are ever-changing, you may want to stay current with a particular condition and its treatments. But if a "cure" is eventually announced, particularly if this happens within a year or so, don't berate yourself for not pursuing that option. Remember, it was unavailable when you or your baby needed it.

To find information, there are many books and organizations that can help (look in the resources appendix and bibliography in the back of this book). Check out other books or call national support group offices for listings of pertinent organizations. Also ask your doctor, midwife or genetics counselor to refer you to resources or give you copies of pertinent articles and book chapters. If you live near a medical school, you can use their library. Or your local public library should be able to arrange interlibrary loans with medical school libraries. Use the resource librarians— they are familiar with all kinds of requests for all kinds of information.

Remember, having information is empowering.

Recognizing the Positive

After your baby dies, trying to find something positive is another way to make sense of your tragedy. At first, you may be too distraught or too angry to even consider anything positive. But when you start to feel better, you can try to assess the salvage from the wreckage. Unfortunately, other people may try to help you find something positive about your baby's death by saying things such as, "At least the baby died before you were too far along ... " or "It's a blessing the baby died because ... " or "Be thankful that at least you know you can get pregnant." This method of comfort may seem cruel to you, but people are simply anxious to help you feel better and hasten you along with well-meaning speeches.

Eventually, when you are ready, you may recognize something positive from the experiences surrounding your loss. Perhaps you will find you have a strengthened marriage, deepened friendships, increased personal awareness, greater confidence or better understanding of and willingness to help others who experience loss. You may even have a new baby, who might not have been conceived if the other baby had lived. These positive things do not make up for your baby's death, but you may derive some small comfort from them. Your own philosophies and outlook on life may determine whether you eventually find comfort in recognizing anything positive from the tragedy of your baby's death.

> The time we had with Jamie was so brief, but now I can look back on that and smile. And I didn't think I'd ever smile about that. Every time I thought about that, it would make me cry. But now I'm grateful that I had that time, that I had him for three days, instead of none.
>
> —Sarah

> Something good has to come out of it, because I don't want her death to be totally in vain. I don't want it to be totally meaningless. So I try to use every opportunity to talk about her and help other people who are going through the same thing. I have a desire for something good to come out of it. I know I'm a better mother than I probably would have been.
>
> —Rose

For some parents, the positives may remain elusive. Holly comments, "I can sort of accept that it was a learning process and that you grow through pain and all that. But I just don't think anybody needs that learning process." Bryn agrees: "I led a very lucky life. I always had the philosophy that, 'Hey, everything works out for the best.' I cannot have that philosophy anymore, because I will never be able to say it was best that he died. I can *never* say that."

Why Me, Why My Baby?

Another way to try to make sense of it all is to figure out "Why me, why my baby?" Aside from autopsy reports and medical theories about *how* your baby died, you need answers about *why* this had to happen at all.

> The doctors said that it was just some stray molecule of bacteria in the air that Rachel breathed, and it gave her meningitis, like she was at the wrong place at the wrong time and breathed the wrong breath. What are the chances? Why did everything come together so wrong?
>
> —Carolyn

Eventually you may find acceptable answers. Upon getting pregnant so easily after Scott's death, Kelly decided that perhaps there was a divine plan at work in her life. Jane simply accepts that God gives her the children He wants her to have, enabling her to accept the fact that "this baby was not the one He wanted for me to have." Originally, Jessie wondered what she had done "to deserve such a horrible thing," but now she believes that there was some unknown purpose. She says, "Maybe her soul wasn't ready, maybe that was just as long as she was supposed to be with us. I do believe that it changed things, that because of her, Kent and I really developed our relationship and stayed together. So it helps me to think that maybe that was part of the purpose."

Perhaps you believe there is no plan, no single purpose. Maybe we are victims of random events in an imperfect world. For instance, Bess believes that David's death "was purely an accident of nature," while Martina concludes, "I don't think you ever find out why it happened. You just know it did and you've got to live with it." Sarah has decided to stop asking, "Why me?" because "it doesn't get you anywhere."

Whatever your conclusions, you will probably acquire some understanding of why this happened and come to the realization that you don't control your life as much as you thought you did. While this can be an unsettling thought, most parents learn to live with it.

Anniversary Reactions

You may find that you have particularly bad days at certain times of the year. These "anniversary reactions" are normal responses to the grief of anniversaries relevant to your baby's life and death. Years after your loss, whether you feel resolved or not, you may experience anniversary reactions one or more times a year—around the baby's due date, birth date, death date or holidays. Anniversary dates are special *and* painful.

> On the anniversary date of his birth, we always try and do something together as a family. I remember on the day that would have been his third birthday, being struck with the fact that there will always be somebody missing. There will always be one less child in my life.
>
> —Sarah

> I wish they didn't have Mother's Day! That's the day I really acknowledge that I have two kids. I'm the mother of two kids, not just one.
>
> —Cindy

Right after your baby dies, you may feel especially blue every week on the day of your baby's birth or death. As time goes on, you may feel depressed on a certain day of each month. You may feel sad on your own birthday or wistfully think about how old your child would have been on the first day of every school year. You may feel particularly forgetful, disorganized, clumsy or even be prone to accidental injuries, so use extra caution during these stressful times.

This baby was born on Christmas Eve, and the first year I was anxious about it, but I think, really, for the first three years, Christmas was *very* hard. I think when Thanksgiving hit I just immediately tightened up. I knew I had to manage these things and I would work even harder to get my Christmas stuff done, and as Christmas approached it got worse and worse and worse. I just don't like that time of year anymore.

—Meryl

In October, I'm real mellow and mopey, and on her birthday it's like, we know it's that day. We take the time to remember that she was with us at one point... . It's just like a signal in your body. And I'll break down and cry over nothing. October is like a lead balloon.

—Erin

Perhaps you fear anniversaries that loom in the distance, like Yolanda who says, "I'm afraid that after my due date it will really hit me that I don't have my baby, because that's when I should have him in my arms. I'm bracing myself."

If you have a surviving baby or babies from a multiple pregnancy, birthdays and death days may coincide or fall close together. Every year at this time you may wrestle with mixed feelings. While you want to be happy, your sorrow can dampen any festivities. You may feel disloyal since you're unable to devote yourself entirely to either celebration or mourning. While this can seem impossible to resolve, you can find ways to honor all your babies. Set aside time and make plans, however private, that accommodate your feelings and recognize the special ways each child had touched your heart. Accept that this will be a bittersweet time.

Anniversary reactions can be discouraging, especially as time goes on and you feel as though you're putting your life back together. You may be surprised by the appearance of these emotions. But remember, even resolution will not spare you from occasional sadness. Some call this "shadow grief"—the dull background ache that stays with you; anniversaries simply bring that ache to the foreground.

Anniversary reactions can also be unpredictable. It is important to give yourself permission to have bad days whenever they appear. You are entitled to your own special pattern of grieving.

Thinking about What Might Have Been

At times you may catch yourself thinking or wondering about what the baby would be like now if he or she had lived. At first these thoughts are painful, but eventually, as you let go of your emotional investment in these fantasies, hopes and dreams, they can take on a feeling of wistfulness or curiosity. You may feel this curiosity when you see children who were born at the same time as your baby who died, or in a pensive moment with a subsequent child as you realize the experiences you have missed with the child who died.

In resolution, you can let go of idealized versions of "what might have been." You will embrace the fact that all babies have their imperfections and temperamental idiosyncrasies. The baby who died would have been demanding and difficult to manage at times. If you lost one, some or all the babies from a multiple pregnancy, you can also let go of your perfect images of twins, triplets, etc. With resolution, you can accept that having all your babies would not have made everything ideal.

> We think mostly about what he'd look like and what he'd be doing now. Every year when school starts and at Christmas time I think about how old he is, and I've thought that I'll be thinking about that when he would have graduated from high school, that he would have gotten married, maybe gone to college.
>
> —Martina

> I'll always grieve the "firsts." What would have been the first step, the first word, the first day of school.
>
> —Cathryn

If you are raising a surviving baby or babies from a multiple birth, there are constant poignant reminders of what might have been. If you know that a survivor is identical to one who died, these reminders are particularly graphic. Even with fraternal multiples, they were still *chronologically* identical and you may frequently envision the sibling(s) who would have been doing similar things at similar times. As Shannon points out, "When Bradley is doing something adorable or getting into something or making a mess, I look at him and think, 'Can you imagine *two* of them?'"

As time passes, these reminders may be less painful, but you can still expect to feel wistful, particularly during significant developmental milestones into adulthood. You may also mourn for a sole surviving child who will never know the unique kinship of a sibling who's the same age; eventually, you will visualize more realistically the bond that they might have had.

Keys to Survival

The simple passage of time may prove to be one of your greatest keys to survival. Other resources to fall back on may include your other children, your partner, your family and friends, books, work, religion, hope and an inner strength that you may have only just discovered through this tragedy. To best utilize these resources, be assertive in telling people what you need and pursue the things that help you cope.

The hope of someday having a healthy baby may help you to look ahead. Peg elaborates: "I'm sure that if I hadn't been able to have one that I'd feel entirely different about the whole thing. Having a baby has helped me to deal with it."

If you are raising a survivor from a multiple birth, you may find it exceptionally challenging to grieve for one or more babies while trying to nurture another or others. You may feel "up to here" with baby things along with the most vivid reminders of what you are missing. But having a surviving baby can be a source of healing too. Anya notes, "I don't know what it's like to lose a baby and not have another baby there too. I did have a baby to hold. I've never had a pregnancy and nothing to show for it."

The most significant key to your survival may be a conscious choice to get through your grief without letting it destroy your life. You can decide whether you will triumph over it or surrender to it. Many mothers mention reaching a point where they just decide to stop wishing it didn't happen and start learning to live with it.

> You just realize that's the way life is. There's a lot of things we don't like and a lot of things that aren't fair... . You can't change it, so you just deal with it so you can move on. What else can you do? If you don't, then you lose yourself.
>
> —Cindy

Getting Help

At some point you may decide you would like to talk to a professional counselor. If you feel as though you need help reaching resolution, this is an excellent reason to go. You may decide on counseling if you feel as though sufficient time has passed and you still have intense emotional reactions or your thoughts, behavior or physical symptoms are interfering with your ability to progress through grief. (See "Getting Counseling" in chapter 9 and "Counseling" in chapter 12.)

> For a long time I thought this was as far as I could get, that's just how it was for me. Now, I feel like I need to get to a different place, need to move on. It doesn't feel like I want it to be, like, a part of my life. It's still too painful. I want to go to a better place, be at peace with it. So I'm back in therapy.
>
> —Laura

Points to Remember

- Resolved grief is marked by acceptance and integration of the loss into your life: Intense grief has mellowed into bittersweet or peaceful feelings and you acquire a renewed interest in relationships and pleasurable activities. Resolution allows you to live for a new future instead of dwelling on the past or what might have been.
- Resolution also includes sadness, love and remembrance.
- Unresolved grief is accompanied by an inability to accept your loss, repression of or continuing feelings of grief, and the baby's life and death occupying a central part of your life.
- The journey to resolution takes time and has many ups and downs.
- Resolved or not, eventually you may feel that there was a purpose or some positives that arose from your baby's death.
- Whether your grief is resolved or unresolved, anniversary reactions are normal, even years after your baby's death.
- Even in resolution you may wonder about what your child would have been like and what might have been.
- If you feel stuck, counseling may help you move to a more comfortable place with your grief.

8

Making Peace
with Agonizing Decisions

If you faced life-and-death decisions for your baby, resolution of your grief may seem incredibly difficult. Whether you interrupted your pregnancy or continued it in the face of serious disability or certain death for your baby; whether you opted for the risks of selective reduction or the risks of refusing it; whether you turned away from aggressive medical intervention or embraced it—your grief has the added component of the illusion that you were ultimately responsible for your baby's fate. For most parents, this decision weighs heavily on their hearts and becomes central to coping with their baby's death. This chapter offers additional support to these parents.

Decisions Parents Face

Perhaps you enlisted the aid of reproductive technology. You greeted the news of conception with joy, only to be faced with decisions regarding the risky business of a pregnancy with multiple babies. If more than two or three embryos were implanted, you may have to consider selective reduction in order to improve the chances of *any* of your babies surviving. You may have taken a leap of faith and tried to carry all the babies, but none of them made it. Or perhaps you chose reduction, but all the babies died. Either way, or if there are severely disabled survivors, you may feel punished for your decision.

Even if reduction leads to the birth of healthy babies, you may still wonder if it was necessary or the right thing to do. If one of multiple babies has died later in the pregnancy, you may have had to decide whether to induce labor early, or continue to carry your babies, dead and alive. There may be risks to the remaining baby(s) either way. Any of these decisions can seem humanly impossible to make. Becoming a parent feels bittersweet at best.

Perhaps you were faced with decisions about interrupting your pregnancy. If your health was in danger, you may have had to decide whether to terminate or risk grave illness, permanent impairment, even death. If your baby was diagnosed *in utero* with a disabling condition, you may have had to decide whether to hope for the best or to spare your child from a difficult, distressing life. Perhaps you wanted to try to carry your baby to term and then let go, but you were told that maximum intervention would be used to keep the infant alive, without regard to pain or suffering. With the threat of mandatory neonatal intensive care, you may have felt the better option was to make plans to let your baby go early.

If your baby was diagnosed *in utero* with a fatal condition, you may have felt torn between your desire to hold on to this child as long as possible and your desire to protect the child from suffering. Perhaps you wanted to get past the nerve-wracking suspense and anticipation of waiting for the baby to die. Or perhaps, knowing that your little one could live for a while yet inside you or briefly after birth, you may have felt reluctant to interfere. As your child's death was a certainty, figuring out what was "best" may have felt like both an exercise in futility and a chance to do something meaningful.

Perhaps you were faced with decisions concerning premature delivery. If your or the baby's health was endangered, the risks of continuing the pregnancy versus the risks of your baby's prematurity had to be considered. If the infant was born so early that intact survival was unlikely, you may have had to decide whether the baby should be resuscitated, or be allowed to stop breathing naturally or go into cardiac arrest.

If your baby sustained brain damage before, during or after birth, you may have faced the decision of refusing mechanical support. If your baby was born with a serious birth defect, you may have had to decide between letting your baby die quickly and naturally or risking painful, life-threatening or possibly unsuccessful surgeries. Maybe you had to decide when to stop further treatment or when to disconnect artificial life-support systems.

Or perhaps you put your trust in modern medicine, made the decision to "go for it" and your baby died anyway. If your baby endured painful procedures and surgeries, you may feel like any suffering was so pointless. Particularly if your child never recovered enough to leave the hospital, you may be experiencing a crisis of faith in authority, technology or God.

In our culture, there is considerable social pressure to reach for miracles and employ the most technology possible to save a life. Carrying multiple babies to near term is considered a brave undertaking where surely, healthy babies are the reward. Parents who take on the care of a severely disabled child are looked upon as "courageous." Extensive and invasive medical treatments for critically ill newborns are referred to as "heroic measures." In contrast, selective reduction, pregnancy interruption and refusal of aggressive medical intervention are generally *not* considered "heroic." As a result, parents who choose these options often feel judged, isolated and unsupported. The purpose of this chapter is to point out the heroism in questioning medical technology, the virtue of rejecting the goal to save every life, the sensitivity in recognizing the complexities of a situation and the wisdom in choosing to let go. Indeed, it takes a lot of courage to meet death head on.

If you faced such a decision and chose to continue your pregnancy or to enlist medical technology to the fullest extent, the following pages can offer comfort to you too. You still made a difficult choice and may wrestle with doubts and a heavy sense of responsibility. Also, the bottom line and the other focus of this chapter is that *your* decision was *best* for your baby, you and your family. Parents—not doctors, not judges, not juries—should have the right to make these personal and heart-wrenching decisions for their babies.

> It seems ironic to me that it takes these very tiny babies—my daughter Emily weighed 760 grams at birth—to magnify these huge ethical mysteries. Often I think the bizarre footrace between technology and human beings is best illustrated in the neonatal unit, where huge machines dwarf very small children and big questions hover over us all.
>
> —Maris

Wrestling with Life and Death Decisions

To make a truly informed decision, parents need a lot of information about quality of life issues, as well as the emotional, spiritual, financial and logistical difficulties of each choice.

If you were pregnant with multiple babies, you needed to know whether selective reduction would significantly improve the chances of carrying healthy babies to term. You needed to know about the risks of the procedure itself, as well as the risks of continuing the pregnancy. Also, you may have considered the toll on your own health and the realities of parenting and caring for multiples. Many parents recognize that it's a shame to have several babies at once, only to be unable to give them the attention and nurturing they need.

If maternal health was at stake, you needed to know if continuing the pregnancy would lead to serious or permanent damage. Is the mother's life in danger? Would the mother's difficulties lead to serious problems for the baby or babies?

If the baby was facing severe challenges, you had many questions about how difficult life would be. How much would the baby suffer physically or emotionally? What kind of life was in store for this child? Would he or she be able to live at home?

If you had to decide whether to pursue treatment for a life-threatening disease or birth defect, you needed to know how difficult that would be for the baby. How painful would the treatment be? How long would it take? How many surgeries or hospitalizations would there be? What are the chances treatment would be successful? Would treatment cure the baby's underlying problems or merely "save" a life? What might the child's quality of life be in the near future? In the distant future?

You weighed these costs and benefits to judge what was best for your baby. You also thought about the logistics of obtaining experimental treatments and caring for a critically ill infant, particularly if it required hospitalization in a faraway city. The financial realities, short-term and long-term, needed to be considered. Finally, you thought about the emotional consequences and strain on you, your marriage and your other children. Even with plenty of resources, the burden still can test the limits of human endurance.

Considering all these factors can be difficult and confusing. It may have been a challenge to gather and sort through the information and various options. You may have felt rushed, making it even more difficult to think clearly or quickly. You may wish you could have felt more sure before you gave your final answer. You might worry whether it was reasonable to rely on your gut reaction or your doctor's advice.

It is important to remember that whether you had two minutes or two years, emotional turmoil would accompany whatever decision you made. After all, you had to make an impossible choice between "terrible" and "horrible." Also remember, the decision-making process doesn't end with a decision. It is *afterward* that you can deliberately comb through all the facts, come to terms with it and gain confidence. There is no deadline for the post-decision part of the process.

> Though all of the facts and logistics were important, what guided us most was an innate, gut-level sense that human beings are not machines, that our body parts are not indiscriminately interchangeable, that our society spends too much of its resources in flight from death and that there are times when death, no matter how painful it may be, how unnatural it may seem, must simply be met. We felt that a heart incapable of functioning was one of those cases.
>
> —Claudia

The Decision

Even as you balanced the rational arguments, your decision was mostly a personal, emotional and heart-wrenching one. For many parents, the choice boils down to two things. First, which do they fear more for their child, death or a severely challenged life? Ted recalls, "For me, the decision crystallized and I *knew* it was right, when the doctor pointed out that *there are some fates worse than death*." Secondly, how much suffering should this child's life entail? Molly recalls, "I remember walking into the intensive care unit where they put Peter on monitors until we made our decision and seeing him all hooked up, I *knew* I couldn't do that to him." Claudia agrees, "We were haunted by the possibility that if we chose surgery, Jacob might die without much knowledge of our love for him. He might have died without being held for any length of time by us and just having known and been cuddled by machines. I felt that if we could hold him and be with him, then at least if he died, he would know that we loved him."

Above all, you chose what you believed was best for your child. Rightly so, you relied on your values, intuitions and projections to guide you. Only you could weigh all the factors, the risks and benefits according to your basic philosophical or spiritual beliefs. While you may worry that you were under too much stress to make a good decision, your emotional duress actually played an important role in your judgment. It enabled you to make the decision with your heart and gut, not just your mind. Your decision was right for your baby.

Each of these parents faced difficult decisions: Ruth suffers from hyperemesis gravidarum—severe nausea and vomiting throughout her pregnancies; Louisa was carrying four embryos and faced losing all the babies; Avery's baby was diagnosed with Trisomy 21 (Down syndrome) in the first trimester; Maria's baby was diagnosed with anencephaly in the second trimester, was carried to term and died shortly after birth; Kaye's baby was diagnosed with Trisomy 21 and severe fetal hydrops early in the third trimester; Lena's baby was born fifteen weeks early and died within a few hours; Claudia's baby was born with hypoplastic left heart syndrome and died three and a half days later; Grace's baby was born with multiple midline birth defects and died twenty-seven days later. Each mother describes the critical aspects of her decision.

> I get very sick when I'm pregnant and with my last pregnancy, I was the sickest. I threw up every 15 minutes around the clock. They tried IVs but I was so dehydrated, they couldn't get them in. Finally at 9 weeks, I felt like I was dying and they really couldn't give me any answers and they didn't know if the baby would make it. So the doctors and my family really pressured me into terminating the pregnancy. I wish that they had given me a little more time to think about this decision, but they started things going right when I said, "Well, maybe we should. ..." But as time passes and I get more information I can see that I may not have survived this pregnancy with the treatment I was getting. The way things were, how could I expect to keep going?
>
> —Ruth

> After years of infertility and then losing a baby to SIDS, I knew that at 40, this was our last try to have a child. We were thrilled to discover that IVF worked. I was pregnant at last, only to find out that I was carrying four babies. The odds were overwhelmingly against me being able to carry all of them, even to viability, much less near term. For us, the choice boiled down to having two or having none. I focused on the fact that selective reduction was a way to *save* two little lives. Still, I was bonded to all four babies and enduring the reduction was an absolute nightmare ... an *absolute* nightmare.
>
> —Louisa

I had always been a "right-to-lifer." I knew I could never have an abortion. That is, I knew until I was put into the position of having to choose between keeping my baby, knowing he had Down syndrome, or aborting him. ... The most helpful information in choosing abortion was the information I received from a friend of mine. Her first child was a Down syndrome baby who died at age 4. I called Ann to share my grief and to ask her advice. She reminded me of the "ripple effect" of keeping this baby, even if he were a "healthy" Down baby. She said, "I loved my little girl, but with my next two pregnancies, there was no question that I would have aborted had the tests shown another Down syndrome baby." Ann's honesty gave me the strength to abort our baby boy. I am so thankful that I could talk to someone who experienced Down syndrome firsthand. My mind was made up before my husband came home. ... As my due date approaches, I miss our baby Jeffrey so much, but I am sure deep in my heart that I did what was best for our baby, my family and for me.

—Avery

I wanted Kristina's death to be natural and out of my hands. I wanted to protect her, love her and get to know her before and until nature said, "It is time." This waiting to see how things will turn out was the only decision I felt I would be able to live with for the rest of my life.

—Maria

I went to medical school because I wanted to be a neonatologist. But after a couple of rotations through the NICU, I was horrified by the suffering of these tiny babies. So I switched my specialty to family practice. But here I was, ten years later, faced with the prospect of delivering a multiply handicapped baby to an NICU. I KNEW I couldn't do that to her. I just couldn't. To protect her from suffering, I *had* to let her go.

—Kaye

For quite a while I wondered if we did the right thing taking Steven off life support. I thought "Gee, could he have been saved and lived a normal life?" They said most likely he would be mentally retarded and have cerebral palsy and he'd be a sick little child all of his life. Part of it was a little bit selfish—I didn't want to deal with that all my life. I do often wonder though what would've happened. But I wouldn't change that decision.

—Lena

The most important factor in our decision was Jacob's welfare. We tried to do what we thought was best for him. We did not feel that the life of pain and uncertainty offered by the surgeries was one that we would choose for ourselves, and we did not feel comfortable choosing such a life for him.

—Claudia

I had to think what was best for him. I firmly believe James would have fought for his life if that is what I wanted, but was that the best for him? Was forcing life on a body that was so incomplete the best I could do for him? I wanted him to be happy and free. ... He was a kind, peaceful person who gave peace to all who knew him. I didn't want him to lead a long, unpeaceful life of struggle. I couldn't ask that of one so small. The best I could do was to let go. The hardest thing I could do was to let go.

—Grace

Facing Death

After the decision has been made, the parents are left with the task of facing death. Even if one is absolutely certain that this is best, death is not easy. As Maribeth recalls, "It's so hard to hold your baby in your arms knowing you've chosen not to do everything possible to save his life. I will never forget that feeling."

I worried that my baby would feel pain from the abortion or know that I was rejecting him. A few days after the abortion my husband came across an article that I found reassuring. Babies at that stage of development don't "think." Also, their nervous system is not sophisticated enough to register pain. I wish I had known that before the abortion. ... For me the abortion was living hell. I felt I was being tortured for 5 hours. I wish someone could have told me what it would be like. The physical pain was mild, the emotional pain was a black horror.

—Avery

I was scared of what she would look like, I was scared of "losing it" in the delivery room. ... I was scared of a lot of things. The worst time in my life was walking into that hospital knowing it was time to say hello and goodbye. ... Looking back I would have grabbed her right away to feel her life. Kristina did move a couple of times in my arms but she spent her first five minutes in the warmer before we held her. I was afraid of death but I'm not now.

—Maria

It was days and hours of saying goodbye forever to a baby I loved who would never be. It was willing James to live, fearing he would die; fearing he would live, willing him to die.

—Grace

While waiting for death can be an agonizing time, it is also a time for cherishing your child's existence. Whether you had a few hours or a few months, before or after birth, nurturing your baby can be an important way to cope with the fact that death is imminent. As Barbara recalls, "My husband is afraid Virginia suffered, but for me, it was twenty-three days I got to be with her and hold her." Mahalia agrees, "I saw a little person in my arms ... and it helps knowing that I protected her till she died."

However, not all parents have the chance to nurture their infant. The baby may have been so sick or died so quickly, there was little opportunity or time. Particularly if you interrupted your pregnancy, labor and vaginal delivery may not have been an option, resulting in missed chances to be with the baby and collect memories. As Teryn tearfully suggests, "I would've liked more choices laid out, maybe the option to have the baby vaginally so I could touch the baby. I don't have that peace, because our baby was terminated; no memories, nothing to hold on to." This too must be grieved.

Making plans for my child's upcoming death is a notion I would have embraced if it had only occurred to me during the frenzy of our son's short life. I never realized having the baby near me 24 hours a day, getting the opportunity to bathe and feed him and certainly arranging to be with him when he died could be important later on. Only after did I learn I could have taken more control over these sorts of "details."

—Rachel

It's a Child, Not Just a Choice

My husband went with me for my CVS. We saw the "fetal material," "beginning of the pregnancy" and all the other clinical terms the medical personnel use when viewing an ultrasound. However, what my husband and I saw was our baby. Following the procedure we took home a photo from the ultrasound to show off and to hang on the refrigerator. ... Waiting for the results, I assumed I would feel relief and could relax with my pregnancy, knowing very early that everything was fine. Two days later I was informed that my baby, a boy, had Down syndrome.

—Avery

Unfortunately, health care providers are only just beginning to consider and understand the emotional trauma involved in interrupting or reducing a wanted pregnancy. Parents are not always encouraged or able to collect keepsakes and hold the baby, things that are so important for grieving and healing. In fact, you may not have even been encouraged to mourn. You may find yourself only thinking in terms of "we terminated the pregnancy" rather than "our baby is dead." Teryn reports, "We were told it was the 'best choice' without anyone acknowledging that it was a *child*."

As such, it is particularly important for you to affirm your baby. Doing things like naming, creating memorials and collecting mementos can help you find a special place in your heart for this child. (See "Remembering Your Baby" in chapter 5.)

Living with the Decision

I have seen death
I have held it gently in my arms
and I have kissed it goodbye
with tear-stained cheeks
To know this pain was my choice
adds a new dimension
It brings peace; it brings guilt
I want to lay it aside
and just grieve for my son
but the guilty verdict pounds
in my soul
It will take time ... time.

—Maribeth Wilder Doerr

You will not necessarily find death easier to accept just by virtue of having chosen it. Having a choice doesn't lessen your grief. After all, you did not want your baby to die, death was simply the only way to secure what was "best." And you are left behind with your doubts, perhaps some guilt and with a heavy sense of responsibility.

If you chose to continue the pregnancy, you may wonder whether this option subjected your baby (or babies) to more suffering. If you decided to utilize medical intervention, you may feel like you walked a fine line between trying to relieve suffering without prolonging an unduly dismal or painful life. Even if those around you applaud the choice, you may still second-guess your decision.

The Doubts

While some parents may have felt that there was only one way to go, others feel torn. With all the options being terrible, you may have felt it was an impossible decision to make. Even after all is said and done, you may still harbor some doubts.

Since you feel so badly, you may wonder, would the other choice have been better? But really, you feel badly not because you made a *bad* decision, but because you had to make a tough, *painful* decision. Moreover, none of the options offered total solutions. Each one held its own risks and created its own problems. The alternatives were equally or even more grim, not better for your baby. Most likely, you would feel equally bad or worse if you had chosen the alternative.

> I never want to have to make a decision like that again. What were the choices? Let her die slowly of heart failure *in utero?* If Joy was born alive, watch her die by inches and be tortured in the NICU? Sometimes I torture myself with the knowledge that I cooperated in her demise. I only know it was an act of love.
>
> —Kaye

You may wonder later, "If I had more time, would I have made a different choice?" But even with all the time in the world, you probably would have made the same choice. You made the best decision you possibly could—under terrible stress—weighing all the information at hand and balancing many factors, including the welfare or your baby, your marriage, yourself, your other children and even your future children. Even if you felt pressured by the biases of your health care providers, relying on their judgment is still a reasonable way to decide. If you feel that the decision wasn't all yours, you can still come to accept it.

You may feel obsessed by "What if?" for a while. This is a natural part of the grieving process. Wrestling with your doubts can be a way for you to evaluate, solidify and embrace the beliefs and principles that guided your decision. While second thoughts can be unsettling, they are normal and can help you accept that the decision you made was right for your baby.

> Much of my own healing has come from learning of families who chose aggressive alternatives. I see our philosophical differences and this has become a source of comfort. Their feelings about "life at all costs" are not right for me; my "do nothing" choice [is] unthink- able to them. And we are both right. ... Each family must determine what is right for them.
>
> —Rachel

If you were pregnant with multiple babies, you may have received a lot of pressure to employ selective reduction. Because of the lack of reliable statistics, it may have been supremely difficult to weigh the risks and benefits. You may have assumed that carrying fewer babies is always better, without being forewarned of the risks of any multiple pregnancy or the reduction procedure, not to mention the emotional toll of relinquishing much loved and wanted babies. To top it off, whatever your decision, you'll never know for sure how it affected the outcome. Also, you may be haunted by media images of families with multiples, and think to yourself, "I could have done that."

To be in this position is terribly difficult. Even if you would not change your decision, you may regret that it could not have been a truly informed choice. But part of the reason these decisions are so agonizing is *because* of the lack of information and guarantees. You did the very best you could with what you had. And remember that television and magazines tend to idealize multiples, and belittle the risks, hardships and craziness of the pregnancy, NICU and parenting. (Also refer to "Thinking about What Might Have Been" in chapter 7.)

The Guilt

Guilty feelings are very common in parents who employ selective reduction, interrupt a pregnancy, refuse aggressive medical intervention or disconnect artificial life-support systems. While SIDS, stillbirth or miscarriage are usually regarded as "accidents of nature," the act of *choosing* to let a baby die can lead to self-blame.

If you made difficult decisions that led to your baby's death, it is important to remember you did not wish for the baby's condition that presented those options. And you did not enter into this decision lightly. You made the best choice you could, after searching your heart and soul for the answer. Even if you've heard about other parents who "went for it," this does not undercut the validity of your decision. Your decision, not somebody else's, was right for your situation.

You may reproach yourself for not being able to face the prospect of raising a sickly or impaired child. Try to keep in mind that parents who already have firsthand knowledge of what that's like tend to feel less guilty about deciding to let go. Whether they have prior experience parenting a child with disabilities or were raised with a disabled sibling, their experience has taught them about the hardships and suffering that can occur. They can be more sure that letting go is an act of kindness for the child.

If you employed selective reduction you may feel particularly angry at yourself for not trying to carry all the babies. Or perhaps you refused selective reduction and you're angry that you didn't consider the risks of multiple gestation seriously enough. Try to remember that whatever your decision, you were trying to guess what route would lead to the best outcome, without any definite signs to show you the way. In making your decision, you did reach for a greater good. Also remember, your decision came from how much you loved and wanted those babies, not the opposite.

It may also help to remember that guilt is a nearly universal feeling among bereaved parents. A large part of your guilt arises from the simple fact that you could not prevent your baby's problems. It is normal to *feel* guilty; this does NOT mean you did anything wrong. Instead of being angry at yourself for the decisions you made, be angry that you were put in the position to make a choice between "terrible" and "horrible." (For more ideas and support, see "Guilt" in chapter 6 and "Coping with Harsh Judgment" in chapter 12.)

Sometimes I still feel a little guilty, that I killed my baby, but I think there will always be a part of me that questions that decision. And maybe that's OK. It's a horrible decision to make.

—Kaye

The Responsibility

Because these decisions deal heavily in matters of the heart, parents are the most appropriate decision makers. It is a burdensome responsibility to bear but your baby would want you, not strangers, to decide.

I told my mom, "I don't want to have to make this decision. I'm not God. I'm not qualified to make this decision." And she said, "God doesn't call the qualified. He qualifies the called."

—Kaye

For me, it was a huge relief when a friend pointed out that my decision was based on my intuitive knowledge of *Jacob*, what he was like, what he could tolerate. This made the decision right for *him*. I might have made a different decision if I'd carried a different baby for nine months.

—Claudia

There are several reasons why you, the parents, benefit from making your own decisions:

- Every situation, every parent, every baby is unique. What may be right for another baby or another family is not necessarily right for yours.
- In the midst of tragedy, you may feel terribly helpless and ineffective. Having choices over what happens to your baby can help reinstate a sense of control.
- Making important treatment decisions is central to being a devoted, nurturing parent. This was your chance to be your baby's best advocate.
- It is you, not the health care providers, who must live with the decisions that are made, for years to come.

Although you may wish someone could have made these difficult decisions for you, parents who are not given choices often regret it. Even now, some hospitals do not let parents have many options. What happens instead often depends on medical staff opinions and preferences. Fortunately, this is slowly changing and most health care providers now realize that instead of being told what to do, parents need to be given alternatives, as well as enough information, support and time to make the right decisions for their baby and their family.

Indeed, if you had been barred from making these decisions, you would probably feel even more angry and depressed. Faced with this possibility,

Grace recalls, "It was unsettling to think that even if I believed in letting nature take its course, the medical ethics committee could overrule that decision and do extraordinary things to James if they felt his life was worth saving."

Also, consider this: You were responsible—not irresponsible. This was probably the most serious, complex, intense and far-reaching decision you'll ever have to face. No one else could have been more agonized and soul-searching with regard to this baby. The urge to hold on to your baby at all costs can be so strong and yet your sense of *what is best for my child* prevailed upon you to give your child wings. This takes a lot of courage and faith. And as John points out, "I really view it as probably the most unselfish thing that I've ever done."

No one else could have done this for your baby as carefully, thoughtfully, purposefully and solemnly as you did. You were the right person to make that difficult decision. (For more reading and support, consult "Books for Bereaved Parents," "Personal Accounts" and "Books on Medical Ethics" in the bibliography.)

> We didn't want to let go of this baby, we just got him, we just met him, we just found out how much we love him, we don't want to let go. But to be good parents, to look after his needs, maybe this is what's best for him.
>
> —Claudia

I Wanted So Much for You
For Kristina

I wanted so much more for you, my sweet little baby.
I wanted to change your diapers, not my life.
I wanted to nurse you, not my grief.
I wanted to dress you up, not bury you down.
I wanted to hear the sounds of you crying for me at night,
    not my own sounds of crying for you,
        my innocent, misconceived baby.

I wanted to see you grow, not the grass upon the grave.
I wanted to see you asleep in the crib, not in the casket.
I wanted to give you life, not death.
I wanted to show you off, not alone go on.
I wanted to comb your fuzzy hair, not save a lock of it.
I wanted to pick up after you, not put down my dreams for you.
I wanted to hold you in my arms, not this doll.
I wanted to walk you late at night, not my fears.
I wanted so much for you,
    my newly born, newly gone—child.

I wanted so much more
I wanted so much
I wanted
I wanted you.

—Maria LaFond Visscher

Points to Remember

- Although there is considerable social pressure to reach for miracles and save lives, there can be wisdom and heroism in letting go. Some fates *are* worse than death.
- Having a choice does not make death easier to accept. Making a decision only gives you the illusion of having control over the death of your baby. In reality, your baby died because of problems over which you had no control.
- Rightly so, you relied on your values and projections to guide you. Your baby would have wanted you, not strangers, to make this decision.
- Your emotional duress played an important role in your judgment. It enabled you to make the decision with your heart and gut, not just your mind.
- It is normal to feel badly about tough, painful decisions you had to make; feeling badly does not mean you made a bad decision. Had you made the other choice, you'd probably feel worse.
- Deal honestly with your deepest feelings of doubt and guilt. Facing your feelings will allow you to come to terms with them, to reassure yourself and to feel less defensive with other people.
- Instead of being angry at yourself for the decision you made, be angry that you were put in the position of having to choose between "terrible" and "horrible."
- You were responsible—not irresponsible. This was probably the most serious, complex, intense and far-reaching decision you'll ever make. No one else could have been more agonized and soul-searching. You were the right person to make that decision.
- Whether you decided to fight death or accept it, your decision was right for your baby, you and your family.

9

Especially for Fathers

Both mother *and* father must grieve in order to come to terms with their baby's death. However, most couples are struck by the difference between their grieving styles. While individual differences are to be expected between any two people, the gulf between men and women is consistent and wide.

This gulf occurs largely because we admire people who can keep a "stiff upper lip" in the face of great tragedy. Men especially have been expected to react this way, and when women have cried, it has been excused as part of their inherently hysterical nature. These shaming attitudes have stifled men and patronized women.

Fortunately, there is a trend toward shedding those smothering values, manners and rules of relating. As we begin to accept emotions as intrinsically human and essential to decent civilizations, we are starting to view subdued reactions with pity or suspicion. As we become more enlightened, the man or woman who can cry without shame will be respected, even envied.

This chapter examines the father's grief and considers the traditional pressures and expectations our culture places on men. Provided with these insights, fathers are encouraged to question social expectations and claim their grief. This chapter can also help a father and mother understand their emotional differences, bettering the chance that their relationship will survive this crisis.

Social Expectations

A father's expression of grief is affected by the interplay of a complex set of factors. Since early childhood, he has learned about expressing grief by what he's been told, what he's observed and what's been expected of him. These social influences have shaped him according to his gender and his personal predisposition toward certain emotions and temperamental characteristics.

While women are allowed to be emotional, men are supposed to be in control, brave, rational, independent and productive. From very early on, boys are taught to be ashamed of expressing need, crying openly, being weak or afraid and having affection for other males. "Real men" aren't supposed to weep or lean on others. Men may also find it difficult to verbalize their thoughts and feelings. As John says, "After Jacob died, it just seemed so hopeless to talk about. I couldn't find the words, so why try? There was no handle, it's just a nonverbal hurt."

Because we live in a culture that values male stoicism, bereaved fathers generally exhibit a narrow range of emotions, seek and accept little support and are not encouraged to cry and talk about their babies. A father's grief may appear to be more mild and brief, but this perception is partly due to the fact that men's grief is more invisible. When grief doesn't show or when the mourning period seems short, it does not necessarily indicate the true intensity of the father's feelings. He may be profoundly bereft, but subdued as he conforms to social expectations.

In addition, isolation for the father can be tremendous because according to social expectation, everyone focuses on the mother, as if he is unaffected. He feels left out when friends and relatives inquire only about the mother's condition. He flinches when others compliment his ability to "hold up," because inside he feels so torn down. He may be expected to return to work without any drop in productivity. He may not have male friends who can listen to him talk about his feelings. Francisco notes, "I feel emotionally isolated from my male friends, in contrast to my wife whose female friends talk about this stuff so freely."

In short, cultural pressures and shame discourage men from the very feelings and behaviors considered necessary for working through grief. The message to men is that they aren't supposed to grieve. At the very least, grieving men feel inhibited by these social expectations.

Unfortunately, men pay a high price for maintaining this stoic front. Bereaved fathers, widows, sons, brothers and friends are at particular risk for crippling psychological and physical problems that can threaten happiness, health, even life itself. Overall, male survivors have more accidents, more disease and a higher death rate than female survivors. For men and women alike, the quality of grieving is related to the quality of life.

Invisible Grief

When a father's grief is invisible, where does it go? Underground. Some or all of his grief may be stored deep in the subconscious so that he is unaware it exists. Subconscious grief will find indirect expression in his behaviors, reactions and physical illness. Stan operated this way. When he was 18, he lost his grandmother, an uncle and his father. After that, he vowed he'd never grieve again. Ten years later when his baby died, he said, "Stuff happens. That's the way it is. You tolerate it, make something positive out of it, accept it and move on." Unfortunately, he needed everyone around him to have the same attitude so that he could keep the lid on his grief. He became very controlling and angry, particularly with his wife who felt entitled to her feelings. He also started to drink heavily, a common anesthetic for men like this.

Another father may keep most of his grief in the back of his mind. He knows he has it but finds it too overwhelming or painful to face. Nick was like this. He filled his days with work and other activities, but his feelings of grief did come to the surface now and then, especially at night. Sometimes he brought them out, but usually he was ambushed by them. Nick worried about losing control, and he often felt isolated as others around him failed to acknowledge his pain.

As Stan and Nick help to illustrate, there are five common styles of filing grief away:

- Silence
- Secrecy
- Action
- Anger
- Addiction

Often, two or more styles accompany each other. For example, Stan used silence, anger and addiction. Filing a lawsuit is action with anger. Sequestering oneself in the workshop, greenhouse or on the hiking trails can be secrecy and action. Nick was like that.

Incidentally, these five styles are not for men only. Plenty of women use them too. Both men and women are influenced by a culture that values emotional restraint. This section focuses on men and the social conditioning that pushes fathers away from their feelings and toward these indirect ways of dealing with grief.

Silence

From infancy, many boys are shamed, rejected and reprimanded when they express needs, want affection or show fear, weakness, sadness or disappointment. "Big boys don't cry." "Don't be a sissy." "Buck up, buddy." These are just a few of the sayings proffered to boys. Boys are even encouraged to cut themselves off from physical sensations such as pain, cold or anxiety. Many athletic coaches scold shivering boys to quit being wimps, get out there and *play!* Is it any wonder, then, that many fathers cannot acknowledge their feelings because the shame associated with "letting" themselves have those emotions or sensations is too painful? They avoid the feelings to avoid the shame.

By withdrawing into silence, you protect yourself from the "sissy" feelings associated with grief. Feelings such as yearning, anxiety, fear, despair and insecurity are kept at bay, and you don't have to deal with them. As far as you are concerned, those emotions don't exist. Since friends and family generally don't ask how you are doing, your silence is reinforced. Unfortunately, by burying your feelings, you place yourself at risk for any of the health and emotional problems associated with repressed grief.

Secrecy

Even if a boy's family allows expression of a wide range of feelings, he quickly learns that his peers are not so accepting. Also, he may notice how other men in the family tend to keep feelings private. Or perhaps in a family that denies emotions, a boy bravely acknowledges his feelings, but keeps them to himself.

In this style, grief is expressed but only privately. You may set aside time for visiting the grave or writing in a journal, but may try to cover up your whereabouts. You may wait for opportunities to be alone, and then you open up and cry. While this is much healthier than silence, you miss out on the benefits of social support, recognition and validation.

Action

Particularly when death is unexpected or sudden, as when a baby dies, some men jump into action. You may orchestrate all the funeral arrangements, mobilize legal action, engage in hard physical labor or become deeply involved in a hobby, sport or project at work.

The day I miscarried, our cat disappeared. We knew we couldn't get our baby back, but by golly, Mark was gonna find that cat. He took a week off from work and was consumed by making phone calls, canvassing the neighborhood, distributing flyers and searching through animal shelters. I really believe that because of the sheer force of his efforts, our kitty was returned to us by kind strangers. And that was his way of dealing with our baby's death.

—Winnie

By taking action, you can try to push away the feelings of helplessness and reestablish feelings of competence. Diving into activities is a way to feel in control. Being in charge, taking up projects and making decisions are ways to strike back at the unfairness of the universe. To be competitive at work and at play is a way to fight back the feelings of fear and vulnerability.

Sometimes action is easily justifiable in terms of producing results or a product to be proud of. But action must be balanced with facing painful feelings of grief. Otherwise, those feelings are never handled or resolved. Instead they are buried and can require tremendous amounts of energy and perseverance to keep at bay.

Anger

Some men get stuck in anger. Anger is a valid response to your baby's death, but when mismanaged, can become hurtful to you and others. You may be easily frustrated when things don't go as you've planned. You may overreact to petty annoyances and find yourself slamming doors or throwing, pounding or swearing at things. You may be easily aggravated by your partner, other children, friends or co-workers and do hurtful things that you regret later. You may experience back and shoulder pain, indigestion or headaches. Anger turned inward can result in depression—feelings of hopelessness, worthlessness, powerlessness or fatigue that won't budge. You may feel less effective at your job or in your relationships. Sarcasm, cynicism, paranoia or forgetfulness can be indirect expressions of anger.

Anger as a coping style is a way to avoid deeper feelings of grief, including sadness, hurt, fear and despair. Though anger can make you feel powerful—and is socially acceptable, expected and is considered masculine—you pay a high price for avoiding feeling broken. Immersing yourself in aggressive activity consumes time, energy, emotion and thought, and keeps you from truly grieving. When you run away from despair, you also run away from healing. Instead of dwelling on memories, you dwell on lawsuits; instead of coming to terms and moving on, you hold on—to blame, revenge, resentment, bitterness and ultimately to your grief. (For more support and ideas on how to deal with anger, refer to chapter 6.)

Addiction

Addiction is simply a way to keep a lid on emotions. Substance abuse, such as with alcohol, drugs and food, can alter emotions by altering brain chemistry. Other behaviors such as gambling, adultery, ravenous sex, competitive sports and fervent religion can provide an emotional fix by immersing you in a drama that distracts you from other parts of your life.

Some addictions look good, even admirable from the outside. Long-distance running, working overtime, getting a charitable organization off the ground, becoming an expert surfer on the information highway—in moderation these activities can enhance your life. But anything can become destructive when the push to excel takes you away from your relationships, any of your responsibilities, your health and, of course, your feelings. With sports, you may find that you cannot take a break, even if it means risking or sustaining serious injury. Overtime at work can win you fame and fortune, but your family and friends become strangers. Charity can bring you praise and recognition, but true charity begins at home. Surfing on the Internet can be a fascinating way to expand horizons, but done to the exclusion of *real* life, your horizons are actually only as broad as a fiber-optic wire.

Everyone needs diversion. Excelling in something can bolster feelings of confidence. The trick is to find a balance so that all the important areas in your life get the attention they deserve. Balance also lets you participate more fully and contentedly in those things you enjoy. When anything becomes compulsive, take it as a sign that you are hiding from pain—pain that won't heal until it is faced, expressed and coped with. Addiction helps you hide; it does not help you cope.

All of these styles—silence, secrecy, action, anger and addiction—mask fear. Although it is natural to feel vulnerable and afraid, you may be largely conditioned to shut down those emotions. You may consider it unacceptable to feel depleted, insecure or yearning. Ironically, by wearing a mask of invulnerability, you don't have the opportunity to face and conquer your fears. You also dampen all of your feelings, including joy, comfort and generosity. Although you may appear to be strong, happy and productive, you may feel like a hollow shell, held hostage by your fears, your emotions, your inner self. While you may think you are controlling your emotions, in reality, your emotions are controlling you.

Reclaiming Your Emotions

You may already have considered that the traditional images of manhood need revision. But to forge a new identity that balances strength and gentleness can be difficult. Relinquishing the limits of male behavior and shedding the in-control, aloof, rational and independent veneer can be a frightening prospect.

Realistically, before you can shed old ways, you must acquire new ways so that you can manage the feelings that come up. Here's an analogy: Although it may be in your best interest to move out of a dilapidated old house, you must first find a new house to move into so that you're not left completely vulnerable to the elements. So it is with your emotional life. It is only fair to expect yourself to give up old ways after you've begun to master and trust new ways. Do take heart—by simply deciding on change, you are more than halfway there.

Facing Grief

Along with the frightening prospect of shedding traditional masculine ways of dealing with emotions, there is plenty to fear about grieving. You may worry that your feelings will be detrimental to your family and other relationships. You may fear losing others' respect. Perhaps your biggest fear is that you will fall apart and lose control of your emotions, your mind, your life.

It may help to try putting catastrophic thoughts into perspective. While opening up may lead to a flood of pent-up emotions from your present as well as past losses, grief is not a bottomless pit. Instead, imagine a tunnel. It may be dark and cold inside, but there is a light at the end. Milling around at the entrance can keep you from getting on with your life. You can't go over it or around it. You just have to go through it. If you get stuck in the middle, it isn't quicksand. You are the one who controls whether you move forward. Getting through the tunnel does require you to fall apart in order to release your deepest feelings. But falling apart is temporary, and unleashing feelings helps you to regain control over your life. Eventually you'll be able to function even better for unburdening yourself. Your relationships will benefit, and others will respect how emotionally centered and healthy you are.

By viewing grief this way, you might even agree that it's the brave thing to do. Loss changes you whether you grieve or not. If you let yourself mourn, you can change for the better, rather that succumbing to the pitfalls of suppressed feelings. You can even play an active role in your grief. There are many suggestions throughout this book on ways to facilitate your grieving process.

Coping with Grief

All of the suggestions for coping, grieving and healing contained in this book can apply to both mothers and fathers, but fathers may be more skeptical or reject many of these ideas outright. Because of the focus on emotions, fathers may see many of these suggestions as more in tune with how women grieve. And they are correct. Even if a mother tends to stuff or deny her feelings, the language of emotions is more in tune with her socialization and cultural expectations. She may take more of this book to heart, while her male partner may shrug it off. As John says, "I think men are into production and with grief, there's no product. You go through it, you're miserable and what do you have in the end? Nothing! It's like, why even bother?"

Grieving *can* be debilitating, but it is far more debilitating to suppress grief, for this silently cripples your strength, drains your energy, injures your health and sabotages your happiness. Suppressing feelings turns them inward, increasing their power to control you. The more you try to avoid grief, the more it runs your life, because every move you make has to keep you detached, tough or in denial.

> For me, when Eli died, I had all these feelings that were hard to identify and incorporate—generalized feelings of anxiety and anger and none of the books talked about that. I was a wreck. Finally I realized it all boiled down to powerlessness and fear—that my life was being torn apart and there wasn't a damn thing I could do about it. After that realization, it seems like I settled down and coped a lot better.
>
> —John

If you think you cannot afford to take the time or energy to grieve, try to make a conscious effort to set aside a little time or to gather a small amount of energy to devote to this endeavor. Avoid filling your calendar. Decline commitments and reduce the number of activities you're involved in. Try to make this a priority before you are forced to by some crisis— failing health, faltering career, disintegrating relationships or marginal sanity. Grieving can be as simple as reading books on bereavement, writing about your feelings, visiting the grave, talking with someone you trust or thinking about the baby while you do mindless chores or swim laps. These acts can help bring feelings to the surface whereupon you can face them, air them out and release them. By setting them free, you free yourself.

Finding the Words

If you haven't had much experience with, encouragement for or exposure to dialogue on emotions, you may find it very difficult to talk about your feelings. You may be able to talk about the facts, but this is not the same as talking about how it affected you. When you share information about your baby's death, try to also mention how you feel. For instance,

- Your baby's heartbeat stopped near the end of the first trimester—how did you *feel* when you found out that miscarriage was imminent?
- Your baby died when the pregnancy was interrupted—how did you *feel* about that decision?
- Your baby was tiny, only twelve inches long—how did you *feel* when you saw your baby?
- Your baby was stillborn at thirty-five weeks—how did you *feel* when your baby was born still?
- Your baby died during surgery—how did you *feel* when you received the news?
- You discovered your baby's lifeless body—how did you *feel* when you realized the baby was dead in your arms?

To vent your feelings, practice using the words that get to the core of your emotions: I feel … . I wish … . I miss … .

Label your emotions in connection with events: I feel angry when … . I feel sad because … . I felt powerless when … .

Find a safe, supportive person who can listen to you. You need someone who is nonjudgmental, patient with your grief, accepting of whatever you say and unafraid of anger or tears. A good listener recognizes the healing effect of talking, crying, dwelling on memories and expressing painful feelings. A supportive listener also sets aside plenty of private time for you so you have a chance to air out feelings, to fall apart and come together again, or to gain a new insight.

Finding Your Tears

Our culture equates being in control of the situation with controlling tears. When someone gets misty eyed, we assume that they have lost control of everything, not just their tear ducts. In just the past few years, this attitude has begun to change. There is research showing that tears are a biologically necessary way of relieving emotional stress—there is evidence that tears remove stress-induced toxins from the body. Holding back tears can increase stress, resulting in a variety of psychological and physical symptoms, including exacerbation of preexisting conditions such as high blood pressure, allergies, ulcers, colitis and cardiovascular disease.

Unfortunately, if a man has been taught that crying is foolish, he may be so inhibited that he is incapable of crying. If you feel like you need to cry but can't, it may help you to set up specific situations that will encourage you to let go. First, set aside a chunk of time when you know you won't be disturbed or distracted. Second, arrange for privacy, a place where you can howl without feeling self-conscious about others hearing you. It is important that you have space and solitude so that you don't feel anxious or afraid of interruption or discovery. Finally, in this place you can keep or take those things that remind you of your baby. These things might include a grave marker, photographs, clothing, a blanket, toys, stuffed animal, a poem or books about bereavement, particularly personal stories written by fathers (see *Anna: A Daughter's Life* by W. Loizeaux in the bibliography). You might look at something you've written or made or planted in your baby's memory. You could listen to music that holds special meaning for you.

When you are in your private space, focus your thoughts on significant days in your baby's life or your time as a father. Remember what it felt like to see the ultrasound image, hear the heartbeat or feel the baby kick. Remember your dreams, hopes and wishes for this child. Remember what it was like to see or hold your baby. Think about what you are missing, your regrets, your sorrows. Tell your baby the things that you wish you'd had time or opportunity to say. Imagine what your baby would say to you in response.

You can also try writing or painting or drawing some of your thoughts and emotions. Use any of your creative outlets to express feelings—music, dance, woodworking, blacksmithing, sculpture, weaving, design, gardening, carpentry, cartooning, poetry, photography, to name a few. You could even try something you've never tried before. Take up a creative art that perhaps you were discouraged from as a boy. Your untapped creativity can be a pathway to emotional healing and centeredness. Embrace whatever outlet feels right for you.

As you allow your deep feelings to surface, don't edit or inhibit them. Any feelings are real and should be permitted to find expression. Let your voice do what it wants. Let your body do what it wants. While a part of you may be shocked, embarrassed or afraid, allow yourself to do what you need. Let it flow. If you feel choked up, panting rapidly can make crying easier.

If you are afraid that once you start crying, you won't be able to stop, your fear is unfounded. No one has ever cried forever. It is more realistic to expect yourself to cry until you are tired and relieved, which for many people usually means five or ten minutes, but could mean an hour or more. This may seem like forever, but it isn't. Also, you may feel like you are crying "all day" when in reality, you are crying for short periods of time, off and on all day. Whatever your pattern, rest assured that crying jags will lessen in frequency and duration as you work through your grief. When you set aside a regular time and a special place to unleash your deepest feelings, you are taking a huge step toward healing and wholeness.

Attending a Support Group

There are many benefits to the father who attends a bereaved parent support group. Particularly if you are a novice at dealing with deep and painful emotions, you can derive a lot of comfort and encouragement from such a group. Some of the benefits are listed below.

- You can establish a connection with others who truly understand what this is like.
- By listening to others talk about their grief, you may be better able to get a handle on many of your own bewildering feelings. Listening can help you find the words for your emotions.
- You can reduce feelings of isolation as you observe that you aren't alone and that your feelings are normal and common among other bereaved parents.
- You can receive comfort from others. As you recover, you can begin to offer comfort as well. This can enhance feelings of confidence and purpose.
- Regular attendance can give you a dependable, predictable and secure anchor that can offer sanctuary and steadiness during this stormy time.
- If you join an all-male group, you can get additional benefits such as special attention to certain subjects that you may not feel comfortable discussing in a mixed group. You may also feel more explicit and implicit permission to cry. Many fathers feel like there is special respect from men for the strength behind their tears.

If you cannot find a men's group to attend, you can ask for a special "men only" meeting of your parent support group. This meeting can be a natural opportunity to launch a regular men's group. (For more information, refer to the section "Parent Support Groups" in chapter 12.)

Getting Counseling

It is common for fathers to feel overwhelmed by their grief. If facing emotions is new for you, you may feel stuck or jammed up and resist letting your feelings flow. Or you may worry about being consumed by your sorrow. Or you may show signs of repressed grief, such as depression, backaches, illness, addictive behaviors or excessive irritation and anger.

Many fathers benefit from counseling. Talking with an objective, supportive listener can help you come to terms with your baby's death. Therapy sessions are a safe place for you to feel and express a wide range of emotions, a place where you can tackle your fears, worries and sadness.

With gentle guidance, you can learn new ways of coping with feelings and dealing with problems, skills which can put you in good stead for a lifetime.

Shop around for a therapist with whom you feel comfortable. Look for someone who validates your feelings, helps you stay on relevant topics and guides you by posing questions or offering suggestions. After you find a counselor you like, give it a fair try. You may need to attend several weekly sessions before you can settle in and feel like you are making progress. New insights and breakthroughs usually come in spurts, so beware of bailing out during lulls before a storm. (For more information and support on this topic, see "Counseling" in chapter 12.)

Going into counseling is not an easy step. Making and attending your first appointment can be one of the most difficult and frightening things you'll ever do. But if you have any inkling that counseling might help you, do it. If at any time you discover that counseling is not right for you, you can always stop.

A Father's Unfinished Grief

Because of social expectations and the pressures of life in general, you may feel that you cannot grieve for long. As your attention gets diverted to other concerns and activities, you may find it easy to let your feelings submerge. You may feel as if you are ready to move on, and there will be plenty of implicit and explicit encouragement for this. But for many fathers, grief does not end after a few days or weeks.

There are ample clues that you may harbor feelings that are looking for expression. You may feel angry at life, sensitive to criticism, disinterested in your regular activities or resentful of others who seem happy. You may lack confidence in your ability to set and reach goals. You may feel generalized anxiety or feel more cautious, reserved or lethargic. You may try to bury yourself in work, sports, hobbies or religion. You may try to find comfort in excessive alcohol, drugs, food or sex.

You may also notice that certain holidays or anniversary dates are particularly hard for you to endure. Family gatherings may be surprisingly difficult, especially if there are other babies. While emerging feelings of grief can be discouraging or unsettling, do try to take the opportunity to work through some of those emotions. Writing in a journal, talking to other bereaved parents or seeing a counselor can be helpful at these times.

Half Moon Pass

Here I am again
    on top Half Moon Pass
Warm sleeping bag awaiting me
    some distance behind
Half Moon—a good place
    to be alone
    six months after tragedy

Half Moon—a good place
   to scream and holler
   into noisy wind
      and deafening quiet
Half Moon—a good place
   to see forever
   as if a vast expanse
      were a help
So I sit here alone
   except for myself
   and the Keeper of this Vista
And I comb through tangled
   and flowing memories
Looking to tend the wound
   looking for a place
   where it stops or starts
But grief is playing that familiar trick
   and the only thing to touch or feel
   is a bucket full of numb
So with exasperation climbing
   I undress
      to the freezing touch
      of unattending wind
And in bitter angry madness
   I pass sentence on grief itself
   "If you will not feel the pain,
      I'll match you numb for numb"
The sun is giving up her reign
And I'm floating in a sea of goosebumps
   feeling righteous
   and of one accord
I spy a place where lightning has struck
   ten miles between me and the growing faraway
      fire—going to work
Watching, waiting—numbing it
A question lurks its way
   to the surface of my mind
      "John, would you rather freeze or burn,
         Which death would be most kind?"
I can't decide tonight
So I elect my sleeping bag
   and the arms of solace there
Believing tomorrow wiser
   in this battle with despair.

—John E. Hicks
In Memory of Eli

Points to Remember

- As a father, you may feel overlooked. You do need to grieve in order to come to terms with your baby's death. When others around you fail to acknowledge your grief, you may feel isolated, misunderstood and feel compelled to keep your grief secret.
- Differences between how fathers and mothers *express* grief largely come from the different social expectations placed on men and women. As a man, you've been socialized to subdue grieving emotions. Be aware that your grief may be more heartfelt than it appears to be from the outside.
- Nowadays, many men are reclaiming their emotional lives and opening up to formerly forbidden feelings. With this new tide of information and social support, many men are gaining respect for facing and coping with their emotions.
- Even if you have felt unable to grieve before for lack of permission or practice, you can try to do things differently this time, to face and cope with your feelings. This can benefit your emotional and physical health, improve your marriage and other relationships, and increase your energy and happiness. Also, this honors your baby.
- Find other men to talk to. Men's support groups can be particularly affirming for you.
- If you are feeling stuck, you might benefit from counseling. Seeking professional help is a sign of your courage and willingness to face yourself.
- While the mother's grief may be generally more intense, you have many of your own fatherly perspectives that can arouse feelings that the mother may not share or understand. Tell her about your point of view. She will be reassured by this evidence of your feelings.
- Remember that although you and the mother should expect to grieve differently and hold different perspectives, you can still have a harmonious relationship. Tolerate, accept and be unthreatened by your differences. They are normal and necessary.

10

You and Your Partner

Most couples notice that their relationship is affected after their baby dies. Some feel closer and draw together in sorrow. In the process, they learn more about each other's sensitivities and strengths, and their intimacy and mutual support may be enhanced.

Other couples pull apart and withdraw into blame, displaced anger and misunderstandings. For some, this tragedy becomes a catalyst that breaks up an already troubled relationship. For many couples, a baby's death drives a needless wedge into an otherwise healthy partnership.

As a couple, you may alternate between intimacy and isolation. This may be the first tragedy you've faced together, and you may discover new ways of being there for each other. But sometimes the stress of grieving can make you so needy individually that it can be difficult to support each other. Many of the grieving emotions, such as anger and depression, make it even more of a challenge to be supportive. Often you will grieve very differently from each other, making it hard for you to empathize or accept each other's feelings.

There are things you can do to make sure your relationship survives. Remember that before you were parents, you were friends and lovers. Care about your partner, care about what he or she is feeling, care about what he or she needs. In addition to caring, *sharing, acceptance* and *reassurance* are the ingredients that can help a relationship survive.

Sharing Thoughts and Feelings

Communication in a relationship is normally challenging, and after a baby dies, the stress of grieving can add tension to your relationship. Misunderstandings flair up easily. You may hesitate sharing your thoughts and feelings about the baby, for fear of burdening each other. It takes energy to communicate, and you may wish your partner could just read your mind or understand you with minimum effort. You may find it difficult to cope with your partner's emotions because you are struggling with your own.

Couples who share thoughts and feelings, however, offer each other valuable support. In particular, a father who talks about the baby and his emotions is a source of comfort to the mother because this lets her know she is not the only one who grieves for her baby. Although it may appear that he is making the mother sad, the father is really inviting her to share the grieving feelings she already has. Sharing feelings reduces the parents' isolation and can help both of them cope better.

Even if you have difficulty expressing your feelings, you can be supportive by listening and allowing your partner to express his or her feelings. Knowing that someone is there to listen and hold you when you cry can be a tremendous support.

> I never felt like I was burdening him with my tears. I needed to talk about it and I needed to cry about it, and he never left me feeling like he didn't want to hear it. Other people tire of hearing your problems, but he never gave me that feeling. He always was willing to listen no matter how many times he heard it.
>
> —Sarah

Many bereaved mothers report that a mutual willingness to listen and an open attitude become invaluable qualities in their relationship. Mourning a baby's death is a shared trauma. Talking about it does not add to the burden, it lessens the pain. By being available, listening and sharing feelings, parents can enhance each other's coping and strengthen their intimacy.

Accepting Your Differences

Parents are often dismayed to discover that they grieve differently. Distinct styles can be attributed to normal variations in personality, socialization, philosophy, coping style and, in the case of women, postpartum hormonal changes.

Mothers and fathers also grieve differently because they usually feel different levels of bonding to the baby. During pregnancy, the mother usually feels a closer connection with the baby. For the father, the baby is much more abstract until birth. Particularly when the baby dies early in the pregnancy, the father usually feels a much lesser bond than the mother. As the pregnancy progresses, the father can see the growth occurring, feel fetal movements and, especially after birth, the fatherly bond deepens. Even so, it is difficult for fathers and mothers to feel the same intense connection with the baby.

> Since this baby was full term, this was the first pregnancy that my husband could identify with. The others were miscarriages, and as each miscarriage occurred, it became the norm to him, I think. He was always concerned about me, but he never ever mentioned the pregnancies. He could never identify with me as to how I felt. All these losses I was on my own, and it was something he could never understand, but with this one, he did.
>
> —Meryl

When the baby died, my husband hadn't really adjusted yet to the idea that we were having a baby. I don't think he felt like a father. He was always supportive of me and willing to listen but the fact that he didn't feel much grief has made it a more lonely experience for me. Now, 3 years later, I doubt he ever thinks about it, so I hesitate to bring it up. I don't want to impose or look foolish.

—Winnie

Because men and women are socialized differently, even if they feel the same sense of connection with the baby, it is natural that they will grieve in different ways. Women are generally expected to be more nurturing and expressive, while men are expected to be strong and unemotional. Although this is not the rule, many couples experience these dynamics: The mother cries and dwells on her memories of the baby, and the father quells his grief and often busies himself in his work. As far as she can see, he is uncaring and has forgotten about the baby. She feels angry at this callousness and isolated as she grieves alone. From the father's view, she will never get over her grief. He impatiently wants her to snap out of it so life can get back to normal.

My husband says I scare him because I grieve too intensely. We try to find a happy medium where we can talk about it without frightening each other.

—Rosemary

Another common dynamic in couples is grieving alternately. If they both fall apart, who would keep everything else together? Somebody has to go back to work, the bills still need to be paid, the pantry needs to be stocked, the other children need care; life does go on. When one of the partners is having an especially hard time, the other often puts grief aside. Sometimes couples switch off daily, sometimes weekly or monthly. Other couples don't switch until a year or so after the baby dies.

At first, I never saw him cry. I'd talk and talk about the baby and he'd hold me and I'd ask him, "Why don't you cry?" and he'd say, "Well, it's over with, he's dead, what's crying going to do?" And finally one night about three or four months after, he cried and then I was better. I could be strong for him. I just held him and let him cry. It was a big relief to see that, gee, he does care, he is human, because I couldn't figure out why I was so depressed and crying when he was handling it just fine, which he really wasn't.

—Desi

In one sense it has drawn us closer, but we've been so focused on self-survival that we've grown apart. He denied his grief for quite a while and wanted me to move on. Then it hit him hard a year later.

—Holly

Just as partners often take turns grieving, they may also take turns being enraged or anxious or depressed. It's as if the partnership can only tolerate a certain amount of a certain emotion, so when one partner feels something intensely, the other partner tones it down. For example, you may notice that the more agitated you feel, the more calm your partner becomes. This in itself can be aggravating because you may feel invalidated by the lack of mutual feeling.

First, recognize that you are holding the lion's share. Eventually, you may see evidence of that feeling in your partner after you've taken your turn. As you let go of an emotion, your partner can have room to feel it. Second, check your emotional boundaries. Give yourself permission to have your feelings and give your feelings permission to be different from your partner's. You are entitled to your feelings whether anyone else agrees or not. Third, take complete responsibility for your reactions. They arise out of your perceptions and your body. No one can "make" you feel a certain way. Instead of blaming your partner for making you so angry, crazy, fearful or sad, see those feelings as your own reactions, arising out of your own issues. Instead of seeing yourself as a victim, claim creation of your feelings. In doing so, you will also claim the power to face and deal with them.

If you can understand where these differences come from, you may feel less threatened by them. Acceptance is also easier if you remember there are no right or wrong ways to grieve, and no two people grieve alike. What's important is finding what's right for you.

It is also important to avoid judging each other, for instance: "Since he feels this way, he must not care much about the baby" or "She will never get over this if she keeps feeling that way." By simply accepting your partner's feelings, you are acknowledging that he or she is entitled to his or her feelings, just as you are entitled to yours. Remember, accepting another's feelings doesn't negate your own. You may not share your partner's feelings; you may not always understand them. You may even feel angry or disappointed at your partner's reactions. But by accepting each other's silences and tears without judging or placing blame, you encourage nonthreatening communication. You also provide the kind of support and understanding so necessary to promote healing and to enhance your relationship.

Attending a support group may help you to understand your feelings and open lines of communication. By listening to other parents, you can be reassured that both you and your partner are reacting normally to your loss. By listening to each other share thoughts and emotions in a group, you can get insights about yourself, your partner or your relationship. You may be able to start a healthy dialogue on your feelings about the baby and your grief.

For instance, Carolyn remembers the time her husband casually mentioned to the group that he thought about their daughter Rachel while he painted the house. Although to an observer this may seem unremarkable, he had never told Carolyn about this, and she found it comforting and reassuring to discover that he did think about the baby. (For more information on differences, refer to chapter 9.)

> I felt like my husband should be grieving and showing his grief exactly the same way that I was. That if he were grieving, that it would somehow lighten my load. When I heard another parent in group say these same things, then I started realizing it was just absurd. I was expecting him to do the work for me and angry at him for not being an identical twin.
>
> —Liza

Reassurance

Before the baby died, your relationship may have been open and sharing, relatively effortless. Unfortunately, grieving can create chasms that can easily widen, and you may fear that your partner will abandon you. Ironically, these concerns can make you withdraw even more as you try to protect yourself from the hurt. Or you may try to protect yourself with blame and anger, using these emotions to push your partner away. Unconsciously you may operate on the principle "I'll quit before I'm fired" or "I'll leave you before you can leave me!"

> We had mostly grieved at a similar rate and style for the first couple of months, and then it seemed as though I felt a lot more alone. Kent was handling it in his own way and I was handling it in my own way, and it was becoming a problem in the relationship.
>
> —Jessie

> I expected John to be the one person I could hang on to in the storm. But through the thick of it, we were both staggering under our own burdens and we couldn't possibly pick up another pound. As a result, we each staggered alone for a while.
>
> —Claudia

Grieving alone, although necessary at times, can be difficult and sometimes frightening. Do try to build bridges, not walls. Reassuring each other of your love and devotion can guard against fears of losing each other. It is reasonable to ask your partner if she still cares about you or to ask if he blames you. In turn, you can reassure your partner that you still love her or that you don't blame him for your baby's death. You both need to be sensitive to each other's needs for this kind of reassurance.

> It really helped that my husband kept telling me that I was important and kept telling me that we were there before the baby and we would still be there after the baby and that kind of thing, always telling me how much he cared for me.
>
> —Bryn

We kept hearing that everybody who said they'd lost a baby said they split up and we thought, "Oh, we can't do that! We've lost something already." So we got a lot closer.

—Martina

Tolerating Change and Conflict

After your baby dies, you will change and so will your partner. If changes make you uneasy, you may feel unsettled, scared or anxious. You may be irritable, inflexible, withdrawn or quick to anger. It can help to remember that you need time and space to adjust.

Many of the changes you and your partner are going through can give rise to conflict. Naturally, your differences can put a strain on your relationship. Some of these sticking points may involve

- searching for and adopting new philosophies, perspectives, goals, desires and assumptions about your life, its meaning and direction
- questioning your religious beliefs and faith
- having a new awareness of your needs and emotions; wanting to become more assertive and expressive
- dealing with a resurgence of grief from past losses
- having varying and incongruent intimacy needs
- having varying and incongruent desires for another baby
- having disagreements about handling your other children's feelings and behaviors
- having disagreements about how much information to share with other people, such as information about difficult decisions, experiences, feelings and other personal matters
- experiencing the end of the "honeymoon period" that existed around the time of death
- enduring the simple stress of grieving for your baby, along with the normal feelings of anger or depression
- walking differing paths of grief—you cannot always grieve together or be supportive
- harboring negative reactions to your partner's coping style, religious views or need to dwell on memories and mementos
- experiencing differences in how easily each of you adapt to change
- having different levels of tolerance for conflict or distance

Acknowledging these changes and conflicts and their often temporary and normal nature can help you weather them. It may also help you and your partner to openly discuss these matters. Just airing your feelings and differences can reduce some of the tension in you—and your relationship.

Resisting the Urge to "Fix It"

Changes and conflicts are normal and natural. Experiencing these rough spots does not mean there is something wrong with you or your relationship. Growing pains are part of the grieving process. They are a part of marriage. There is no way to make either grief or marriage smooth or painless. Terri remembers when someone told her that life's upheavals were *supposed* to be hard. Just hearing that affirmation helped her to let go of her struggle to figure out a way to make it all easy. When you are in the middle of a lake, you're better off putting your energy toward learning how to swim rather than trying to bale out the water.

Also, it is natural to want to help ease your partner's emotional pain. But remember, just as you appreciate it when others *don't* try to fix or smooth over your feelings, your partner will appreciate it when you simply listen and accept. While you may believe you have some answers, remember that these answers may not work for someone else. Resist preaching your insights, perspectives and attitudes to your partner. If you do share what has helped you, speak personally and nondirectively: "I did this and it really helped me." Or "For me, it helps to look at it this way." Avoid being prescriptive and presumptuous, as in, "You should try this because it helped me."

Keep in mind that your partner may not embrace your ideas. What is right for one person can be counterproductive for another. The best help you can offer is to be a nonjudgmental sounding board. This will encourage your partner to find his or her own special way toward healing and growth.

Sex and Intimacy

For some couples, sex provides the intimacy and reassurance they need from each other. However, for many couples sex becomes a tension point. When a couple is drained emotionally and physically, when they feel depressed or angry, or when communication breaks down, sex may be the last thing they desire. For many parents, the link between sex and conception is painfully obvious. For others, the association between sex and affection makes them feel hurt by their partner's lack of desire. Mothers must also cope with natural postpartum physical and emotional changes that can make them less responsive.

Negotiating your sexual relationship requires more sharing, acceptance and reassurance. Be sensitive to your own and each other's emotional needs during this stressful time. By talking, listening and holding each other, you can maintain feelings of affection and intimacy without the pressures of intercourse. You can find comfort in spending quality time together, including dinner for two, going for long walks and sharing other activities you enjoy. In time, as your grief becomes more manageable, your sexual relationship can become more comfortable.

Handling Anger

Anger is a natural facet of grief. Unfortunately, you may aim it at those you love most. When you are simmering, minor mishaps can explode into World War III. If you notice that you are having a lot of big fights over little issues, you may want to sort out your feelings. Do you need some constructive outlets for your anger? Try writing a letter, pounding a pillow, running around the block. Do you have some underlying fears that need to be addressed? Acknowledge your vulnerability and lack of control over your life right now. Do you need encouragement? Anger is often accompanied by feeling unworthy. Tell your partner or a good friend that you need to hear what they like about you. Think how much you would enjoy returning the favor.

Perhaps most of all, you and your partner may need to somehow get out of the vicious cycle of anger and withdrawal. You've lost your precious baby and it is natural to feel angry. Particularly when you and your partner are aggravating each other, it is normal to withdraw rather than stay vulnerable. Stepping back can be a way to protect yourself. Putting up a wall of anger can be a way to keep your distance too.

But how can you get out of a vicious cycle of anger and withdrawal? First, you have to want change. For some couples, shouting matches or simmering silence contain the only emotional connection they feel comfortable with. If this is your style, you may find it especially difficult to call a truce. Before you file for separation, though, remember that you will take this style with you into future unions. So you might consider learning how to manage conflict now and reap the benefits.

In an intimate relationship, anger and withdrawal often mask underlying feelings of hurt and fear. So, the antidote is to address the hurt and fear by REASSURING YOUR PARTNER THAT YOU ARE COMMITTED TO STAYING IN THE RELATIONSHIP. The next time you want to nip escalation in the bud, or pick up the pieces, try saying something like, "I'm not going anywhere. Even though you wish I would, I'm not leaving you." You needn't say anything mushy or speak of love. After all, while you are aggravating each other, an "I love you" will ring false. Endear yourself by exaggerating faults. "Even though I'm the worst on the planet, you're stuck with me no matter what." Or acknowledge your partner's fantasy of your disappearance. "I'm coming home whether you want me or not." Gather up your courage to try it. Find the reassuring words and style that work for you.

When you basically trust and like each other, there is hope. If you think you would benefit from counseling, do it. Go alone if your partner won't join you. As you learn to manage conflict, all of your relationships will benefit. (For more on coping with anger, refer to chapter 6.)

Can Our Relationship Survive?

Many couples experience stress after their baby dies, but their marriage survives. Sophie, Rose, Bess and Clara talk about the difficulties they encountered.

The first month or so after Stephanie died, Cal was very supportive and did as much as he could to help me physically as well as emotionally. But there was some point after a month or so—maybe he had deferred some of his grieving because he was so busy taking care of me—where he kind of lost his patience and there was a lot of tension between the two of us. We got some counseling at that point. And it went through my head that events like this either really cement a marriage or blow it out of the water entirely: "Which one are we going to do?" So then I'd get scared that my marriage was also falling apart, but then I began to understand that Cal was dealing with his own grieving and his own stress. He'd been so superattentive to me that he finally was worn out and couldn't do it anymore.

—Sophie

I hated my husband. I felt like he wasn't sympathetic and he wasn't grieving like I thought he should be. I didn't really see him for about six months because he was trying to bury himself by keeping busy, school and work, thirteen hours a day.

—Rose

We never really blamed each other for what happened, but there was just stress. There was so much unhappiness for having lost the baby that I think we took it out on each other. Then he, trying to handle grief his way, would go elsewhere sometimes, and that was very, very difficult. I became very dependent on him and then when he wasn't there, it hurt me more and I became very angry with him. I remember that spring I asked him to move out of the house, and then we got back together and went to counseling.

—Bess

Right after the baby died, there was this honeymoon period where we felt, "We're alive, I love you so much, we'll try again soon," and then you start drifting apart into your own grief and grieving so differently, and that incredible closeness goes away. But then we came back together eventually.

—Clara

For some couples the stress may break apart an already floundering relationship or create problems that seem too big to overcome. Poor communication habits that existed before the pregnancy may flare up and ignite smoldering long-standing issues such as sex, money and relatives. Mira recalls, "After Matthew died, we simply stopped talking and we had nothing in common anymore. We lost each other." Anya remembers how she and her husband drifted apart: "My husband never talked about her, ever. He never showed his feelings, never held her, did not want pictures, never cried."

> As soon as we got home he said the cruelest words a person could say: "If you hadn't gone skiing, we'd have a healthy child." I felt so guilty. I thought I'd murdered my own baby because I'd gone skiing. That was the beginning of the end of our marriage.
>
> —Lena

If you are both determined that your relationship will survive this tragedy, it probably will. It might be useful to read self-help books written for couples interested in improving relations (see "Books for Couples" in the bibliography). Many couples benefit from counseling. A therapist can help you understand why you are withdrawing or quarreling and help you sort out the underlying fears and tensions. Keeping your relationship going is hard work, but the payoffs of strengthened communication and deeper commitment can make the struggle worthwhile. Faith advises marriage counseling for anyone having trouble: "It saved my marriage. And after my baby died, the last thing I needed was a divorce, to lose my husband too!"

Many couples are reassured by the fact that they came through this experience feeling closer than ever. You may have opened up new lines of communication or discovered things about each other that enhance your intimacy or commitment. You may even realize a sense of accomplishment—if your relationship can survive this, it can survive anything.

> It was wonderful for our relationship. It's an awful thing to say, but it's really true. It brought us so much closer together and we've managed to keep close. It was a real binding kind of thing, finding strengths we didn't know each other had.
>
> —Sarah

Parents without Partners

If you are a widow or widower in addition to being a bereaved parent, your sorrow may feel too deep to comprehend. You may feel confused, not knowing who your tears are for, or you may feel disloyal when you cry more for one loss than the other. You may long for the understanding hugs of your baby's other parent as you grieve your baby's death; you may long for that baby to be safe in your arms, so you can hold on to a piece of your partner's living legacy. As if dealing with one or the other loss isn't unbearable enough, to lose both can seem especially intolerable and cruelly unjust. Be sure that you get support for both of your losses by talking about each one, reading books specifically for each or attending support groups for each.

If your relationship has broken through separation or divorce, or if you didn't have an established relationship, you may long for the commiseration of your baby's other parent. You may feel isolated and lonely as you grieve. You may also feel like the accommodations you made in preparation for being a single parent were all for naught. You may feel you are being punished for your decisions or being denied the chance to prove that you could succeed.

The pain you feel upon your baby's death can bring up grief you may have experienced during the breakdown of your partnership. After the baby dies, you may feel a greater bond to the other parent. You may consider reconciliation as he or she is a tangible connection to the baby you miss. You may even have fantasies of achieving another pregnancy with this person in an effort to recapture what you've lost. In fact, the desire for another child can make your single status a huge source of frustration.

To add to your isolation and frustration, others may fail to offer you the sympathy they might offer a couple whose baby has died. Attitudes such as "being a single parent is tough to manage" and "children are better off with more than one parent" can make people see your baby's death as "a blessing in disguise." Or you may project those attitudes onto others when they act uncomfortable around you.

If you are single, don't fall into the trap of idealizing grieving within a partnership. Grieving is something that you must do largely on your own, whether you are in an intimate relationship or not. Isolation and loneliness are common feelings for any bereaved parent. Remember that even in a normally close and sharing marriage, partners will grieve as individuals, often incongruently and at a distance.

Do seek out support from others. Support groups and newsletters can help you feel less isolated. Organizations such as Pen-Parents and SHARE have access to the vast network of bereaved parents and they can put you in touch with others who are in similar circumstances. Having friends or a therapist to talk to can be key to your healing.

Points to Remember

- As a couple, you may notice that your baby's death affects your relationship—sometimes for better, sometimes for worse.
- Change and conflict are natural and inevitable. Weathering change and resolving conflicts are far more beneficial than avoiding them.
- Key ingredients to help your relationship survive this tragedy include caring about each other, sharing thoughts and feelings, accepting your differences and reassuring your partner that you are committed to the relationship.
- Partners have very different needs for sex and intimacy. In time, as your grief becomes more manageable, your sexual relationship can become more comfortable and easier to negotiate.
- Anger is a common grieving emotion and can lead to a cycle of outbursts and withdrawal. Reassure each other that you aren't going to leave the relationship.
- Allowing feelings and being honest will build intimacy and strengthen your marriage.
- Constructive ways to resolve conflicts involve listening, acknowledging feelings, stepping back when your partner ventilates and setting aside time for planned discussions.
- If you are both determined that your relationship will survive, it probably will. If you think couples counseling might help, try it.
- If you are without a partner, seek out support from others. Support groups, newsletters and bereaved parent organizations can put you in touch with people who are in similar circumstances.

11

Your Family

Your Baby's Grandparents

Not only do I grieve the death of my grandson, I grieve for my daughter. I don't want her to have any pain because she's *my* baby, and I can't make it better.

—Pearl

Many grandparents endure a double sorrow. They grieve for the grandchild who will never grow up and they grieve for you, their child, who suffers the death of a baby. They may also feel as though they've lost you, so immersed are you in sorrow. Your parents may feel very helpless or inadequate because they cannot lessen your suffering. They may feel the same anger that you experience and may want to blame someone for their grandchild's death. If they have ever lost children of their own, they may relive that pain now. In any case, you may feel as though you have to protect them from your despair.

My mother cares so much, I feel like I can't give her a whole lot of my problem. … She'll just feel so awful herself. It's not that I couldn't say anything to her, but I just thought, "Why?" It won't help me, it won't help her and I'll feel like I have to take care of her.

—Meryl

It's easier to talk to somebody who's unrelated because relatives have so much emotion themselves. I felt I had to protect them, you know; my mom lost a grandchild. We didn't talk about it that much. They were there, but no one really talked because we didn't know what to say to each other.

—Erin

At a time when you want to depend on your parents for emotional support, they may not be able to give it for one reason or another. They may withdraw, frightened by the way your baby's death forces them to face their own immortality. Some simply do not understand the grieving process you must go through. If they have trouble dealing with emotions, they may try to smooth over your feelings of despair. Others may have lost babies of their own, but if they were not encouraged or allowed to grieve, acknowledging your grief would require them to examine their own. For many, that's too painful. Instead, they may try to belittle your baby's importance or try to talk you out of your feelings in order to protect themselves from their own sadness, and you from yours.

Even more difficult, some grandparents may not readily recognize the baby as a grandchild, particularly if there are other grandchildren. If your baby died during pregnancy or early infancy, they may not have had a chance to develop a grandmotherly or grandfatherly bond. While they may feel sorry *for* you, you may wish they could feel sorry *with* you. You may be very hurt when they make comments that appear to discount your baby's life, or when they don't say anything.

> My mother came in the hospital room and was trying to be real cheerful and happy and perk me up and make me feel better. She didn't really let down too much around me. She did with my sister. With me she was trying to be the "good mommy" and that kind of stuff. I felt like she didn't have to do that. I cried when anybody came into my room, and they did too, and she didn't need to be so … . The crying made me feel better!
>
> —Hannah

> My mother-in-law was furious that we sent out announcements of our baby's death. She said, "It wasn't even a baby you lost." It turns out she had a miscarriage but never grieved and was told, "Just have another baby and forget it."
>
> —Clara

> I wish that my mother could talk about David more. She could say, "I know it's that time of year and I'm thinking about him too," but she can't. My husband and I are pretty much the only ones who ever think that February is difficult. Sometimes I wish someone would acknowledge that he existed.
>
> —Bess

> The first Christmas after I miscarried, I was 15 weeks into another pregnancy but I was consumed with thoughts of the baby who should have been a couple months old, cradled in my arms that holiday season. My parents were focused on the new baby and gave us a couple of baby gifts but I had my husband open them because I couldn't bear it. … To commemorate this baby, I hung a special ornament on their tree, without saying anything. I didn't want to "spoil" the celebration, even though I really felt like screaming.
>
> —Winnie

When your parents aren't supportive, avoid telling them what they are doing wrong—criticism is rarely productive. Instead, make suggestions for what they can do to help. You may be afraid to tell them what you need for fear they won't respond, and then you'll be even more disappointed. However, you have a right to at least try. If it is difficult to talk to them, you could write a letter, buy them a "grieving grandparents" booklet or send a photocopy of a chapter or article on supporting bereaved parents. Emphasize that you find it most comforting when people listen and let you cry without judging, advising or fixing. Remind them that they can't, nor should they try, to ease your pain. If they cannot be supportive, focus on friends or other family members who can be there for you.

Sometimes grandparents become more supportive if they are included in acknowledging the baby's life. Show them your mementos and any pictures you have. Invite them to the funeral or send a formal announcement. Ask them to memorialize your baby in their own way, perhaps by making a donation, planting a tree, lighting a candle or including the baby in their prayers. Point out that your grief will last a long time and that you'd appreciate their sensitivity. You may also decide to forgive any misguided efforts on their part because you know they mean well.

Some grandparents are able to be supportive without much prompting. Your parents may be educated about grief or may naturally react sensitively and compassionately to your needs. Or they may be responsive to your suggestions.

> My mom thought of things like getting him an outfit, donating my extra milk to the La Leche League. That was very helpful, being able to do what I could as far as the mothering role I wanted to be in at that time.
>
> —Kara

Other Relatives

You may feel close enough to some of your siblings, cousins or even aunts or uncles to consider them friends. If you normally rely on these family members for companionship or support, you may be able to count on them being there for you. However, in many families, babies are born concurrently and you may be desperately jealous that your sister has her arms full and yours are so empty. If you find it difficult to be around or talk about other babies in the family, do let those parents know how sad, envious or resentful you feel. Chances are, they want to know how to handle this difficult subject when you are around. If you bring it up, they'll probably be eager to hear what you have to say.

While some relatives will surprise you with their sensitivity, others may disappoint you with their callousness or evasiveness. Differences in emotional outlook or religious and philosophical viewpoints can drive a wedge into a relationship. After Avery interrupted her pregnancy, her sister was openly critical and their relationship sadly disintegrated. Winnie and her cousin suffered miscarriages within a month of each other but the circumstances were so different that they could hardly speak about it. Winnie says, "We've always felt close, but this was not something we could share. Her pregnancy was her fourth and unplanned. She felt relieved and relied on her strong religious faith, so she could say, 'Oh well, it's for the best.' This was my first baby and I was in utter despair." (For more information and ideas on getting the support you need from relatives, see "Friends" in chapter 12.)

Other Children in the Family

How other children in the family respond to the death of their baby sibling will depend on several factors, including:

- their level of understanding about death
- their relationship with the baby
- their reaction to the parents' grief
- the support and reassurance they receive

Explaining Death to Children

In the past, discussing death with children was considered insensitive and unnecessary. Parents avoided talking about death to spare children from sadness. They often answered questions with misinformation to protect the children's innocence. However, by telling children stories such as "Grandma went on a long trip" or "Spot went to sleep and won't be waking up again," their well-intentioned remarks only added elements of fear, rejection or anger to the sense of loss. A child who is told, "Grandma went on a long trip" may wonder, "Why did Grandma leave me without saying goodbye and why can't I visit her? Doesn't she want to see me?" A child who is told, "Spot went to sleep" may worry, "If I go to sleep, will I be able to wake up?" A child who is told, "Billy is with God" or "God needed another angel" may be fearful or angry toward a God who takes people away forever. In these attempts to spare children the pain of grief, parents may unwittingly intensify disturbed feelings.

Nowadays, most parents recognize that children can cope better when they are informed. Informing your children, however, can be difficult to carry out if you are wrestling with your own emotional issues. When you were growing up, death may have been a taboo subject in your family. If your parents didn't encourage or allow you to ask about death, you may find it difficult to tolerate your children's ponderings. You may feel anxious and unable to answer questions calmly and openly. Recognize the source of your discomfort and let go of your family's judgment. If you let yourself wonder about death, you'll find it easier to welcome your children's questions.

Even if death was always handled openly and appropriately in your family, talking to your children can still be hard.

There are a number of books about near-death experiences and angels that can help make death seem less mysterious, frightening or gloomy. Children's books are good resources too (see "Books for Parents and Children" in the bibliography). Reading stories together about death and grief can open up discussion.

There are no perfect words to explain death to children. The words you use, however, should be honest, informative and age-appropriate. When your children ask questions or make confusing or false statements about death, take the cue and answer, clarify and reassure them. If the time or place isn't right, tell them you'd like to discuss this at a better time and then make sure you bring it up again within a day or two. Putting it off won't make them forget about it. If they don't ask again, they might need you to broach the topic for reassurance that it's OK to talk about.

Try to answer questions directly and simply. Instead of offering complicated, elaborate explanations, let the children ask more questions so you can see where their line of curiosity is going. Accurate information empowers your children to master their ideas and feelings. Avoidance, half-truths and euphemisms may damage your children's confidence in you and contribute to fears about death and what it all means. If your children know they can ask questions and get honest answers from you, they will learn not only about death, but also that they can confide in you. This in turn will encourage them to ask more questions about whatever they find worrisome or confusing.

You will not overwhelm your children if you take into account their need for information and reassurance. If you are not afraid to talk about death, they will not be afraid to hear about it.

> After the twins were born, my daughter (age 4) saw Bradley and kept asking "Now, when are you going to have the other baby, Mom?" The first thing that came to mind was, we'll just tell her the doctors made a mistake but then we thought, "No, because we don't want her to have a mistrust of doctors." So we just told her that when Jeffrey was born he was too small and too sick and he went up to heaven. She seemed to handle it OK, "Oh, all right." Even now (1 year later) she'll say "Isn't it sad that Jeffrey has to be up in heaven and can't be with us?"
>
> —Shannon

Children's Understanding of Death

Children's ability to understand death depends on their level of intellectual development—the way they view the world and relationships between things and events. Until adolescence, many children need to experience and think about things in tangible ways. But death is not tangible. Dead is not something they can be for a little while to see what it's like. It's not something they can do to see how it works. As a result, children have difficulty understanding death the way adults do—that death is when the body is no longer alive, that it is irreversible and depending on beliefs, the person either ceases to exist, the spirit goes to heaven or to another plane of existence, or the person goes on to be reincarnated as another living being.

Most children acquire an inaccurate understanding of death, but this is not necessarily a problem. They may simply have a unique way of looking at it, a way that causes them no concern. Other children may have some misconceptions about death that frighten them. Rather than focusing on how accurately your children understand death, try to address any concerns or fears they may have. (See "Providing the Support and Reassurance Your Children Need" later in this chapter.)

Attending the Funeral and Other Rituals of Mourning

In the past, many parents felt that siblings should be spared from attending the baby's funeral or graveside services. However, children who are not allowed to participate in these rituals may feel excluded from the family at a time when they need to be surrounded by loved ones. Being a part of the family, seeing how others grieve and hearing others talk lovingly about the baby are comforting and help them sort out their feelings about the death. They may also gain understanding about where and how the dead are buried or ashes are spread, instead of being left to think about scenes from cartoons or horror films about skeletons rising from dusty, crumbling graveyards. If you can explain to them what the baby's funeral or service will be like, you may be able to encourage them to attend. You may be able to encourage them to go to some family gatherings and to forgo others. It is better to err on the side of allowing children to be a part of rituals and family gatherings, rather than excluding them.

Understanding Your Children's Sense of Loss

If your children knew there was a baby but the baby never came home, they may wonder where the baby went. But children vary widely as to how much they look forward to a new baby. Unlike parents and older children, many younger children cannot form an imaginary bond with the baby. Without emotional investment in the idea of having a new baby/sibling/ companion/rival/roommate, very young children will not grieve the death of this invisible baby because there is no loss felt.

If your children looked forward to playing with or helping you with the baby, they may feel deeply disappointed. If your baby lived for several months and your children had time to develop a bond with the baby, they may grieve. Even so, your children do not share the same anticipation or fantasies as you and will not grieve as intensely. In fact, your children may have harbored some resentment or jealousy as they watched you fuss over the baby or the nursery. Your children's apparent lack of concern for the baby after a few days may strike you as callous. But if allowed and encouraged, your children will grieve according to the unique sense of loss they feel.

If you suffered a miscarriage or pregnancy interruption, your children may not have even known that you were pregnant, especially if they are young. Even so, your children will respond to the family disequilibrium caused by the baby's death. The disruption of familiar routines and the changes in you—from playful, responsive and easygoing to sad, withdrawn and irritable—can be very distressing to young children. Children are naturally egocentric and easily assume that they are the cause of your anger or despair. Even if you try to hide your feelings, children are very perceptive and may become more confused and anxious by your reticence.

Providing the Support and Reassurance Your Children Need

From infancy through adolescence, children often show their grief, confusion or anxiety by changes in their behavior. If your children are upset you may notice:

- regression in abilities, including motor skills, toileting, talking, schoolwork
- regression into infantile behaviors such as baby talk, chewing on toys
- increased separation anxiety, clinging, not letting you out of sight, not wanting to go to school
- disrupted sleep or appetite, increased night waking
- increased irritability, obstinacy or aggression, including fretfulness, tantrums, biting, stealing
- diminished resistance to illness
- recurring headaches, stomachaches, nervous habits, tics and other physical manifestations of tension or anxiety (make sure you ask your doctor to look for physical causes for any of these symptoms)
- restlessness, disinterest in play, difficulty concentrating, overactivity
- increased emotional sensitivity, including crying spells, easily hurt feelings, empathy with people or characters in stories or television
- increased perfectionism, including outrage at failure or frustration, refusing or being afraid to try new skills, being overly compliant

- frequent or repetitive questions about the baby, death, illness, etc.; or never asking any questions at all
- withdrawal from you or others, turning away
- decreased adaptability, including low tolerance for changes in routine, new foods, contact with other people, even familiar ones

Your children's behavior and questions are a barometer of their feelings and how they are coping. Whenever your children are acting out, there is an underlying problem that needs to be addressed. Common underlying concerns around death and grief include:

- concerns about how the baby died
- fears of sleep
- concerns about dead bodies
- fears of separation or abandonment

In addition, children may act out when they are having difficulty coping with feelings, particularly anger and guilt. By understanding the concerns and issues your children may be wrestling with, you will be in a better position to offer support. By dealing with the underlying problem, you can help your children find real solutions that diminish the need to act out.

Concerns about How the Baby Died

Your children may ask many questions about the cause of death. While children are naturally curious, their questions usually arise from a need for reassurance. Even as adults, we want to know the cause of death when we see an obituary of someone who died relatively young. By knowing the cause we can vow to avoid it or be relieved that we don't run that particular risk. Similarly, your children will benefit from honest answers. Answers can reassure them that they are not in danger of dying too.

If your baby died from an infection or other illness, your children may equate sickness with impending death. The following are indications that your children may be worried about illness.

- They ask many or repetitive questions about illness, disease, germs, health.
- They ask many or repetitive questions about why the baby died.
- They are concerned about getting sick or being around sick people.
- They have more (or a lot fewer) physical ailments or complaints.
- They are worried that you will get sick.

Give your children as much information as they need about the baby's illness or birth defects. Even if you don't know the cause of death, you can still answer that somehow the baby didn't grow right, or was born too early, or that the body didn't work properly. Avoid simplistic explanations like "The baby had a bad tummyache," or your children may fear for their lives the next time their stomach hurts. Emphasize to your children that it's obvious that they are growing just right, were born right on time and that their bodies are working beautifully. Emphasize the difference between weak, little babies and big, strong, healthy kids like them and grownups like you.

> Luke asked tons of questions about what made his brother die. I
> think he was worried that the same fate might befall him. So I
> assured him that babies aren't as strong as older kids, so he decided
> that for a baby to survive the first year, to make it "past zero" to 1,
> was very difficult, but that since he was 4, he was out of danger. He
> would reassure himself by saying, "It's hard to make it past zero."
> —Cathryn

If you decided to interrupt your pregnancy or refuse medical intervention, it can be a challenge to be honest without distressing the children. Telling young children that you allowed the baby to die because the baby was too sick or didn't grow right can cause them to worry that if they get sick or do something wrong, they're next. Even though your role as decision maker may be paramount to you, be careful to emphasize that the baby died because of severe illness or deformity and offer those details. If they ask why the doctors couldn't fix it, you may explain that doctors cannot fix everything. You may even broach the fact that letting go was the only way to protect the baby from suffering. You may want to wait until the children are older before you reveal the entire matter of difficult decisions. Either way, you can explain that death brings release from suffering.

With older children and adolescents who can understand the ethical or religious dilemmas, it is best to reveal your decision. Be sure to explain how difficult it was and how you arrived at it. They may feel angry or unsettled, and you may want to emphasize that you did not make this decision lightly. Most important, talk about the differences between the regular problems of kids like them, and the catastrophic problems of babies like yours. You might even have frank discussions about how they feel about extraordinary measures to keep them alive should they encounter serious illness or trauma, such as cancer or head injury. Reassure them that you will abide by their wishes.

If your baby died in an accident or under frightening circumstances, you may want to postpone revealing what happened until your children are old enough to handle the information without feeling scared or vulnerable themselves. If you decide to conceal certain details, you must make sure that others respect your wishes, and that your adult conversations are in private. You can still explain in broad terms why the baby died. Cathryn, whose baby Kevin died in a particularly horrifying situation, talked generally to son Luke about why death occurs. She told him that Kevin died because his body stopped working—no more beating heart, breathing lungs, thinking brain.

Fears of Sleep

Particularly if your children hear people equating death with sleep, or if they have a chance to see the baby after death, they may conclude that death is similar to sleep. There are several signs that your children may be confusing death and sleep.

- They are restless at nap time or bedtime.
- They wake up in the night and can't get back to sleep.
- They ask you why the baby won't wake up.

To reassure your children, you can explain that death and sleep are totally different, that sleep is necessary for a healthy body, and that your body stays alive when you sleep, and then you wake up. In death, the heart and breathing stop, and then the body dies and can't become alive again. Your children may have difficulty understanding it all, but the message that sleep and death are completely different should sink in.

Concerns about Dead Bodies

If children resist attending the funeral or graveside service, or if they seem preoccupied with dead bodies, burial, cremation or afterlife, it is important to help them sort out their fears. For example, are they concerned about the baby suffering? Are they afraid the body may burst out of the casket? Do they worry about skeletons and ghosts? Your children may acquire scary ideas about death from movies, television, comic books or friends; children are prone to misinterpreting what they see and hear, to confusing fantasy with reality.

You can reassure your children by answering questions honestly, giving whatever details they require. Let their questions be your guide and keep in mind children's need for reassurance that death is a natural end of life and a quiet, peaceful existence. If you decided on burial, you can talk about the body returning to the earth; if you chose cremation, you can talk about the body returning to the air. Some children are satisfied with the idea that the physical body stays in the earth or turns to ashes while the spirit goes to a peaceful place. Your own personal beliefs can provide a comforting framework for your children, even if the abstract idea of "spirits" is hard to grasp. For younger children struggling with the concept of death, emphasize that a dead body cannot move or feel anything, including loneliness or pain. Talking to your children about these stark realities may be difficult and sorrowful but you may also benefit from these reassuring reminders that your baby is not suffering.

Fears of Separation or Abandonment

When a new baby arrives, most children have trouble dealing with this separation from mother and all the attention given to the baby. When a baby dies, siblings have to deal with the physical separation *and* a change in both of their parents. Plus, children may wonder, "If the baby can go away, then what's to prevent Mommy and Daddy from going away?"

During this difficult time, your children need reassurance that you can still take care of them, that you still love them, and that eventually you will feel better. You are your children's main source of emotional support, and they need you to be there.

There are several clues that your children are having fears of separation or abandonment. Regression into infantile behavior may be a way of trying to regain the safe feelings of earlier times, when you took care of so many of your children's needs. If your children feel neglected, they may make bids for your attention by becoming more annoying, fearful or clingy. Many children can also become more aggressive, angry or withdrawn. Be alert to any of these signals that your children need more reassurance and attention from you. Even when your children are irritable, a hug or a gentle reminder that you love them may be soothing. With your comfort and empathy, they will regain confidence and security sooner than if you ignore these bids for attention or insist that they "act their age" and be as independent as they were before the baby died.

If your children exhibit any of these behaviors when you leave them with other caregivers, they may need extra assurance that you will return. Also beware of your own anxieties. If you are worried about their safety or care in your absence, your children may pick up on this and not want you to leave. This unwitting, inadvertent collusion is common between parents and children.

When their world has turned upside down, some children have an increased need to feel in control. They may still have fears of abandonment, but instead of clinging, they assert their preferences and ideas in order to gain some feelings of competence and mastery. Obstinacy and tantrums are common. If you notice that you and your children are getting into power struggles, try offering more choices and letting your children be in charge of some things. At the same time, continue to meet your children's needs for attention and dependence. Even if your children seem self-reliant, they still need reassurance that you are available.

Children also need reassurance that they are not the cause of their parents' distress. When you feel sad or upset about the baby, it is important for you to be open about it and to assure your children that your feelings are due to your grief over the baby's death.

It is also important to avoid the trap of attending to your children only when there is a crisis. If you feel like you're in a cycle where the more angry you get, the more aggravating the children are, you may need to step back and find ways to spend relaxing, enjoyable time with them. Otherwise your anger may be the only emotional connection your children can elicit from you. As strange as it may seem, anger is better than nothing and children will figure out quickly how to provoke it.

Unfortunately, when you are in the depths of grief, it can be very difficult to be a responsive parent. It is hard enough to deal with your own grief, let alone the day-to-day needs of your children. Ultimately, by taking care of your own emotional needs, you will be able to reinvest in nurturing your children. So, when parenting becomes overwhelming or draining, rely on your partner (or other adults your children enjoy) to take up the slack. Or find someone to help you with the mundane chores so you can be available to your children at critical times. Try to make sure your children don't feel abandoned.

> After William died, I found it very difficult to be a nurturing mother to my girls. I was grieving so much that I had nothing left for them. I felt guilty about that, like I wasn't a good mother, but I pretty much left their care to my husband for the first couple months. And then, eventually, as I felt better, I was able to be an attentive mother again.
>
> —Eva

Helping Your Children Express Feelings

Allow your children to vent their feelings, including fear, anxiety, sadness, anger, guilt or relief. You can teach them to express feelings safely—by talking or physical and creative activities that pose no danger to anyone or anything. By encouraging this expression, you are helping your children cope with these feelings and this will reduce their need to act out in destructive ways.

If your children cry, let them sob as much as they want. Remember, you needn't fix it. Resist saying things like, "There, there. Everything's okay. Don't cry." While this is considered comforting, children hear it literally and get the message to buck up and swallow their sentiments. Try something affirming like, "You have lots of tears today, don't you?" If you allow tears, your children will know that you also allow feelings. If they don't feel like crying, reassure them that this reaction is fine too. People can be sad without tears.

There are many other ways to encourage expression of emotions. You can try sharing some of your feelings and engaging in dialogue. Some children may be able to talk about things; resist the temptation to push those who are reluctant. It is also important to provide opportunities for drawing pictures, painting, sculpting clay, writing stories, dictating letters or playing out emotions in dramatic scenes with toys. These methods can help your children master feelings that are especially confusing or distressing. Encourage physical activities to let off steam. Find a place in the house where screaming can be permitted—and very acoustically satisfying—such as in the bathroom with the door shut. Read stories about death and grief—this can help your children clarify emotions and feel less isolated or abnormal. When your children are able to express feelings, they can learn to identify and handle them in constructive, healthy ways.

Dealing with Anger

When a promised baby sibling doesn't materialize, children may feel anger toward their parents. Young children tend to see their parents as all-powerful. If you promise a baby, you should be able to bring one home. Your children may reason that you caused the baby's death or somehow sabotaged this promise. They may even take it personally, assuming that you did this to disappoint or aggravate them.

Children need answers as much as adults do. If you can explain that the baby's death was a cruel twist of nature, that no one is to blame, that you are angry too, you can help your children direct their anger away from you. You can help your children express their anger and disappointment by encouraging them to draw pictures, talk about their feelings, dictate a letter to God or Mother Nature or pound on pillows. (See chapter 6 for more on expressing anger.)

> We kept telling our 6-year-old son that it was OK to be angry, but then when he would get mad, we'd tell him to stop it. So, finally, he regressed to wetting his pants and biting, and I realized that not only did I need to allow him to express anger, but I needed to give *myself* permission to express anger.
>
> —Amy

Dealing with Guilt

Children often believe that things happen because their actions, thoughts or wishes are powerful enough to cause things to happen. This egocentric thinking may make your children feel responsible for the baby's death. Before the death they may have felt competitive or resentful that the new baby would get all the attention. Your children may have wished that the baby would never be born, or would go away forever. When the baby dies, your children may worry that their thoughts were indeed powerful enough to cause the baby to go away forever. They may feel horribly guilty and yet be unable to admit it.

This self-centered thinking may also lead your children to feel responsible for your grief. When you are feeling mad, your children may naturally assume that they did something bad to cause your anger. If you are sad, your children may think that they did something to disappoint you. To compound this, your children may worry that you are upset because you have figured out that their wishes caused the baby to die.

To help assuage any of your children's feelings of responsibility for the baby's death, you can provide assurances that nobody is to blame, that thoughts or wishes or unrelated actions cannot make bad things happen. In addition, your children may benefit from repeated explanations of the possible or definite physiological reasons for your baby's death.

Let your children know that they are not responsible for your grief. Be open about your feelings of grief and explain that you are upset because you miss the baby. Even if you try to hide your feelings, children are very perceptive, and your underlying feelings will not escape their notice. You needn't share your private, overwhelming emotions with them, but if you can talk about your feelings and explain why you cry, you can reduce their confusion or anxiety. The more information they have, the better they will feel. They need to know that you aren't upset with them, and that they aren't to blame. Your children will also learn about loss and grief and may even see your sadness as assurance that if they died, you would grieve for them too.

Your children may have other fears or worries about death not covered here. If you become concerned by any behavior, it may be helpful to talk with a family counselor who is knowledgeable about how grief affects families. The counselor can help you figure out what your children need to get through this family crisis. Stanley Greenspan's book *The Essential Partnership* is another excellent resource for ideas and support on helping your children deal with feelings.

Telling Teachers and Caregivers

Be sure to alert your children's teachers and other caregivers that a baby sibling has died. This knowledge can help them to be more understanding, patient and sensitive to you children's needs for extra attention, guidance and reassurance. You might even share written materials on talking about death, children's grief, behavior changes and how to help children through this tough time. If you are tempted to make suggestions, remember, you'll be more likely to make an alliance if you are sympathetic and offer written information in the spirit of helping them gather insights—"I know my child has been a handful lately with all that's going on. I hope this helps make your job easier." Also let them know how much your family appreciates their support.

Reassurance for Specific Age Groups

Children react to death and grief according to their level of maturity. It can be helpful for parents to understand the special needs of toddlers, young children, older children and adolescents. The age ranges are guide-lines only, as your children may very well have special needs described under any of the age groups.

Toddlers—Under 3 Years

It is difficult to know how much children under age 3 understand about the baby in Mommy's tummy or what it means when Mommy and Daddy come back from the hospital without the baby. Nevertheless, toddlers are especially affected by family disequilibrium after a baby's death. Whether your toddler grieves or not, he or she will notice the changes in your behavior. You can help your toddler cope by trying to be as consistently nurturing and patient as possible. You may be very grateful to have a little one at home, but even so, nurturing and patience can be difficult when you are grieving. Try bringing a friend, relative or favorite baby-sitter into your home to help you with household chores so that you have more energy to meet your toddler's needs.

> Having Lisa made me feel very much better. If I had had a miscarriage before having her, I probably would have thought I'll never have a baby. But I had one at home to come home to. I was so thankful to have her. I felt empty inside, but I didn't feel like I was empty-handed.
> —Jane

If you have a surviving baby or babies from a multiple pregnancy, you may be grateful to have a baby, but you still need to grieve. Anya recalls, "That made it harder in some ways. Because I had Kim to focus on, I put off working through some of my feelings about Rachel, so I think it dragged out for a longer period of time."

Even in infancy, your surviving baby or babies will notice your grief and preoccupation. Remember, your grief itself will not harm your baby. *Suppressing* grief is far more harmful to your capacity to nurture your children. It is normal to be alternately preoccupied with the baby(s) in your arms and the baby(s) who dwell in your heart. The trick is to find a balance between grieving and parenting, month to month, day to day, hour to hour. Just as each baby who died deserves to be mourned in his or her own special way, each baby who lives deserves to be celebrated, held and cherished like any other newborn.

Understandably, you may not have the emotional resources required to meet your surviving baby's needs. Go ahead and enlist the help of another caregiver—your partner, a friend, a relative, or hire a teenager who enjoys babies. Use this time for yourself and your grief. Pore over your memories and mementos, regrets and dreams. Write in your journal, gather keepsakes, visit the grave, cry. Taking the opportunity to grieve now, as best you can, can prevent grief from surfacing later in ways that are more damaging and difficult to manage. Grieving now can also make it easier for you to deal with the ongoing challenges of raising a survivor. Enlisting the aid of other caregivers is a nurturing support, on many levels, to both you and your baby. Even if you don't have help, you can get into the daily routine of setting aside time to focus on the baby or babies who died. This simple act can free you to be an attentive parent for the rest of the day.

> Perhaps the best gift I gave to my other children and myself after Teddy's death was to grieve as wholeheartedly as I was able and to

seek as much support and help with this process as was available. It was very hard to do, yet very necessary.

—Lisa

Young Children—2 to 7 Years

Many young children think of death as life under different circumstances. People don't simply disappear. They must have gone somewhere else, and surely they will return, or at least you can retrieve them from wherever it is they have gone. To young children, death may be reversible, and some children may associate it with sleep. You may be barraged with questions like "When is the baby coming back?" or "Can we go get the baby from the hospital now?" or "When will the baby wake up?" You need to patiently explain that being dead means the baby won't come back, that the baby's body cannot move or breathe anymore. In attempts to understand what you mean, your children may raise new concerns such as "Where is the baby?" or "Why can't we go there?" or "Why did the baby die?" or "Am I going to die?" or "Are you going to die?" Your children may seem obsessed with playing out scenes of death or making up songs about babies dying. While this behavior may seem morbid or even maddening to you, this is your children's way of trying to master the meaning of your baby's death.

Even if you carefully explain the cause of death in physiological terms or the fact that the body is buried but the spirit goes to a higher plane, it is important to remember that young children cannot always interpret these explanations correctly. Because they are unable to grasp abstract concepts, children this age are mystified by death and may worry about whatever they cannot understand. They think about death in concrete, egocentric or magical ways, and sometimes these can provoke anxiety. If you have children this age, it is especially important to be aware of the fears that children commonly have about death so that you can reassure them.

Answer questions honestly, in terms your children can both understand and cope with. You might try saying, "Dead means we can't see the baby again." If your children are not frightened by the idea of a body failing, you can try saying, "The baby died because his (or her) body couldn't stay alive and breathe." You can go into as much detail as your children's curiosity requires. However you explain it, make sure your children feel reassured and know that you won't disappear next, or that their body is not likely to fail in the same way, without warning.

I tried to explain to Kristen [age 28 months] about how the body stops working, but she yelled, "No, no, no." Maybe that was too much for her to handle, so we just left it that "died" means we can't see them anymore and that I wasn't going anywhere.

—Terri

Older Children—6 to 12 Years

Most older children are curious about death. They are concerned with rituals, where the body goes, where the spirit goes. They may still consider themselves somehow responsible for the baby's death.

> It was really hard on my 10-year-old daughter. She had been wanting a brother or sister, but then when I was pregnant she said, "I don't want a brother; they're mean." So when Gregory died, she blamed it on herself. So next time I was pregnant, she said, "I don't care what—if you have a monkey, Mom, that's fine."
>
> —Martina

Children this age are often more able to hide their feelings because they want to maintain control or seem grown up. If you hide your feelings, they may take that cue from you. If you are more open and share some of your feelings, this may encourage them to vent their own.

Adolescents—Over 10 Years

Adolescents usually have sophisticated ideas about death, but may still have many questions and concerns about the physiological and spiritual aspects of death. They may feel some embarrassment about pregnancy and sexuality and perhaps guilt about any feelings of resentment toward the baby. Adolescents can seem so grown up, yet it is important to remember that they are naturally self-centered and immature and may say cruel or insensitive things. Adolescents can benefit greatly from your honesty and sharing feelings, as well as your acceptance of their feelings.

As Your Children Grow

As time goes on, children may seem to have recovered from the baby's death, but memories of one kind or another may surface from time to time. As children grow older, they become more sophisticated in their ability to understand death, and the death of a younger sibling may take on new meaning. For a 3-year-old girl whose baby brother died, the typical questions are: "When is the baby coming back?" and "Where did he go?" and "Why can't we see him?" When this girl is older, she may ask more detailed questions concerning the physical and spiritual nature of death, and she may be concerned about the rituals of burial. As an adolescent, she may have thoughts and questions about how her life might have been different if her brother had survived. As children acquire new understanding about death and the meaning of the loss of a sibling, they need to have continuing support and information from their parents.

Points to Remember

- Grandparents often carry a double sorrow as they grieve for their grandchild and for you, their own child.
- Many grandparents have difficulty supporting their grieving children. It may help to include them as much as possible in affirming and memorializing your baby.
- If you are close to other family members, you may or may not be able to rely on them for support. If there are other babies in the family, be honest about your feelings so that these parents might be more sensitive to your needs.
- Children grieve according to the loss they feel. Young children, in particular, are primarily affected by your grief and the family imbalance resulting from the baby's death.
- It can be difficult to nurture your other children when you are grieving. Have others help you with household tasks, so you can be more available to your children.
- Children need information and clarification about death and grief. Otherwise, they can fear death or feel responsible for your sadness or even for the baby's death. By being honest and by sharing some of your feelings, you can help them understand and cope.
- Children often need help expressing their feelings in constructive ways. Try to be a good example; children learn a lot by watching you handle your own feelings.
- Children need reassurance that you are still there to love and take care of them and that you are upset because the baby died, not because of something they have done.
- If you feel unsure about what to tell your children about the baby, err on the side of honest disclosure. In general, secrets are more damaging than the truth.

12

Support Networks

Friends

The most supportive friends are those who recognize that your baby's death is a significant and tragic loss. They try to understand what you are going through, they listen whenever you need to talk and they accept your behavior and your emotions without being uncomfortable or judgmental. Having this kind of support can help you cope with your baby's death.

You may even find that the support you get from friends is more soothing or affirming than what you get from your partner or family members who may be immersed in their own grief. As Shannon points out, "I lost a baby but my husband lost a son and my mother lost a grandchild. So, it doesn't feel like they can be real helpful to me. It feels more helpful to have sympathy from a friend or a nurse—someone I can *lean* on. It seems special too, because it's someone who doesn't necessarily have to care, but they do."

Friends who are able to anticipate the moments that might be particularly painful for you or who can alert others to your sensitivity are always good to have around. Even if you tend to handle things by yourself, you may feel better just knowing that someone else sympathizes and cares.

My sister and my friend Sally, they were just always there and I could act how I wanted to act, be distracted, things like that. Just to know they were aware of things. Like when we went out to eat, Sally would tell people what happened so they wouldn't come rushing up and say, "Oh, what did you have?" She just did anticipatory stuff that turned out to be real helpful.

—Hannah

As a result of your loss, you may discover the true meaning of friendship, as some friends stand by you through thick and thin. Sadly, some friends won't align themselves with your sorrow, perhaps because of their own discomfort. However, you may be touched by the kindness of casual acquaintances, particularly those who have experienced loss and grief. You may even form long-lasting bonds with these people, who can turn out to be more supportive than old friends.

Prior to aborting our baby, I wish I could have known the outpouring of love and support we would receive. Even people who may not approve of abortion for themselves respected our decision. The flowers, food, cards, notes and visits were so loving and so appreciated. Also, many women "confessed" to me their abortions from their pasts.

—Avery

When Friends Turn Away

To us she was real, but to others Claire was just "stillborn." I think people just brush her off as insignificant.

—Henry

It surprised me how few people will cry with you. I don't know where this idea of strength comes in, that you're strong if you don't cry.

—Bess

Unfortunately, supportive friends can be few and far between. After your baby dies, you may discover that many friends do not recognize the importance of this baby or the significance of your loss. They may be supportive at first, but soon wonder why you aren't feeling better. Holly recalls, "There's that period where everybody's very attentive and then they all fade away and people expect you to be better or they don't want to bring it up." In particular, you may sense these attitudes from people who are unfamiliar or uncomfortable with death and grief. You may find your loss more difficult to bear for several reasons.

- People expect you to have minimal grief. ("Aren't you over this yet? Gee, you can always have another one.")
- Rituals—naming, baptism, funeral, memorials—are often considered unnecessary. ("What's the big deal? This really wasn't a baby.")
- You may feel alone in your grief, that you are the only one who cares about this baby. ("Why are you so upset? You never even got attached to that baby.")

Unsettling Remarks

Most bereaved parents have endured insensitive, rationalistic statements from well-meaning people who are trying to erase their pain. Here is a small sampling, and how it can feel to hear these remarks.

"You're healthy, young. You can always have another baby."
But you want *this* baby.

"Be thankful that you already have a healthy child."
   But children can't replace each other.

"I know just how you feel. My dog died last summer."
   They presume to know how you feel or belittle your grief by making comparisons.

"Your baby is a little angel in heaven."
   But you don't want a little angel. You want a baby in your arms.

"This is nature's way of weeding out the defective ones."
   But why did this have to happen to you and your baby?

"I've known other people who have handled this well, never cried."
   Handling this well means expressing grief, not repressing it.

"You're lucky it happened now instead of six months from now."
   How on earth can your baby's death be "lucky"?!

"At least you know you are fertile."
   It is hardly a comfort to know you can conceive but can't keep the baby.

"At least your loss was final. When our house burned down, for months we kept remembering more things we were missing."
   But you too will always miss your baby and remember what might have been as the years go by!

   Other unsettling remarks may make light of your baby or your loss or may aggravate your grief by pointing out others' tragic losses.

> I had my share of insensitivity. An elderly neighbor said, "Isn't that funny, this other lady could have quadruplets and you couldn't even have one."
>
> —Bryn

> Somebody asked me, "Why did you name him? It was just a miscarriage!"
>
> —Kelly

> When the twins were born prematurely, somebody told me, "Well at least you have two extra income tax deductions for this year."
>
> —Anya

> A friend told me, "My mother lost a baby and she *never* got over it." I was ready to kick her in the teeth. People say really stupid things to people who are grieving, and I understand why—because they don't know what to say.
>
> —Sophie

Someone said to me, "Don't worry, I know a woman who had
thirteen miscarriages before she had a baby." I thought "Oh God. I
don't want to hear that!" She was trying to help, but that was not
really the right thing to say.

—Peg

As Camilla testifies, even when a baby has severe problems, parents
have so much love and care invested in the child that death is still very
difficult to bear.

When Kacey died, many many people said "It's better this way."
They didn't take care of my Kacey—they didn't stay up with her all
night, they didn't take her to sometimes 3 or 4 doctor or therapy
appointments a day. They didn't hold a screaming baby—knowing
there was nothing that could be done but to love her and make sure
she was as comfortable as possible. She will always be in our hearts.
Don't ever tell a grieving parent "It's better this way."

—Camilla

While most people have good intentions, there may be some who are
abrasive or malicious. Try to remember that these people have problems
and push blame or resentment on you as a way of avoiding their own pain.
They may make remarks such as "What did you do to deserve this?"
Remind yourself that you certainly do not deserve their incrimination for
something beyond your control! You need to take care of yourself by
avoiding people who cannot be compassionate.

Coping with Harsh Judgment

There was one instance where someone felt we had "murdered"
our son and that hurt. This person had never walked in my shoes.
Even though every other person felt we were courageous and right
to do what we did, this one instance stays with me ... the one
comment I can't forget.

—Maribeth

Was it euthanasia? Murder? Abortion? It will always make me feel
lonely and defensive. And I resent that because I don't want those
feelings to tarnish the precious few months I had with my only
daughter.

—Kaye

When you make the decision to let go and say goodbye to a much-loved
baby, you may worry that some friends and family will judge you harshly.
Even if you try to keep it a secret, most social and family circles exchange

information freely. As a result, it may be impossible to completely avoid judgment and harsh remarks. So how do you face everyone? Eventually, as your grief softens and you come to accept that the decision you made was best, it will be easier to be around others and talk openly about your experiences. In the meantime, however, you needn't withdraw until you resolve your doubts. You only need to learn to survive others' comments. To do this, try the following suggestions.

- Gather insight into what drives those who judge you harshly. Many judgmental people are limited by simplistic thinking or their own emotional issues. They may cling to a black-and-white view: *Life is good and death is bad.* There are others whose capacity to reason shuts down when they hear the word "baby." Remembering these shortcomings can help you deflect harsh comments.

- Learn to shrug off harsh remarks. When people try to lecture you, question your decision or belittle your grief, you may feel hurt, angry or defensive. But you don't have to. You can choose which reaction to have. You can take unkind remarks to heart and feel distressed, or you can shrug them off. If you typically react strongly to situations, you may find it difficult to remain calm. If you are sensitive to others' disapproval, you may find these comments hard to ignore. Especially in the thick of your grief and doubts, it is normal to be upset by unkind remarks (see the following suggestion). But with practice, you can learn to disagree with and disregard others' judgments. You can reassure yourself by saying "It doesn't matter what they think. It wasn't their body, their baby, their family, their decision." As the lovely Eleanor Roosevelt said, "No one can make you feel inferior without your permission."

- Face your feelings. While shrugging off harsh remarks is a valuable skill, the other side of the coin is to examine the feelings that are brought up. Recognize that others' judgment is most distressing to you when you harbor feelings of doubt, guilt and anger—painful emotions that you may be trying to avoid. So when a remark stings, take the opportunity to dwell on these feelings, so that you can work through them. Then, over time, you won't be hypersensitive to every utterance. And when you do meet with judgment, you won't take it so personally, for it no longer sets off an echo of remorse inside you.

- Remember, you don't owe anyone a list of justifications. You don't require anyone else's approval or forgiveness. And you needn't try to change others' views—just insist that they respect yours. Even if some people don't accept your decision, they can refrain from being hurtful to you. If necessary, avoid them while you heal.

When Friends Focus on the Surviving Baby

Parents who experience multiple birth and loss may endure especially awkward moments, particularly when they are able to bring a baby home. When you have a surviving baby or babies, it is natural for you to be excited about showing them off. People will be happy for you and they may be unsure of how to react toward your loss. Shannon points out, "I don't blame people for being happy for us because it was such a mixed thing. I think people find it hard to say 'We're sorry about your baby and oh, congratulations, by the way!'" In addition, others may refer to "the baby" when to you, she or he is "one of twins." "The twins" to others will always be "the triplets" or "the quints" to you.

Unfortunately, some people may expect or encourage you to relish the survivor(s) without mourning for the child or children who didn't make it. Others may even express relief that some, or all, of multiple babies died early in pregnancy because they feared for you having to carry so many. If death occurs later, they may consider it a blessing because of the emotional, physical and financial challenges of raising multiples. If you have battled infertility, people may chide you to just be grateful for any older children you might have. This lack of sensitivity and support can leave you feeling isolated, misunderstood and angry.

> People focus on the fact that we have Bradley. That's so frustrating. I never really respond except to say, "Yes, we thank God." But what I *want* to say is, "Yeah, we are really lucky but we also have two cribs sitting up there, we'd gotten excited about the idea of two babies, and we were looking forward to two babies. *We still lost a baby!*"
>
> —Shannon

> Sometimes people treat us like our triplets were not real because they were not with us for very long. ... No one knows what to say to us. Our older son is our greatest comfort—but having him doesn't make us feel any better about losing Cory, Carly and Allex. I love my son more than anything, but don't tell me "At least you have him."
>
> —Georgia

Mothers who've experienced different kinds of loss report that losing all the babies from a multiple pregnancy is in some respects easier than having some survive. When all the babies die, there is a greater understanding of the mother's need to grieve. When one or some babies survive, there is a pressure from all sides to focus on the living. There may be little acknowledgment of the babies who died, minimal patience for feelings of grief, undermining of attempts to remember the dead and lack of appreciation for the efforts and challenges involved in caring for survivors. At best, people overestimate how busy you feel.

> There is nothing so horribly un-busy, too peaceful than that first year or more. ... One baby is just not a totally full-time deal. When you expected to be flat-out all the time with twins, every little bit of peace and quiet or spontaneity is so awful because you know you wouldn't have had time to think about it or do this or whatever, if they were both here.
>
> —Jackie

As such, if you are raising one or more survivors, it is important for you to resist the pressure to consider yourself so lucky, or that the baby or babies who died were simply a nice bonus that just didn't work out. Don't let others persuade you to forget. Ignore their judgments on how you are doing. Surround yourself with people who understand and appreciate what you are going through. Another supportive resource is CLIMB—Center for Loss In Multiple Birth (see appendix C).

Educating Friends about What You Need

> This has been a real learning experience for both of us, to find out that all the supposedly comforting things we used to say to our friends who had miscarriages, those are really some of the worst things to say.
>
> —Mark

Even if your friends have good intentions, you may feel isolated and angry because they don't know how to comfort you. Remember, your friends want to be supportive, but like most people they are uninformed about grief and what bereaved parents need. It can be easy for you and even your well-meaning friends to fall into cycles of misunderstanding.

- When friends make unsympathetic remarks, you may conclude that they are minimizing your baby's importance. Perhaps they just want you to feel better and mistakenly believe that they can ease your pain by rationalizing your baby's death.
- Your friends' silence may lead you to believe that they don't want to be burdened with your sorrow. Instead, they may avoid talking about the baby because they think that will protect you from your despair and help you forget.
- While their misguided efforts can appear uncaring, your friends simply may not realize that certain statements sound hurtful or unfeeling to you.

- Your friends may feel helpless because they want to be supportive but aren't sure how. You may believe some of them are belittling your grief, but most likely they are simply uncomfortable around bereaved people.
- Your friends may be uncomfortable with their own feelings too. Rather than honestly expressing their emotions, people often repeat trite sayings that they have heard before. Instead of saying, "I don't know what to say," they may offer platitudes. Instead of saying, "My heart aches when I see you so upset," they may urge you to buck up. When they aren't being honest about their feelings of inadequacy or helplessness, you will naturally feel less welcome to be honest about how you're really feeling.
- When your friends talk about others who have lost babies, you may wonder why they are insensitively deepening your sense of hopelessness. Yet they are only trying to let you know that you aren't alone, that there are others who have survived what you are going through.

Naturally, if you interpret your friends' actions as uncaring, you will feel uncomfortable sharing your emotions with them. Even if you realize they are trying to help, you may find it difficult to tolerate their blunders when you are feeling so vulnerable and sensitive. If they avoid the subject, you may feel awkward or afraid to talk about your baby. You may think you have to protect *them* by not bringing it up, especially around friends who are pregnant or have babies, or during celebrations or the holiday season. It is a challenge to confront friends or suggest what you need when you are feeling so sad and helpless.

> You feel so insecure you don't feel like you've got a right to stand up and say, "You know, that's really inappropriate. How dare you say something like that!" I wanted to wear a shirt that said "Please Be Nice to Me."
>
> —Bryn

With some of our friends who were clearly uncomfortable with this event in our lives, I remember feeling isolated. Initially they supported me, but with that really bad period of depression I was getting subtle—and not so subtle—hints from people that it was time to get on with things, and I didn't feel *ready* to get on with things. I think I only heard that from people who hadn't experienced any kind of death of anyone close. Mostly I avoided people who made me feel that way.

> —Jessie

A lot of friends were afraid to talk to me for fear they would upset me. I could've talked to any of them, but they really didn't understand and I didn't want to depress them. I probably tried to hide it more when I was around them, act like I was handling it.

—Rayleen

Friends backed off, and I understand that now. It was too close to home, especially for people that had little children. They acted as if, "I don't even want to *think* that *my* baby could die." So when this happened to me, it made it real to them, they backed off and they didn't come around for a while.

—Cindy

It is common for bereaved parents and their friends to disengage from each other. Parents often retreat if they sense that their grief is an imposition, and then they notice their friends back off even further. An irony about grief is that when you withdraw, you may need people's support more than ever, but people sense your withdrawal and leave you alone. If you feel as though your friends and family have backed off, remember, they take cues from you. Don't fall into thinking, "If they really loved me they would know what I need." They can't read your mind. *Tell* them how miserable you really are and how much you need to talk about the baby. Instead of waiting for them to bring it up, you can initiate conversations about how painful this is and how much you miss your baby.

Here are some other suggestions you might try sharing with your friends.

- Tell them that you will cherish their sympathetic ears for listening, their shoulders for tears, their calls and their hugs.
- Let them know it's okay to ask questions. After all, you *need* to talk about what happened. If you cry, this means they asked a very *good* question. Thank them for asking.
- Confess that you need specific, detailed offers of help because you don't have the energy to assign tasks and you don't want to impose on anyone. "Call if you need anything" is too intimidating to follow through on. It's much easier to say "Yes" to "When it snows, can I shovel your walk?" or "How about I take your kids to the park tomorrow?" or "Can I drop off lasagna and fruit salad on Friday?" Remind them that if offers are turned down, to make them again in a few days.
- Explain how you would rather have them bumble through with honest expressions of their feelings than avoid you, cheer you up, fix things or offer advice. Reveal that the best words to hear are the very ones they are censoring as they desperately search for the perfect thing to say. The best—and most

honest—words are things like "I can't imagine how awful this is for you," or "I want to say the perfect thing to make you feel better but I'm not sure what that can possibly be," or "I'm so sorry your baby died."

- Ask them to use your baby's name and to acknowledge your baby on anniversaries and holidays. Remind them that even if you get pregnant again, your focus may still be on the baby who died.
- Tell them that you'll appreciate their patience and support as you find your own way through grief.

Even though it can be difficult, you do have the right to let people know what helps and what doesn't. You can give them something to read (including this book), write them a letter or tell them in person. It takes energy and courage to confront people, but sometimes that is the only way they will know how to support you. Friends and relatives are usually grateful to know what you need. They truly want to help, and they appreciate your guidance. Surround yourself with people who can be responsive and compassionate.

It was about three to four months until I saw my family, and they obviously didn't want to bring it up and it was never really discussed. Looking back, that's something I would do differently. Now I'd probably say, "Hey, look, I want to talk about this."

—Dara

I say to my friends, "I feel like everybody is tired of listening, but I still need to talk." When I say that, it makes them feel like they aren't one of *those* people, and they want to listen.

—Claudia

I want to tell my friends, "Just say you're thinking of us, that you care, put your hand on our shoulder, don't probe, don't try to make us feel better, don't stay long, maybe drop off a meal and leave. It just helps to know you're thinking of us."

—Courtney

Parent Support Groups

A support group can be a valuable source of comfort for parents who have experienced the death of a baby. Other bereaved parents, unlike many friends and relatives, can be sensitive and knowledgeable.

Attending a support group is comforting in many ways. In a positive, accepting group atmosphere, parents can share their grief with others who truly understand. They can talk about their baby and their feelings. Others can validate how significant and painful their loss is, reassure them that their feelings are normal, give them insight on ways to cope, and help them to discover that they are not alone in suffering such a loss or having to have made such difficult decisions.

> It felt like a lifeline, knowing others were surviving this devastating loss. It was a place to talk, and that helped me work through the guilt.
>
> —Jessie

> It helped, just being able to air out some feelings and just the fact that I was doing something positive, was getting out, just somewhere to go every other week, being a part of something. I would have been a lot more desperate if it wasn't for the support group and friends made there, if I couldn't have had anyone to talk to.
>
> —Rose

> The group just made me feel normal in a state where you don't know what to do. I felt like no one could possibly feel this bad, and then I would sit there and hear these people saying the same things that I was thinking myself. It was an incredible comfort.
>
> —Liza

> I just needed a supportive forum in which to voice feelings of anger and isolation, to know the feelings I had were typical. And it's helpful if you go for a period of time to watch people work through their grief and know that there is a point when things begin to improve.
>
> —Holly

Most support groups are free, sponsored by hospitals, hospices, churches or mental health agencies. Most meet for two hours once or twice a month. Parents may attend as many meetings as they wish. Some groups bring in speakers and then open up for discussion, while others devote the entire time to open discussion. A facilitator may be there to offer information and help guide the discussion, but parents determine the issues by sharing the feelings they are struggling with. If parents do not wish to talk, they should feel welcome just to listen.

Many parents attend support group meetings without their partners. Schedules and babysitting sometimes make it possible for only one parent to attend. Or one partner may not feel a need to attend or may feel reluctant to share private feelings with others. If your partner is reluctant to go with you, you might encourage him or her to attend one or two meetings, just to observe and support you.

Going to your first support group meeting can be scary. You may feel anxious, especially at the thought of sharing your feelings with strangers. It can help to go with someone—your partner, a friend, a relative. Or you can even call the facilitator or another bereaved parent who attends and ask him or her to look for you. These people know how difficult that first meeting can be.

> I wanted to talk to people who had lost a child because I thought that would be helpful. My husband also believes only they would know exactly what it was like. I did seek out people like that. But I never attended a support group. Looking back, I would've benefited from that, but we just couldn't quite get it together. We just missed a lot of connections, and I didn't have the energy to pursue it. I think if somebody pursued it with me, I probably would've gone. Maybe even if somebody had sent me a letter that said, "This is the next meeting exactly and why don't you come?" I needed a push.
>
> —Hannah

Because grieving the death of a baby is so different, parents who experience miscarriage, stillbirth or infant death find that pregnancy/infant loss support groups are far more helpful than general bereaved parent groups. If you made decisions like interrupting the pregnancy or refusing medical intervention, you may feel uncomfortable about the possibility of others judging you. You could contact genetic counselors in your area and ask for a referral to a support group specifically for parents who faced difficult decisions. Or suggest that they sponsor such a group.

Do remember that any well-run support group will embrace and offer compassion to *all* parents, whatever the circumstances of their loss. Also consider that as you struggle with pangs of regret, any judgment you feel may be your own. By attending a "regular" support group, you can see that other parents cope with feelings of guilt. The "What have I done?" and "What if … ?" are universal questions. You may find special comfort in this.

> After Kevin died, we went to a bereaved parent support group several times, but their children were so much older, even in their 20s, and they had so many memories and so many other people knew their child and grieved with them. It was hard because Kevin never had a chance to form other relationships besides with me and his dad. He didn't have any friends who also knew him and grieved too. That made us feel worse.
>
> —Cathryn

Some parents do not feel the need to attend a support group. They may feel they are getting enough support from other sources, or the idea of a group just doesn't appeal to them. Other parents may go once and get turned off by the experience. If you go only once, however, you may not be giving it a fair chance. Most groups have open attendance, so the composition can vary from meeting to meeting. Talking and listening to other parents may be more helpful after your shock and numbness have worn off. If you still feel reluctant or skeptical, you may want to go a couple of times or talk with the facilitator about your doubts.

> We went once, two weeks after Jessica died, and I didn't like it. They had all lost their babies less recently than me. Then, at two months, my husband started school and I had no support. So I went to the group by myself and met another woman who was struggling with spiritual stuff too, so I called her. She's been my biggest support ever since.
>
> —Rose

Even if you do not like the idea of a group, it can be a good place to meet another parent to connect with. You can continue this relationship outside the group, offering each other the reassurance and understanding that are so helpful. Many parents who lack the support of other bereaved parents feel an extra sense of loneliness and uncertainty about their grief.

> It would've helped just to know that I wasn't the only person it happened to. That it wasn't this big mystery and we weren't bad people and that kind of thing.
>
> —Hannah

> To see what other people were going through would've given me permission to express my feelings. At the time I was just completely ignorant of what other parents experienced. There wasn't any information out, there wasn't anything that said, "This is a significant loss, this is real and these feelings you're having are normal." I was just real hungry for information and I didn't know that much about what to expect.
>
> —Anya

To find a support group in your area, ask your doctor or contact the social worker at a local hospital, hospice or mental health agency. Newspapers sometimes publish a listing of area support groups. Or you can call or write to one of the national organizations listed at the back of this book. If you are too shy or overwhelmed to make inquiries, ask someone else to make the phone calls. A good friend would be pleased to assist you with this.

If there are no support groups in your area, you may get a sympathetic health care provider to start sponsoring one. If you live in a sparsely populated area or if a support group doesn't appeal to you, you can correspond with other parents through organizations such as Pen-Parents and SHARE (see appendix C). Ask your doctor or midwife to put you in touch with other couples who've been through a similar experience. However you make the connection, another bereaved parent can be a lifeline. (Also refer to "Attending a Support Group" in chapter 9.)

Counseling

Many parents benefit from individual counseling as well as a support group. Each has its own unique benefits. Attending a support group can help you feel less isolated, offer opportunities to strike up supportive friendships and let you have hope for the future by observing how others have coped. Individual counseling can give you a chance to air your feelings at greater length and help you work through other personal issues. Many parents have particular difficulty dealing with anger or feel overwhelmed by guilt, depression or anxiety. Family therapy can also benefit surviving children and your relationship with your partner.

You could benefit from counseling if any of the following apply:

- you think it might help,
- you feel stuck or worry that you are resisting grief or consumed by it,
- you feel you are falling apart or no longer in control,
- you notice that you are engaging in addictive or destructive behaviors (see "Numbness and Shock" in chapter 2 for more signs of repressed grief),
- you continue to find no joy in other aspects of your life and resent others who do,
- your feelings, behavior or physical symptoms interfere with your well-being or your functioning (for instance, your depression prevents you from eating or sleeping, your lack of concentration produces costly mistakes, your headaches or fatigue keep you from enjoying favorite activities),
- you feel isolated or want the comfort of someone who can listen and support you, or
- others—friends, relatives, doctor, clergyperson—tell you they think you might benefit from counseling.

Some people hesitate to enter counseling for fear they will never stop needing it. For many people, getting into therapy implies weakness, mental illness or character flaws. Actually, it indicates personal strength, health and courage because being successful in therapy means facing your feelings, your problems and the truth about yourself. Therapy can help you to

- feel and express a wide range of emotions
- obtain insight into your reactions
- learn new ways of coping
- acquire more skills for working through problems

Eventually, through therapy, you gain the ability to help yourself. When you stop going regularly, your counselor can remain available for occasional consultation.

If nothing else, therapy gives you a chance to talk about your baby. A sensitive counselor can help you express and cope with your feelings. With that special support you will find it easier to come to terms with your baby's death. (Also see "Getting Counseling" in chapter 9.)

> Therapy was essential for me, just to be able to go in once a week for an hour and talk about Kevin and go over and over the same stuff. You don't feel like you're imposing because you're paying them to listen; that's *your* time to do whatever you need.
> —Cathryn

> Counseling really helped me a lot. It was a place where I could go and unload my feelings and learn to cope with them instead of shoving them inside.
> —Clara

If you decide to try counseling, look for a licensed professional who has experience working with bereaved persons. A reputable counselor can be a psychologist, clinical social worker, psychiatrist, psychiatric nurse or clergyperson. You might also want to explore other emotionally healing avenues such as art therapy, yoga, meditation, journaling and massage. To locate specialists in your area, contact professional organizations or check the Yellow Pages listings under "Counselors" or "Mental Health Services." Recommendations from people you know can be most valuable. You might ask:

- other bereaved parents
- your doctor or midwife
- parent support group facilitators
- the social worker or psychologist at a local hospital
- the women's center or parent education department at a local hospital
- your community mental health clinic
- your church or synagogue
- a hospice organization
- the local college, university or medical school counseling center
- a family service agency

If cost is a concern, community, university and medical school mental health clinics operate on sliding fee scales, so you pay what you can afford. Many private counselors will negotiate their fees. Most health insurance or employee assistance programs will pay some or all of the cost. It may help to remember that *you are worth it*.

Health Care Providers

Parents are profoundly affected by the treatment they receive from health care providers. When treated with warmth and empathy, they can be comforted by the fact that someone really cares. Parents are deeply touched by health care providers who can share a tear with them and really validate their grief. Any emotional support where feelings are validated can help with coping.

The pastor, social worker, doctors and nurses kept coming in to check, and I think it was helpful because it made me think, "Well, when you have a baby that's alive, they come in to see how you're doing and how the baby's doing, but if you have a dead one, they don't just leave you out. They treat you like you're human too."

—Martina

The nurse cried right along with me. You know, there's really something to someone giving validity to your feelings when everybody else is trying to make you feel better. Here this wonderful woman was crying and letting me know I had good reason to cry. She didn't try to shut me up. She wasn't in a hurry. She acted like a regular person who was really feeling sad that this had happened to me and she wasn't scared of what I was going to do next. I could be hysterical and it was OK.

—Sarah

Our doctor was there for us in a lot of ways. He was unusually sensitive. When we went into his office just a few days after Meghan died, he said, "I want to talk to you about the emotional side of this," and he made a real point to discuss what we could expect to feel. And he was real open about his own feelings. I remember him crying the night we delivered the baby and saying how hard that was for him, that the reason he went into obstetrics was so he could bring life and not have to deal with death so much.

—Jessie

There are no words that can erase your pain. But you can be deeply comforted by the special attention you receive: your doctor's availability to just listen and be with you, your nurse's gentle touch or any special arrangements made for you. Caregivers may also help by handling some of the paperwork, gathering information on funeral homes or sensitizing others to your special situation. Even little gestures that save miniscule moments of pain can make a big difference.

They did things to make me get well, but also be separate from the maternity ward. Since they didn't have facilities on that floor, they

brought me a portable sitz bath. That they cared was real important. You need to feel that you are important and not just another
one of the patients.

—Bryn

The hospital social worker was so nice, she wanted to listen and she
helped us. We didn't know where to start, how to bury him or
what. We had never had to deal with this, and she helped us
through the whole thing. She called around and she got prices of
things. You know, that's something to think about. She made you
realize that you did have to think of cost and not to feel guilty.

—Kelly

Our pediatrician did stuff that was very helpful in terms of making
sure we didn't get lost in the system. He told the clerks that this
family would be coming to see him, and it wasn't for a pediatric
appointment. So we didn't get to the desk and have someone say,
"Oh, what are you doing here?"

—Hannah

Honesty from your caregivers is as important as warmth, empathy and
sensitivity. You needed to know what was happening and to be told the
truth about your baby's prognosis. If the doctor was perplexed, you wanted
uncertainty rather than phony answers or assurances. To be prepared for
the worst is far preferable to being caught unprepared.

My doctor was very good during the labor, as well as right after
delivery, about keeping me informed of exactly what was happening and what the risks were and what the choices were and what
things he suggested. Later he spent a lot of time talking out some of
the more philosophical and emotional issues about a kid hooked up
to machines. He was very open, direct and supportive.

—Sophie

My OB was open and sincere. He was sad too, and that was very
helpful. When he came in the second night—he had just gotten back
from seeing the baby at the hospital—he came in and flopped down
on a chair and just buried his head in his hands, and he said, "You
know, I don't know what to tell you." I appreciated that he didn't
come in with some big long dissertation on something. He just
didn't know what to say, and that honesty was so nice. He acted
very sad, and I wanted everybody to be very sad.

—Sarah

I feel like no one was really geared towards dealing with a death.
None of them would admit for a moment. I kept trying to find out

how bad it was and my pediatrician talked to me at the hospital and she kept saying, "Things look bad," but she was the only person that would say it like that and try to help me get prepared for the worst. I think everybody else was denying it more than I was. I'm very angry that the other doctors were not honest with me.

—Liza

If Health Care Providers Turn Away

Parents are very impressionable after a baby dies. If your doctors and nurses treated you as if your baby's death was insignificant, you may come away wondering if they are right. If you were treated with aloofness or evasiveness, you may feel that you are not entitled to information. You may wonder if you did something wrong to make your doctors or nurses abrasive, too busy to listen or too uncomfortable to share your grief.

My doctor was saying things like "products of conception" and "Be grateful that it happened early. You were hardly pregnant!" I couldn't believe what I was hearing. Hardly pregnant? My baby was dead and he was telling me this!

—Mariko

Since I was in labor at twenty-four weeks, we signed a paper saying we did not want the baby to be resuscitated if she was born lifeless. Then this doctor said, "I understand you don't want your baby resuscitated," like he was accusing me of not wanting my baby to live.

—Elaine

I saw my doctor just standing up against the wall, so I've always felt like there was some grief there, but she just couldn't share it with me. I've always felt like if she could've shared that, it would have been a little bit easier for me.

—Liza

You may have resented your doctor's cool, clinical attitude. Charlie remembers, "It was *my* wife and *my* baby Kimberlie, and the doctors were looking at it as another fascinating case." Jessie recalls, "The doctor kept calling it 'fetal demise.' I felt like he had difficulty saying 'dead baby.' That really bothered me." Rayleen feels this clinical attitude undermined her dignity: "They come in and just do to you whatever they want and after a while your body is just theirs."

If you needed to recuperate in the hospital, you may not have been given a choice about staying on the maternity ward. You may have wanted to be with the other mothers and babies because you felt that's where you rightfully belonged. Or you may have preferred to be in another ward because you could not bear seeing a mother cuddling her infant. Unfortunately, some staff on other wards do not know how to give sensitive care to bereaved mothers, and you may have felt isolated and forgotten. As Erin recalls, "Nobody knew what to do with me, so they just avoided me. I felt like a freak, that I did something wrong." Hannah remembers being disappointed that no one inquired about her baby's death. She says, "Not one nurse said anything to me about the baby. It was incredible. I thought somebody might say *something!*"

Educating Your Doctor about Grief

Unfortunately, some doctors don't know how to support grieving parents. Grief education is not routinely included in medical training, and death is not a regular feature of obstetric or pediatric practice. Just as parents may feel like failures after their baby dies, doctors may also feel helpless. This mutual sense of failure can make parents and their doctor feel awkward with each other.

You may have to enlighten your doctor about the kind of support you need. Just as friends and family may take their cues from you, so may your doctor. Your doctor cannot read your mind, but if you can explain your feelings and concerns, he or she may be responsive to your needs. If you feel like crying, cry. If you have questions, ask them. If you are angry with your doctor, talk to him or her about your feelings. Your doctor can learn from you about the needs of grieving parents, knowledge that may enable him or her to be helpful to you as well as to others. (See appendix A, "A Note to Caregivers.")

If your doctor is unresponsive to your suggestions or if you do not feel comfortable with your doctor, consider finding another one. Other bereaved parents can offer suggestions as to which doctors handle grief and death sensitively. You can ask for consultation appointments with several doctors and explain your situation and needs. Especially if you plan to have another child, you will want a doctor who is sensitive to your needs for reassurance and vigilant medical care without being patronizing. Changing doctors can feel like another loss, but you deserve a doctor who is supportive.

Family doctors, unlike obstetricians and pediatricians, take care of people of all ages—from infants to pregnant women to the elderly. As a result, they may be more familiar with death and dying. Since they provide continuity of care during pregnancy, delivery and afterward, they may be quite helpful during your grieving process.

You might also consider seeing a certified nurse-midwife. A certified nurse-midwife (C.N.M.) is a registered nurse with a graduate degree in nurse-midwifery who is certified by the American College of Nurse-Midwives. Besides specializing in obstetrics, they act as a woman's advocate within the health care system. Typically, they set aside plenty of time for each appointment, are trained in dealing with your emotional reactions to pregnancy and birth and are responsive to any birth plans you may have. Some midwives work in practices that also include OBGYN doctors. In any case, a midwife will seek out quick consultation and referrals should you want or require them. Because they offer personal and individualized care and emotional support, a C.N.M. may best meet your needs during a subsequent pregnancy.

Spirituality and Religion

Your spiritual and religious beliefs may help you cope with your grief, or they may make you more confused or angry. Even if you consider yourself devout, it is normal to question your beliefs and even modify them according to the lessons you learn about life and death. Rose notes, "It hasn't lessened my faith in God. I know He's there. But it has changed my perception of what He is and how He reacts to this world." Janet agrees: "I used to see God as all-powerful and rewarding, but now I see Him as no more in control or better than me."

Many mothers struggle with the idea that God took away their baby. It is especially difficult to find comfort in the rationalization "God needed a little angel." As Bess says, "That made no sense to me whatsoever—that now I had my personal angel in heaven, that I should be glad for that. I told the hospital chaplain that I needed David here, and he said God needed him more than I did, and I just disagreed with that!" Courtney concurs, "You'd think after a million years of human evolution He'd have enough little angels." Lena notes, "I was so angry at God that I just told Him to get out of my life. It took a while to get back to the church."

Although you may be struggling with your religious faith, your speculation about what happens after death can be a comfort to you. If you believe that people exist after death, you may hope to see your child again someday. Spiritual philosophies about the purpose of life and death can also help you make sense of it all. Perhaps you believe that what happens in your life is part of a divine or universal plan. Believing that someone or something is in control can help you feel a little less vulnerable.

I have this in my imagination that Christopher is up there with my grandparents. I have no idea what happens after death, like if we know anybody, but if we do I'm sure my grandparents are having fun with him and I know he's happy. ... I just have to keep remembering that he is in a better place, and that helps a lot. He has the best baby-sitter.

—Rayleen

I've accepted that what happens is God's will. I felt very strongly that the baby wasn't meant to be. After I'd questioned everything I came to that conclusion and I had to live with that.

—Jane

Maybe God decided that Nicole was too good to be on the earth and go through the things that we go through. Maybe He needed an extra angel in heaven and He took her. Maybe He knew that I was going to get divorced and maybe He figured that two kids would be too much for me to handle. I don't know. I just know that He knows what He's doing and maybe He thought through this experience I could help other people.

—Cindy

I feel like God allows everybody a choice of what their life is. You don't know it after you're born, maybe, and it's not predestination, but I feel like we chose and Daniel chose and for some reason we were his parents, and I would rather have had him for three days than none.

—Liza

Part of what I believe is that we exist as a soul or whatever, as an entity, before we are a body. We decide how and when and to whom to be born and what kind of life to lead, which is not to say it's all predestined and cast in stone, because we make changes as we go, but that we have a purpose for being born, almost like something or some things we want to accomplish. And when those get accomplished, then we usually die. Some people accomplish these quickly and some people take a long time, and I had the sense that Stephanie had some particular things that she wanted to do in this lifetime and she had some things to help us learn and she had a reason for being here. ... She needed to know that she was loved, and she knew that the whole time I was pregnant and she knew that the five days she was here and that she wanted to share that love with us, and then she didn't need to stay around any longer. I also had another sense about her—I have a real issue with letting go of all the way from trivial things to people and relationships, and I think one of the things she was here to teach me was how to let go.

—Sophie

Even if you do not consider yourself to be religious, you may discover some spiritual philosophy that gives you answers and helps you cope. (For more ideas, see "Why Me, Why My Baby" in chapter 7.)

Points to Remember

- Supportive friends can help you cope with your baby's death.
- Many people do not know how to be supportive because they are unfamiliar or uncomfortable with death and grief.
- Friends often take their cues from you. Tell your friends what you need. True friends will appreciate your guidance.
- Some friendships will deepen, others will be lost and new ones will form.
- Attending a support group can help you feel less isolated and can reassure you that your feelings are normal and that you will feel better over time.
- -However you make the connection, another bereaved parent can be a lifeline.
- Counseling can help you work through difficult feelings and help you cope more easily.
- Health care providers can make a tremendous difference in how you cope. Having their support validates the significance of your baby and your grief.
- Religion or spirituality can be a source of comfort. Find some philosophy that helps you cope.

13

The Subsequent Pregnancy: Trying Again

When your baby dies, you lose your innocence. Your firsthand experience with tragedy teaches you that there are no guarantees. Whether your baby died early or late in your pregnancy, before or after birth, you may feel anxious about having another baby. There are a number of issues that you will have to face along the way:

- deciding whether to try again
- deciding when to try again
- trying to conceive
- obtaining vigilant and sensitive prenatal care
- making decisions about prenatal testing
- coping during the pregnancy
- preparing for and coping with the birth
- coping after the birth

This chapter tackles decisions and experiences around getting pregnant and prenatal care; the next chapter looks at coping with the pregnancy, birth and what happens afterward.

Should We Try Again?

One reaction to the death of a baby is to insist on never having more children. The risk of going through another pregnancy or becoming attached to another baby may be too much to bear. You may even consider sterilization for you or your partner. Especially if you have had a number of losses, you may simply feel it is time to move in another direction with your life. At the other extreme, if you think another baby would help you cope with your loss, you may want to get pregnant right away to fill the emptiness and ease your sorrow.

Most parents vacillate between the two reactions, month to month, or even minute to minute. One day you claim, "NEVER AGAIN," and the next day you yearn to feel new life inside you. Or you may be certain you want another baby, but you need to gather your courage before trying again. If you have to deal with the possible recurrence of a genetic defect, you may want more information before making a decision about future pregnancies.

Since Johanna's heart defect was genetic, the doctor thinks there is a 15 percent chance it will happen again, so we feel anxious about another pregnancy. We'll wait until we can focus on the 85 percent chance that it *won't* happen again.

—Courtney

If you've battled infertility or experienced a number of losses, you may wonder "How many times can I go through this before giving up?" You needn't answer that unanswerable question. Just ask yourself whether you can do it *one more time*. Whatever that answer is, that's all you need to know.

When Should We Try Again?

Many parents can't even consider trying again in the months following their baby's death. It feels too risky to set themselves up for possible disappointment. Even parents who are desperate to try again notice that this urge fades over the first few months as their grief intensifies. If you are sure you want to try again, you might consider waiting a few months to see how you feel.

Your Doctor's Advice

If your baby died during or shortly after your pregnancy, there are certain physical considerations that bear on the timing of another pregnancy. After an uncomplicated pregnancy and vaginal delivery, your doctor may advise waiting three to six months, enough time for the uterus to get back into shape so that it can sustain a healthy pregnancy. If you had a Cesarean delivery or complications during your pregnancy, your body may need more time to mend. Ask your doctor about your special needs for physical healing.

Aside from the physical healing, there is emotional healing. Many doctors and psychologists have speculated that after the death of a baby, parents may encounter difficulties relating to the subsequent child. The mother may hesitate to bond during pregnancy, she may be overprotective or she may treat the new baby as a replacement for the dead one. Because of these concerns, many doctors suggest a waiting period of six months to a year, so that the mother can resolve her grief before having another baby.

However, this view is changing as more evidence shows that many mothers do not feel resolved for four or more years. In addition, after a baby dies, it seems only natural that the mother may feel anxious about another pregnancy and overprotective of her children. Finally, many parenting difficulties can be overcome with emotional support, assistance and information on effective parenting. Resolution of grief is not the only key to successful parenting.

Still, many doctors advise their patients to wait six to twelve months. Whatever the time period your doctor suggests, it may seem like an eternity. Jessie points out, "I didn't want to wait a year to start thinking about another baby. I had all this parenting energy and nowhere to direct it." On the other hand, if your doctor tells you to get pregnant right away, you may later resent it because, as Holly says, "It sounded as if, 'Let's just write this one off and move on.' I think it adds to the demeaning of the life that was."

Deciding for Yourself

Most mothers agree that open-ended advice and information are more helpful than a prescribed number of months. With information, you can decide what is best for you as an individual. Deciding for yourself can also restore a sense of control that may have been shattered by your baby's death.

My doctor said to wait until I felt ready. He said, "They can tell you six months or a year, whatever, but you've got to tell yourself when you're ready because some people can't handle it right away and some people have to get pregnant because they can't handle not having that baby." I was glad he said that because I feel that every person is different. Some people need that baby right then and they want to go right back into a pregnancy—I did at first. ... And if they give you six months or a year, whatever, you figure like that's a timeline. If you don't get pregnant after six months or after a year, whatever, something else is wrong. If they leave it up to you, it makes you feel like you *can* do something right.

—Martina

Waiting six months was something I decided for myself, and that made me feel good because that was one little place I could have control. It really seems like it should be an individual decision, because you know what is best.

—Liza

Deciding for yourself lets you take into consideration your own unique needs and feelings. You may want to contemplate the following questions before making decisions.

- Do you want to have all your children before you are 30, 35, 40 years old?
- Do you want your baby to be close in age to your other children?
- Are you worried that it may take a while to conceive, so you should get started soon?
- Do you feel that having another baby as soon as possible may help you cope with your grief and your emptiness?

- Do you need more time to heal physically?
- Do you need more time to research the cause of your baby's death?
- Do you need to find a supportive doctor or a specialist who can help you get answers?
- Do you feel that waiting a while may help you feel less anxious about the next pregnancy?
- Do you feel that waiting may help you to enjoy the new baby more, so you aren't grieving for one baby and preparing for another at the same time?
- Are you anticipating any big changes in your life—school, job, moving, relationships, other deaths and births in your family?
- How does your partner feel?

Getting Pregnant Soon

Some mothers who get pregnant within six months of their baby's death are simply driven to have a baby. For them, the pregnancy can be a very anxious, grieving time, but a healing thing to do.

> I really felt that getting pregnant soon was what I needed. I was aware of what the problems could be, and it's just hard not to. It's not like you totally have control over it. You try to comply with what you know is best—just from a physical point of view, the chances of having a healthy baby are better if you give your body a certain period of time to recuperate. So I waited as long as I could [four months].
>
> —Hannah

For some mothers, the need to become pregnant is overwhelming. They find that being pregnant fairly soon helps them deal with their loss and erases the feeling of failure. Some mothers report a need to "prove I could do it." The advantages of getting pregnant soon include:

- having the feeling that you're moving on toward more hopeful, joyful times
- overcoming feelings of failure, wanting to be able to "do it right"
- overcoming feelings of anxiety about possible infertility
- overcoming some feelings of emptiness (while the new baby can't replace the baby who died, you want a baby in your arms)
- beating the biological clock
- having the new baby close in age to your older child

Many mothers recognize the emotional and physical disadvantages of getting pregnant so soon, but for some the advantages still outweigh the drawbacks. You may decide that you can't feel any worse at this point, so you may as well risk another loss now, rather than later. You may also find it difficult to use contraception because it feels so counterproductive. (See chapter 3, "Sex and Contraception.")

If you decide to get pregnant before three or six months have passed, there may be people who disapprove. Your doctor and your friends may express concern about your physical or emotional recovery or how you would cope with another loss. But remember, it's not their decision to make. It's your recovery, your body, your pregnancy, your children, your life. It's also your decision.

> It was OK except for the fear. It would've been a calmer pregnancy if I had waited at least a year. But then the aching for a baby overtook the fear. I wanted a baby, so forget the fear, we're having a baby!
>
> —Cindy

> I risked it, losing another baby at a time when I was already vulnerable. I thought I could handle it better than if I got over the grieving process, felt happy about my life, got pregnant, lost another baby. That terrified me more. I couldn't face that, whereas, I thought, "OK, I'm at the bottom right now and I think I could handle this." I don't understand this advice about waiting a year. For me I think that would've been much worse.
>
> —Bryn

Waiting to Get Pregnant

The advantages to waiting before another pregnancy include:

- having more time to heal physically
- having more time to heal emotionally
- having time between the babies to help you appreciate their individuality and keep them more separate in your mind
- being less anxious during the pregnancy
- being able to enjoy the new baby more because you are grieving less

You may have your own special reasons for waiting a while. If you've had a string of losses, you may need a break, emotionally and physically. If you had physical complications during pregnancy, your body may need extra time to heal, increasing your chances for a healthy baby. There may be other changes in your life, and you want to feel more settled before you try again. Perhaps you have a surviving twin to care for. Perhaps you are a single mother without a steady partner.

Some mothers who try to get pregnant fairly soon end up waiting because infertility or miscarriage postpones a successful pregnancy. Many mothers concede that their bodies and minds may have needed more time to prepare for another pregnancy and another baby. Jessie and Holly finally had success after working through anger and periods of depression. Claudia notes, "When I accepted that my life is full even if I never have a child, then boom—I got pregnant." Hannah agrees: "I think your mind and body know to some extent when you're ready." Bess eventually had a baby a year and a half later, but feels "glad that it happened that way. By then I felt more positive about the future and carrying a new baby. She fit right in, and I could be happy about her."

Some mothers who get pregnant within six months wish they had waited a little while longer. They discover that grieving intensely, being pregnant and then having a new baby is a confusing, unpleasant combination. Typical of these mothers, Sarah admits, "It was just too close. It was all so blended—exhaustion, grief, hormones, being pregnant again, postpartum blues, everything. That first year was a nightmare, even after Gary was born, not knowing what was the cause for my tears that day. I was a mess."

But waiting can be very difficult. You may feel frustrated, in limbo, unable to move toward your goal of having a baby in your arms. Instead of waiting a prescribed number of months, you may want to take your own special needs and situation into account:

- Educate yourself about the advantages and disadvantages of postponing pregnancy. Ask your doctor and other bereaved mothers; find articles and books to read.
- Consider your physical and emotional needs.
- Take it a month at a time. Avoid any pressure to either wait or get pregnant by a specific date.
- Allow yourself a sense of control over your own life.

Remember, even if you wait more than six months or a year, getting pregnant can still have a healing impact.

When Partners Are on Different Timetables

We went back and forth about having another child. Cal wanted to get pregnant right away, and I said, "No, I'm not ready." And then by the time I was ready, we had reversed positions. He was saying, "Maybe we should wait six months or a year." So there was a lot of stress there.

—Sophie

Unfortunately, it is very common for the mother and father to take turns feeling ready for another pregnancy. This is normal and usually an indication that as a couple, you need more time to gather up your courage. But this can be particularly exasperating if you, the mother, want to get pregnant and he doesn't. After all, you may think, "It's my body and *I'm* ready, so why not?" But because you will need each other's emotional support more than ever during a subsequent pregnancy, you are wise to be concerned that you are BOTH ready before you take the leap.

But how can you convince your partner that it's okay to try again? You can't. Each of you has to convince your own self that it's okay. You can't *make* someone else ready. But if you're the one who's ready, there are things you can do to help your cause.

- Instead of talking, try *listening*. By encouraging your partner to talk about feelings and fears, you may provide the support he or she needs to feel ready.
- Be aware that you may very well share many similar thoughts and feelings. This sense of common ground can make you feel that you agree more than you disagree. It can be illuminating to discuss together the following questions:
    What is the worst thing that could happen?
    What is the best thing that could happen?
    What is the most likely thing that will happen?
  There are no right or wrong, good or bad, reasonable or crazy answers. Every answer is valid and can give you insight on ways to support each other.
- For many couples, a main concern is for the mother's safety and well-being. Perhaps her physical or mental health is at stake. You can offer reassurance by letting your partner know that you share these concerns but are confident that problems won't arise or can be overcome. Perhaps your doctor, midwife or therapist could address some of these issues. Meeting with a genetics counselor may also offer necessary information.
- Being patient can be most helpful. Pressure does little to make anyone adjust or work through things. By simply easing off, you may give your partner the space he or she needs to feel comfortable.
- Be aware that a common dynamic is to strike a balance in the relationship, such that the more obsessed you are with getting pregnant, the more your partner backs off. By reducing your obsession, you may enable your spouse to feel more open to another pregnancy. But how can you stop dwelling on it? If you think about it day and night, try putting your thoughts in a journal. This can reduce their pressure in you. Your obsession may also serve to distract you from your more unpleasant

feelings of grief. Try to set aside time for yourself to remember the baby or babies who died. Go over your mementos or write about the child you're missing. Doing so can help you feel less desperate to move on to another pregnancy. Also recognize that new babies don't fix things—they make things more complicated. Another baby will not fill the emptiness or banish the longing you feel. Alas, working through your grief is the only thing that will bring you lasting peace and happiness.

Can We Get Pregnant?

Once you decide to start trying again, you may feel hopeful because you are doing something positive and moving forward. You may feel as though you are regaining some purpose in your life. You may feel closer to your partner.

Trying again can also be a frustrating, infuriating and nerve-wracking time. You may feel obsessed with trying to get pregnant, as you believe that a baby will fill some of the emptiness you feel. You may feel anxious because you know that this baby will not be the baby you lost. You may feel angry that you have to do this again. As Jessie recalls, "I felt like I'd put in my time being pregnant and I just wanted the baby." You may worry that if you get pregnant, you'll wish you had waited a little longer out of loyalty to your baby or out of fear that you're not ready to love another baby as much.

If you are struggling with infertility, your grief and anxiety can be intensified by the invasive procedures, mechanical timing of sex and disappointment month after month. Even if you are normally fertile, you may worry if you don't get pregnant after a couple of months.

> The monthly thing of finding out you're not pregnant is a grief every month. After Heidi died, the first miscarriage set me back. Then the second miscarriage and D & C—that was like the final blow. That whole invasion of my body ... that was probably the height of my depression, because I was still grieving over Heidi and frustrated about getting pregnant.
>
> —Holly

Trying again can be especially difficult for parents who have lost one or more of twins, triplets, quads or quints. There is something special about raising two or more children who were conceived and born together. You may feel as if you have blown an incredible once-in-a-lifetime opportunity, as the likelihood of conceiving another multiple pregnancy can be slim. When a subsequent pregnancy is not a multiple one, you may feel added disappointment.

There's not even the illusion that the score has somehow been evened. ... you don't get to say, "Well, I'll really grieve and then get pregnant with my subsequent twins."

—Jackie

Losing twins really bothered me more than any other loss. It bothers me just to read about twins or see them. It hurts to think about twins. I had them fixed in my mind as something special. It's something I really wanted. A lot of people think that would be too much work to have two, but I think it would be fun. I always thought it would be fun.

—Peg

Prenatal Care

Working with Your Health Care Providers

When you come in with a subsequent pregnancy, your health care providers may want to shift focus to the future and dim the past. They may encourage you to be optimistic, as if that will help the outcome. They may express concern that you are not bonding to the new baby. They may try to avoid the topic altogether, being uncomfortable with your tears and the intensity of your feelings. There may be times during this pregnancy that *you* might even feel uncomfortable with your grief.

Remember, it is still normal for you to dwell on the past. Even as you carry new life, you may long for your other baby, the "right" baby. Holding on to your memories is how you say goodbye and gradually let go. Grieving is what frees you to enjoy and bond with the new baby.

It is also normal for you to be anxious. To get the reassurance you need, you may want more monitoring than usual. It is natural to want to hear the heartbeat, check your progress and pay more attention to details. And yet, you may be worried about imposing on the nurses, midwives and genetic counselors with incessant calls, interrogations and requests.

So, how can you ask all those questions and make all those demands without alienating everyone? How can you talk about your feelings without raising eyebrows? How can you get the reassurance you need during this trying time?

Here are some ideas for working with your doctor or midwife during your subsequent pregnancy.

- Don't apologize for how you feel. Whatever you are feeling, it's right for you. If you think it would help, ask for a referral to a counselor who is comfortable with grieving parents. But you are entitled to your feelings and you needn't change them or deny them to please anyone.

- Surround yourself with emotional support. Get in touch with other moms going through a subsequent pregnancy. Continue to read books that help you deal with your grief. Keep a journal. Not only will it help you cope with the roller coaster of your grief and new pregnancy, you are making a lovely keepsake, whatever the outcome. All of these measures can alleviate the pressure for your doctor or midwife to be a therapist too.
- Try to empathize with your health care providers. Remember, your relationship may feel more complicated. You are a *bereaved mother*, not just another patient. Most pregnant women are blissfully naive and excited. Not you. You may be fearful, wary, demanding, depressed, angry, withdrawn and untrusting. Your doctor or midwife may feel bewildered and helpless. Grief education is not routinely included in medical training and death is not an anticipated feature of obstetric practice. A mutual sense of failure or anxiety can make you both feel awkward with each other. If you can openly acknowledge how awkward things feel, you may open the way to a more comfortable and honest working relationship with your caregiver.
- Have realistic expectations. We often idealize our doctors. They may seem so knowledgeable, successful and powerful. But they cannot guarantee a healthy baby. And they cannot erase your anxiety. You may feel disappointed in your caregivers when you realize they aren't the life-giving, super-compassionate souls you wished for. No doctor or midwife is perfect. Work with one who is "good enough."
- Be in charge of your medical care. Empower yourself by acquiring information on pregnancy, prenatal care or any other topic that will help reduce your anxiety. Accurate information is always an antidote to fear. You may also find that the more you know, the better in control you feel. Practice good prenatal care and educate yourself about the signs and symptoms of problems that could pose a threat to your baby, for example, preterm labor, placental bleeding, infection, gestational diabetes, preeclampsia, sexually transmitted diseases, fetal distress. Educate yourself about prenatal tests, what they do and how they are done. And if it helps you to read every book and article you can find on birth defects, stillbirth, beta strep, SIDS, abortion, miscarriage, prematurity or whatever, then do it. It is not morbid; it is mastery.
- Don't expect your health care providers to read your mind. Just because you are wearing a sad face doesn't mean they will draw you out. And don't take your cues from the doctor or midwife

who avoids your grief or anxiety. Go ahead and say what's on your mind. Ask for what you need. Do you need reassurance? Do you need information? Do you have concerns and feelings you want to discuss? Do you need longer visits? More visits, more tests, *fewer* tests? Your health care providers can't read your body either. IF YOU ARE CONCERNED ABOUT ANY SYMPTOMS OR SENSATIONS, YOU MUST LET THEM KNOW THAT YOUR CONDITION FEELS SERIOUS AND REQUEST FETAL MONITORING OR OTHER EXAMS TO GET ANSWERS OR REASSURANCE. Sometimes vigilance can avert tragedy (anxiety is good for something!). Not every disaster can be prevented, but you can sure try.

- Make appointments in the practice with those you find supportive. You don't have to "get to know" them all. And should you get the doctor with the unpolished bedside manner during delivery, you can be surrounded by other supportive advocates (see below). If you wish you had more time to talk during appointments, you can ask the receptionist to budget extra time for you or book an appointment during less hectic hours. And if you have concerns that maybe shouldn't wait until tomorrow, DON'T HESITATE TO CALL. They expect calls at all hours and would rather head off disaster than have to deal with it full-blown in the morning!

- Plan for your labor and delivery. How do you want labor managed? Do you want to be induced or left on your own as long as everything looks fine? Will you stay home as long as you can stand the thought of the car ride, or will you check in at the first contraction? What kind of pain relief? (Even if you plan on none, choose what you'd like in case you deliver by Cesarean.) How much monitoring of your progress or baby's heartbeat? Do you want to be kept fully informed about any interventions being considered, or do you want to be spared the details and just informed of your options? Do you want the baby handed to you as soon as possible, or do you want the essential health checks done first? While plans are not guarantees, they can help you feel in control.

- Make arrangements to have supportive advocates with you during labor and delivery so that you have help getting what you need and help with any decisions that must be made. Your partner may fit the bill, but consider additional people. Perhaps you have a friend or know a bereaved mother who would be assertive and persuasive on your behalf or maybe just a comfort to you.

- Plan for your hospital stay. Particularly if your other baby died shortly before or after birth, you may have some strong feelings about the smallest details. It is normal to have flashbacks. You may be surprised by their intensity and find them comforting or unsettling. You might have some choices, whether you want things to be similar or very different. Do you want the same hospital but a different delivery room? Do you want your new baby wrapped in a special blanket or the standard-issue hospital duds? Do you want to be in a different section of the maternity floor? Private room or shared? Do you want to stay as long as possible or leave as soon as you can? It is normal to want to feel close to the baby you miss and yet distance yourself from the tragedy of untimely death. This can be tricky, but you will find the balance that is right for you.

- If you decide to give your caregivers feedback, couch it in terms of what YOU need or needed. After all, you cannot speak for every bereaved parent, but you can say what would help *you*. For example, "I need(ed) this" rather than "You should do this." Your doctor or midwife will feel less defensive and more likely to take your suggestions to heart. As a result, you and other bereaved parents may get more of the support and understanding you need.

You deserve to have a compassionate doctor or midwife who attends to your anxieties, respects your feelings and works with you to have a healthy baby. If your concerns are brushed aside, you may feel more worried or angry and less in control. A dedicated caregiver should be willing to accommodate your needs, thus showing a commitment to you and your baby.

Jessie remembers how attentive and dedicated her doctor was; he even lent her a stethoscope so she could listen to the heartbeat whenever she wanted that reassurance. Rayleen recalls, "When the twenty-seventh week came along, I was just really bothered. My doctor said I could come in every week, every day if I had to. That helped." If complications arise during this pregnancy, you will be especially anxious and want additional care and reassurance. In Peg's case, her doctor's extra attention helped her to comfort herself:

When I was about 30 or 32 weeks pregnant with Justin, I started bleeding and I was a basket case. At that time they had already put a cerclage in [wrapped a string around the cervix to keep it closed] and I was taking terbutaline [medication to stop contractions]. I remember I had a doctor's appointment that day and I was getting ready to go and I started bleeding and I thought, "Okay, take a deep breath, calm down. ... You're farther along than you've ever been before, so even if something happens, you're going to have this baby." And I went to 38 weeks with him.

—Peg

Prenatal Diagnostic Testing

In this age of advanced medical technology, we often assume that the more technology we employ, the better the outcome. With prenatal care, however, it is important to differentiate between tests that identify potential problems in the pregnancy and tests that identify preexisting problems in the baby. Furthermore, tests vary in their value toward improving the outcome. A test is useful when there are remedies or actions to take if a problem is discovered. If there isn't anything that can or will be done, then you might consider the test useless, even detrimental.

There are a number of tests that can make a difference to your baby's health—they examine aspects of the mother's or baby's condition that may be remedied if problems are spotted. Examples include screening for preeclampsia, preterm labor, gestational diabetes or beta strep infection in the mother. In the final weeks of pregnancy, there are tests that monitor the fetal heart rate during contractions or examine fetal movements and amniotic fluid volume by ultrasound. If problems are detected, solutions might include bed rest, diet, antibiotics or induction of labor.

Your doctor or midwife may offer you a number of other tests—alpha fetoprotein analysis (AFP), chorionic villis sampling (CVS), amniocentesis or high-level ultrasound. These tests are not required to ensure a healthy pregnancy, but are available for parents who want genetic or developmental information about the fetus. Unfortunately, with current technology, getting a closer look at the baby's chromosomes or the organ and skeletal development isn't going to lead to prenatal repairs for these problems. In addition, jumping through the hoops of testing does not guarantee that your baby will be all right. These tests are meant to screen for a handful of anomalies, but are not foolproof and cannot identify or rule out many other problems. Most important, these tests do not prevent certain problems; they merely identify them.

Whether to do genetic or developmental prenatal testing on your baby is a personal choice. Your decision may be simple and straightforward, or belabored and complicated as you try to find the right balance between technology and letting nature take its course. Even if it is highly recommended in your case, you can still decide against it. Even if you have zero risk factors, you can still decide to do it.

Your decision will be based on many things, including

- your personal experiences with infertility and previous pregnancies,
- the probabilities and kinds of genetic risks you hold,
- your desire to be reassured or forewarned about possible problems,
- your beliefs about disability and suffering,
- your beliefs about and willingness to interrupt a pregnancy,

- how your partner feels,
- whether you have surviving children to care for,
- your gut feelings and
- your faith in science or Mother Nature or a higher order.

Answers to the following questions can also help you decide:

- How high is your risk for having a baby with birth defects?
- What will each test try to detect?
- When and how is it done?
- Do you have access to experienced specialists who can perform the test and interpret the results?
- Are there risks or disadvantages to the mother or baby?
- How do the probabilities compare? (Balance the chance that your baby will have problems against the chance that problems will be caused by testing.)
- How long does it take to get results?
- How reliable or accurate are the results?
- How will you use the information?
- What steps follow a negative or positive result?
- How much will it cost?
- Are there other ways to get similar information?
- Which feels better to you: doing the test or forgoing it?

You may decide that diagnostic testing gives you some peace of mind, maybe even a glimmer of hope. If your deceased baby had birth defects, you may want to test for possible recurrence. As Janice points out, "At least we could rule out some things, even if we couldn't rule out everything."

Many mothers find prenatal testing reassuring, while others find it invasive and nerve-wracking. When you're trying to carry a baby to term, the thought of taking a sample of placental tissue or amniotic fluid may seem too risky. When you are struggling to be optimistic, testing can rake up fears and undermine already shaky feelings of confidence. You may simply want to avoid having to make any decisions that come with unfavorable test results.

Along with feeling protective, you may also feel fatalistic—that this baby's fate is already sealed and there isn't anything you can or should do about it. As Terri points out, "I figure I'm going to have the babies I'm meant to have. And I'm terrified at the thought of inaccurate results and terminating a normal baby." Winnie concurs, "I just figured I'd hope for the best and accept the rest."

If you have miscarried a baby in the first trimester, an early ultrasound might be all the reassurance you need. It may feel just right to see the heartbeat and then coast the rest of the pregnancy. If you want more information about the baby but hesitate taking samples from your womb, it is reasonable to go ahead with maternal blood tests and high-level ultrasound, which are less invasive and may offer some reassurance. If these exams lead to concerns, then you can choose whether to go on with more invasive testing.

If you decide to forgo some or all diagnostic prenatal tests, your doctor or midwife should support you. Some states may require AFP tests, but it can help to remember that unfavorable results are often false alarms. If your health care providers are pressuring you, they are only trying to provide you with the most sophisticated technology. If there are certain prenatal tests that you don't want, you should be able to discuss your concerns and politely refuse without ruining your relationship. After all, they want what's best for you and your baby. And what's best is for you to decide. (For further reading, consult "Books on Infertility, Pregnancy and Health" in the bibliography.)

I felt like testing promoted the assumption that there were problems that had to be uncovered or ruled out. I just wanted to assume that this baby would be fine. To encourage myself, I'd remember that women have been having healthy babies for centuries without prenatal testing and kick charts to guide their pregnancies along!

—Winnie

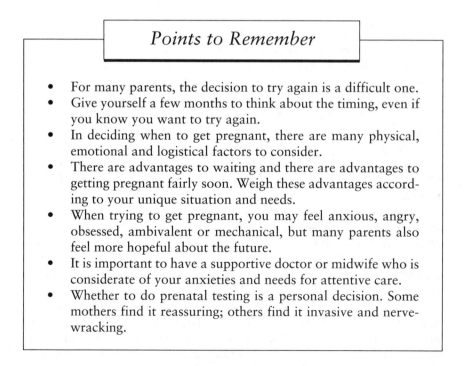

Points to Remember

- For many parents, the decision to try again is a difficult one.
- Give yourself a few months to think about the timing, even if you know you want to try again.
- In deciding when to get pregnant, there are many physical, emotional and logistical factors to consider.
- There are advantages to waiting and there are advantages to getting pregnant fairly soon. Weigh these advantages according to your unique situation and needs.
- When trying to get pregnant, you may feel anxious, angry, obsessed, ambivalent or mechanical, but many parents also feel more hopeful about the future.
- It is important to have a supportive doctor or midwife who is considerate of your anxieties and needs for attentive care.
- Whether to do prenatal testing is a personal decision. Some mothers find it reassuring; others find it invasive and nerve-wracking.

14

Coping during Subsequent Pregnancy and Birth

The Pregnancy

Vulnerability and Control

Some days I thought, "I'm pregnant; the world is great!" Then other days I'd think, "I've already lost a baby. What if it happens again?"

—Cindy

Having a baby die, especially during pregnancy or shortly after birth, will probably color your experience with subsequent pregnancies, making you more anxious that something could go wrong. You don't just have abstract knowledge that babies can die. You can't hide under the assumption that it won't happen to you. It *has* happened to you, and while the chance of it happening again may be remote, it is a possibility.

You may feel angry or disappointed that you can't have that innocence back and enjoy a blissful pregnancy. You may wish that you could relax, but you can't totally ignore what happened before. You may feel you simply cannot expect a pregnancy to result in a baby that will survive. Holly recalls, "All through my pregnancy I thought, 'Yes, I am pregnant, but I don't feel like I'm going to bring anything home from the hospital.' "

Feeling vulnerable is difficult to cope with. You may feel uneasy because you know that even if you take good care of yourself and your baby, your baby can still die. On the other hand, knowing your baby's cause of death can help you feel some control, that perhaps certain things can be done to prevent the same thing from happening again.

No matter how well you take care of yourself during a pregnancy, nothing is guaranteed. I decided that even if you go into labor it's not guaranteed that you're going to have a baby. It's not guaranteed when that baby is born you're going to have a baby. You've just gotta go one day at a time. After you lose one, it's so hard.

—Martina

The doctors had described a place on my uterus where, from my miscarriage probably, my uterus wasn't completely healed, so as the next baby was growing, the placenta was breaking away from the uterus and that's what was causing the bleeding. It was an abruption. Knowing the reason helped encourage me that there wasn't something dramatically wrong with me, that all I needed to do was wait until I was better healed. It made me feel like it was a problem that could be solved by time.

—Elaine

Although you can remind yourself that the vast majority of babies are normal and healthy, the statistical probabilities may offer little comfort. After all, you "beat the odds" when your baby died. While intellectually you know everything is likely to turn out fine, it can be difficult to convince yourself *emotionally*. While you may be certain that others will have healthy babies, you may feel sure that you won't.

If your anxieties seem overwhelming, the following ideas may help calm you.

- Remember that having fears about the baby's health and development is a common experience among pregnant women, even those who haven't faced tragedy.
- Remind yourself that your anxieties and thoughts do not have the power to harm your baby or make your fears come true.
- Try relaxation techniques (see "Relaxation" in chapter 3).
- Talk about your fears to someone who can listen and offer reassurance that your anxieties are normal but most probably unfounded.
- Write about your feelings and worries (see appendix B).
- Reduce your stress in other ways. For instance, give up unessential responsibilities and set aside time for leisure.
- Instead of trying to repress your fears, redirect them toward positive imagery. For instance, Courtney acknowledged her fear of heart defects and was able to counteract them somewhat by imagining her baby's heart forming properly during the first critical months of development.

You can also diminish anxiety by trying to gain some feelings of control. You may want a lot of information and monitoring during this pregnancy. You may make frequent visits to your doctor. You may eagerly wait for the baby to start moving; you may even figure out ways to encourage movement because it can be very reassuring. You may have a lot of superstitions. These are fine to act on as long as this nurtures you and your baby. Or you may find that by giving up some control, you can relax a little because it's out of your hands.

I remember getting scared, thinking she hasn't moved, and I was counting time on the clock. I would count the hours. I'd lay down real still and see if the baby would kick. I remember holding my belly, holding my baby there, and I would talk to her and I just was very hopeful that things would be OK with her.

—Bryn

I had a lot of superstitions. Whatever I did the last pregnancy, I didn't do this time. If I went swimming last time, I didn't go swimming this time. Things like that.

—Holly

With the other pregnancies, there wasn't anything I could do about it and I just knew it wasn't going to work. This time I was more accepting, saying, "Since there isn't anything I can do to make it one way or the other, I might as well realize that there could be a good outcome, not just a bad outcome."

—Meryl

Getting Past a Certain Point

For some mothers, anxiety is tempered by hope. Especially if this pregnancy is uneventful, you may be able to feel some guarded optimism. As your due date approaches, you may dare to feel that maybe this pregnancy will turn out all right.

Depending on when your baby died, you may feel that if you make it past that certain point, you can relax a little. If you didn't make it beyond the first trimester, you may hold your breath until you get well into the second trimester. If your baby died during the third trimester, your anxiety may intensify then.

From my twenty-second to my thirtieth week I was nervous about everything, and time just went so slowly. I can remember thinking, "I have to get through one more week and one more week and one more week. ..." You're waiting and hoping nothing happens, and that was probably the worst time. Once I reached thirty weeks, then I think I relaxed quite a bit.

—Peg

Some mothers find it hard to relax at any point. If you make it past the first trimester, you may worry about making it to full term. Even if the baby is born healthy, you may worry about your baby surviving the first six months or the first year. And even if your child survives infancy, another pregnancy, another baby can rake up all those anxieties again.

You may feel very impatient for your due date to arrive so that you can have your baby safely in your arms. Or you may wish that you could just remain pregnant, that your baby is safer inside you.

The first three months, everything's OK if you don't lose the baby, and then usually the middle months are OK, and then pray from six to nine that you don't go into premature labor, and then pray that you don't have a stillborn.

—Cindy

The whole nine months, I swore it took nine years. It was the longest nine months I've ever been through. But I didn't want it to be time to have her because I just kept having these pessimistic feelings, so why hurry it?

—Martina

Bonding to Your Baby during Pregnancy

After the trauma of losing a baby, many mothers hesitate to bond with the subsequent baby. Your joy and expectations are clouded by fears and pessimism. You can feel totally committed to this pregnancy and you desperately want to count on having a healthy baby, but at the same time you worry about the devastation you would feel if this baby died. Mothers often remain reserved because they dare not pin their hopes on a positive outcome.

While he was still in the womb, I consciously would sit and pat and rub and talk, which I didn't do much with the others, but I kind of thought I'd give him a little extra advantage. It made me feel good, but I also knew that now I was feeling attached and that was hard— on the one hand being told, "Don't get your hopes up too high," but thinking, "There's no way that I can't feel something!"

—Meryl

For a lot of mothers, preparing the nursery and collecting baby things, thinking about names, even feeling the baby move, seems too hopeful. You may wallpaper the baby's room in a pattern that would also be appropriate for a guest room or a den. When you first perceive fetal movement, you may be hit with the stark reality of your baby's presence and how awful it would be if this baby were to die too. You may wait until your last month to think about names. You may wait until the baby comes home before you prepare the nursery.

Sarah remembers how doubtful and cautious she was: "I wanted to pretend I wasn't pregnant. I packed up the nursery. I wasn't into maternity clothes or little pregnancy conversations, none of that. I was going to wait and *see* if I got a baby!" Hannah postponed baby showers and shopping until *after* Michael came home. Lena concurs, "I didn't want to go buy a bunch of stuff and have this one die too." Even after Bryn's daughter was born, she recalls, "I was afraid to buy diapers above the newborn size because, 'What if she didn't make it?' I was still just taking it a day at a time." For many mothers, superstitions add to their caution. Kitty notes, "I've always been superstitious, even with my first. I didn't want to start the nursery too early in case something would happen."

If you have kept the nursery set up, you may be very protective of its contents. Cindy remembers not letting anyone borrow her baby things until she had a baby of her own to use them. If you put the nursery away, you may hesitate getting things out again because preparing for a new baby triggers memories about the baby who died. This may be difficult, but you can grieve for your missing baby while you look forward to another one. Dara recalls, "Bringing out all her baby things brought everything back into focus again, but it didn't feel *worse*."

Not wanting to feel too attached to your new baby is a common experience. As your pregnancy progresses, your confidence may grow and you may allow yourself to feel a greater bond with this baby. Especially in the months after the birth, you will acquire the full depth and joy of maternal love.

Pessimism and Optimism

Part of me was *so glad* I was pregnant and another part of me was so terrified. I thought, "I can't do this again. I was a fool! Why did I think I could go through this again?" I kept trying to be positive. I did have a feeling she was going to be OK.

—Bryn

While vulnerability makes you worried and bonding makes you scared, pessimism gives you little hope. Pessimistic feelings may seem overwhelming, but it *is* possible to have some optimism, maybe not blissful, durable or concrete, but optimism nonetheless. Hopeful thoughts and feelings, however elusive, can encourage you and help you cope with your anxieties. You may feel that pessimism and holding back hope are useful, yet they only offer the *illusion* that you would be prepared for or protected from tragedy. So, if you have any thread of hope, spend some time hanging on to that.

Naturally, this is easier said than done. But there are things you can do that might help. First, remember that your feelings are separate from your pregnancy. Your pessimism, while normal and understandable, does not necessarily bear any relation to your baby's condition. If you are classified high-risk because of your history, you may actually be in the midst of a low-risk pregnancy. Even if you truly are high-risk, be aware that while your emotional reality is in the throes of horrific worry, your physical reality—and the baby—may very well be normal and healthy.

Second, resist the superstition that you will invite curses by having any hopes or confidence. Constant pessimism can cost you dearly in terms of energy and peace of mind. Remember, optimism does not make bad things happen.

If you feel hopes rising, let them flow. Dare to dream about the soft smell of a baby's head. Permit yourself to fantasize about how full your arms and days will be. Go ahead and buy darling baby clothes. You may fear that dreaming and nesting—particularly smoothing baby things or preparing a nursery—will raise your hopes too high. You may imagine that if the baby dies, you would only be more devastated, surrounded by reminders that would heighten your despair. To the contrary, these are the very things that would aid in your mourning and eventual healing. In your darker moments, you can see how these items could be precious mementos of this baby you love. Those little outfits and teddy bears would give you something of your baby to hold on to. Memories of making a place for your baby to come home to would give you more things to reminisce. Remember, even if you don't want to allow it, you *are* invested in and bonding to your baby. You would love and miss your baby terribly whether you had a stocked nursery or a bare one. Although you don't feel like a "normal" pregnant woman, you can dare to nest like one. If it gives you hope, do it.

> When I was about 7 months pregnant, I bought a pretty little baby dress. I was *terrified* to do it—afraid that if I did, this baby wouldn't happen. But after I did it, it felt *great!* It actually made me think that maybe this baby was for real and everything would be all right.
>
> —Clara

> I went back and forth between high anxiety and blind faith. When I bought some maternity clothes, I knew it was an act of faith that I'd even need them. I also found it comforting to look through and collect cotton baby clothes. They gave me hope. Of course, this was balanced against reading a stack of books about prenatal testing, birth defects, prematurity and medical ethics. Looking back on it, it was like having a split personality.
>
> —Winnie

You might also try keeping a journal. Besides the therapeutic value of helping you express and deal with your feelings, a journal can be a priceless keepsake of a special, perhaps agonizing, but miraculous time in your life. A journal can help you endure the pregnancy and prepare for whatever the outcome.

Looking Forward, Looking Back

Many mothers find it difficult to be pregnant and to prepare for another baby while grieving for the baby who died. Some parents who avoid grief believe that it is best to move on to the future without looking back. However, avoiding grief thwarts emotional needs and can make parents less capable of emotionally nurturing their new baby. Others believe that the subsequent baby can somehow replace the one who died or erase the need to grieve. But, as Clara realizes, "Being pregnant is great, but it doesn't fix everything; it doesn't banish my grief."

Although it is challenging, it is possible to manage these competing feelings—to express hope for the future *and* grief for the past. Continuing to work through grief enhances your adjustment to your baby's death and prepares a healthy foundation for your relationship with the subsequent baby. (See "How Do I Resolve My Grief?" in chapter 7.)

During pregnancy, you may imagine the new baby will be similar to the baby who died, as the hope that this baby survives merges with the wish that the other baby had lived. You may even feel that the baby who didn't survive is reborn in some way with the new baby.

> When I was pregnant, I did think about Christopher. I never thought it was the same pregnancy, but it was hard to believe it was another person, another child. It was really hard for me to imagine there could be two of them. I *knew* it was another, but I know I thought about him.
>
> —Rayleen

Intellectually, you know it is not the same baby, but especially before the birth, it is easy to believe that your subsequent baby holds the essence of your other baby. As long as you can appreciate the unique biological and spiritual identity of this new child, imagining similarities can be a harmless way to hold on to the baby you miss so much. After this baby is born and you become acquainted, you will find it easier to keep the babies separate. (See "The Replacement Child" in chapter 15.)

Wishing for a Certain Gender

Most parents have a strong preference for the sex of the new baby. If your only daughter or your only son died, you may hope to have another of the same gender. You may feel disappointed if you don't get your wish. If you do get your wish, you may feel very grateful.

> After Jenni died, when I got pregnant I really, really wanted another little girl. Then I had Dustin, and I love him dearly, but I had my heart set on a girl. I think about trying again, having another baby, but with no guarantees, it doesn't seem like the thing to do.
>
> —Maya

> I had done everything. I had known when I was ovulating, so there was no doubt in my mind it was a girl. Even through the whole pregnancy I was telling people it was a girl. When Chris was born, I remember feeling disappointed and I felt like a jerk because I thought,

"You're disappointed in the sex of your child?" But you wonder, "If I hadn't lost the other baby, I would've had a girl."

—Elaine

I *am* having a hard time accepting that I'm having a boy. I've been trying to realize my motive for wanting a girl and it's really because I want *Carolyn* and since this baby would not be her, I'm getting used to the idea of a boy. But I would like to have another daughter someday.

—Janice

We wanted a girl, not just because Melanie was a girl, but because, you know, the perfect family, a boy and a girl. For some reason I didn't think I was going to have a girl, so when I did I was just really happy. It took me a couple days to really realize that I had a normal healthy baby and it was a girl, everything I wanted.

—Kitty

I was happy when I had Max, because I really never thought I'd have a boy. I always thought I was going to just have girls, that I wasn't meant to have a boy.

—Jane

On the other hand, you may hope your subsequent baby is the other sex, in order to keep them separate or avoid feeling as though you've replaced the baby who holds a special place in your heart. Bryn observes, "I think maybe it's good that I had a girl. If I'd had another boy, I wonder if maybe my memories would have meshed into one." Martina agrees: "We didn't want a boy because we were afraid we'd try to put the boy in Greg's place."

I was thrilled she was a little girl. It was nice because I immediately saw that I couldn't go through with my little fantasy, that if it was a little boy, it would be the same little boy. And that would've been pretty strong because at birth she looked so much like him. ... But sometimes I wish I had another little boy so that I'd see a little bit more of what he would be like.

—Liza

As these mothers illustrate, it is very common to be especially disappointed when an only daughter dies and then to give birth to a son. This may have to do with the mother's "loss of self" being less repaired when a son instead of daughter is born. Or it may be the fear that she has forever lost her chance to have the special relationship that mothers and daughters often have.

Like many women, you may believe that mother-child intimacy is best achieved with daughters. In our culture, it is commonly held and practiced that mothers must push their sons away, starting when they are barely out of diapers, in order for them to reach full masculine maturity. It may help to remember that with the changing image and role of men in our society, there will be less pressure for mothers to do this—and you needn't bow to that pressure, in any case. We are beginning to recognize that when a boy is close to his mother, he is better prepared for the trials of life, better able to express emotions and better able to have strong relationships with others. Both boys and girls need attentive caring and guidance into adulthood. It may help you to read some of the new books that examine the importance of the mother-son bond and the issues involved in raising a boy. (See "Books on Parenting" in the bibliography.)

Strong desires for a certain gender are legitimate. If you are disappointed, it is important that you acknowledge this loss and your emotions. Saying "This is not what I wanted" can help you put these feelings aside and accept your little boy or girl.

Support Groups

Some mothers stop going to their support group after they get pregnant again. To hear about babies dying may make them more pessimistic or anxious during their pregnancy. Jessie recalls, "That was the only negative part about being in the support group. Now we knew 101 ways that babies can die, even things we never used to worry about." For other mothers, going to a support group or at least staying in touch with those parents gives them an opportunity to talk about their anxieties about the new baby, as well as their continuing sadness about the baby who died.

Some hospitals have organized "subsequent pregnancy" support groups for parents who have already experienced the death of a baby. These groups can help parents cope with their anxiety as well as connect them with others who can accompany them through this experience. To find a group near you, ask your obstetric practice, bereaved parents support group leaders or call area hospital women's and parent education centers. You might also look into the subsequent pregnancy newsletter, "PAILS of Hope" sponsored by Pen-Parents (see appendix C).

The Birth

The final weeks of your pregnancy may be an especially anxious time. The "moment of truth" approaches. You may constantly monitor your baby's movements or visit your doctor daily. You may try to keep busy to distract yourself from the worry. Even if you feel too scared to count on bringing home a baby, as the due date draws near you may find yourself hoping and feeling optimistic, even as your anxiety mounts. When you're getting ready for the birth, you may feel an odd mixture of impatience and dread, elation and anxiety, optimism and pessimism.

During the last weeks I felt increasing terror, especially since it was only a year before that I delivered another baby. It was such a blend: it was hard to figure out the grieving, the hormones are going crazy and just being pregnant you're a mess anyway. I can't even compare pregnancies. You go into one pregnancy excited to see your baby and you go into the next one being sure the baby is going to be dead.

—Sarah

I felt anxiety and fear, but also a little bit of investment, looking forward to it. I actually went out a few days before she was born and bought a dress for her to wear home from the hospital.

—Holly

I couldn't wait to have him. I was so anxious for him to be born. I wasn't worried so much about the birth part of it, but just to have him here with everything going right. … I wanted to have this baby. The doctor took my cerclage out when I was thirty-seven weeks and nothing happened. After months of stopping premature labor, we thought, "When we take this out there's nothing that's going to hold this baby back," but nothing happened. I kept waiting and waiting and waiting and finally, a week later, I went into labor.

—Peg

If you are anxious about your baby during contractions, having a fetal monitor can be reassuring. If you deliver by Cesarean, you may want to be awake to feel more in control, or you may wish to have a general anesthetic to spare yourself the anxiety. As Martina recalls, "I didn't want to be awake in case something was wrong." Even if labor and delivery go well and you have a healthy baby in your arms, you still may worry. Bryn remembers, "I was happy, but also afraid and nervous. I got to hold her, but I still couldn't trust that everything was going to be OK."

Many mothers are afraid of losing control during labor or being consumed with grief and thoughts of the baby who died. Similarities between your present and past experiences can haunt you. Bryn recalls, "When she was born, everything I was going back to was my first experience—all the rooms, the doctors, the procedures … I was terrified when my water broke because that's when it all started before." Sophie remembers, "I was afraid I would get real crazy in terms of thinking about Stephanie and crying and sobbing uncontrollably, and that wouldn't help labor at all." But Sophie, like most, found she was able to focus on the present birth. Focusing on the differences between this experience and the other can help you cope and feel more optimistic.

They had the monitor on me and just knowing that her heartbeat was OK, I felt good about it. But I know I was scared too. It's getting close, but you still don't know what's going to happen.

—Rayleen

The first thing I said was, "Is he breathing?" I wanted to make sure he was alive. I think I was so enthralled that this baby came out alive.

—Erin

When Nicole was stillborn it was so quiet. It seemed like the whole hospital got quiet, and you could hear a pin drop, it was so quiet and peaceful. When Emily was born, it was so loud. Everybody was talking and laughing and crying, and so it was a really big difference. I loved the noise.

—Cindy

Coping after the Birth

Just when you expected to be fulfilled with maternal joy, you may be drowning in sorrow. It may help to remember that feelings of sadness are normal for all new mothers. There are physical reasons, such as fluctuating hormones, sleep deprivation and the around-the-clock demands of nursing and caring for an infant. Giving birth is also a first step in letting go and this in itself can feel like a loss. You may worry that the baby isn't safe outside your womb. Feelings of emptiness can be literal as you no longer have a baby inside you. You also may have some grief over the birth—perhaps unplanned interventions were necessary or you were separated from your baby for a while. All of these sources of sadness are part of normal postpartum recovery.

Because you are a bereaved mother, you may be dealing with other issues that can dampen your joy. When you finally bring home a healthy baby, it may feel unreal to you. Your dream has come true, but after months of being afraid it would never happen, it can be quite a shock. And even when cradling your little one safely in your arms, you may wonder when this infant is going to be taken away too. After all, you know for a fact that mothers don't get to keep every baby they bring into the world.

Most significantly, whether you waited two months or two years before getting pregnant, feelings of grief can intensify after your new baby's birth. Even if you feel as though you have put your grief behind you, having this baby in your arms can trigger emotions you've yet to express and work through. You may come to another level of realization that the baby you lost will never be recovered, even by having this baby. As Laura points out, "You always hope deep down that maybe another child could fill the void in your heart."

Some mothers try to suppress their grief so it won't dampen their joy. By stifling emotions, you won't feel sad, but you won't feel happy either. Bryn recalls, "I was so happy and yet I could still not enjoy it. I was not ready to really enjoy anything. I couldn't savor things." If you permit yourself to feel sad emotions, you also open yourself up to feel the happy ones. Finding a balance rather than trying to repress feelings will benefit you and your baby.

Once you have a real living baby and you see that you're actually dealing with a baby, then it really made me start to think about the other babies quite a bit. I went through a period where it was bothering me more than it had before. ... My grief was something I felt I had pretty much gotten over, and then when I had Justin it brought it back to me and I realized, "It still bothers me."

—Peg

Within a couple of days I was really starting to grieve again. I think a lot of it was probably relief, and maybe I had suspended some of the grief during the pregnancy. I remember while I was in the hospital, just crying a lot, carrying her around, just being so happy with her. At the same time, it seems like I really got a lot of that grief out the first month.

—Liza

I thought having another baby would make me feel better, and during the pregnancy I had something to look forward to, but after Alysia's birth, something was gnawing at me. I've been feeling angry and feeling strongly that I should have another baby. Then last week it dawned on me that I want another baby because it feels like a baby is missing—Steven is missing. I wish I didn't miss him so much, and I thought I'd feel better and go forward instead of backward.

—Alison

Instead of trying to leave your baby and your memories behind, you might try to take those memories with you, forward into the future. This can help you feel less discouraged. (See "Remembering, Moving On" in the last chapter.)

Bonding after Birth

If you feel reluctant to get close to the new baby for fear of getting hurt again, rest assured that it may take you a little while to adjust to the reality that this child is healthy and here to stay. Also it may help to recognize that withdrawal offers no protection, as you would be absolutely devastated if this baby dies, no matter how much you try to steel your heart. Take the leap and dare to enjoy your little one. The risk may seem great, but the rewards are immeasurable.

If you have nagging concerns about your maternal feelings, do seek help from a qualified counselor who has experience with bereaved parents. Ask your local hospital, support group or other bereaved parents for referrals. Mothering an infant is such a precious and fleeting time. You deserve to enjoy it.

Another Loss

After Laura died, I had a miscarriage and that was real hard. It was depressing. It made me think, "Maybe I really am not going to be a mother." I felt like a victim, like maybe there was something out there that was going to get me, and that was a bad feeling.

—Hannah

The miscarriage hurt too. It was like, add another one to the list. When I think about getting pregnant—I had a miscarriage, I had a stillbirth, I had an almost-premature baby—I mean, what's going to happen next?

—Cindy

To have these miscarriages that once again you had no answers for and you couldn't control ... the miscarriages really compounded my grief and just made it more difficult to keep going, to function, to *want* to continue. I just would have rather been dead. The pain was unbearable sometimes.

—Holly

It kept building for me, because the more times it happened, then I thought the less chance I ever have of having a baby, that there was nothing that could be done. So I did get more anxious with each one.

—Peg

After your first loss, your greatest fear is that it will happen again. If it does, it can be devastating. You may wonder if it's a sign of deeper problems, a prelude to chronic infertility or an inability to bear a healthy baby. After a number of losses you may feel more anxious than ever when you are pregnant. You may fear that you could never survive another loss. But you are probably more resilient than you think. And you will probably gather up the courage to try again.

Points to Remember

- During your pregnancy, it is normal to feel anxious and hesitant about investing in the baby or a positive outcome.
- Hopeful thoughts and feelings, however elusive, can encourage you and help you cope with your anxieties. Do things that give you hope.
- It is normal to have strong preferences about your new baby's gender.
- During your pregnancy, it is normal to feel that the new baby and the baby who died are similar or somehow the same.
- A supportive friend or partner can help by listening to you talk about your hopes and fears for this baby.
- During the birth, it is normal to think about your previous experiences.
- After the birth, it is normal for you to grieve deeply, as having another baby can act as a catalyst for your emotions about the baby who died.
- Make room for your grief and your joy. Finding a balance rather than trying to suppress emotions will benefit you and your baby.
- Mothering an infant is a precious and fleeting time. You deserve to enjoy it.
- If you experience the death of another baby, you can use what you have learned about grief and gathering memories. You will survive this one too.

15

Raising Subsequent Children

Most parents find that the death of a baby profoundly affects their relationship with the children born afterward. Parents often mention a heightened appreciation for these precious children, overprotective feelings, a desire to be the best parent possible and a tendency to compare babies. These reactions can be, but are not necessarily, unhealthy or detrimental. By educating yourself about the effects other parents have noticed, you can be on the lookout for ways to enhance your relationship with your subsequent children. Moreover, you can be reassured that your feelings are normal.

You may also notice changes in your relationship with your children born before the baby died. When there are one or more surviving babies from a multiple pregnancy, parenting can be especially impacted. Though the next two chapters focus on subsequent children, you may find them helpful in dealing with any of your surviving children.

Heightened Appreciation

Many parents feel an enhanced appreciation for their subsequent children. These children may seem very precious because, after experiencing the death of a baby, parents don't take for granted the health and survival of their children. Kara notes, "You realize things aren't forever and you appreciate everything they do and what they are." You may feel closer to your children. You may really enjoy them and consider them special. Jane elaborates: "I view Jenny as a child that wouldn't have been if I hadn't lost the other one." Like most parents, you may consider this appreciation to be one of the positive lessons learned from the death of your baby.

You may feel vulnerable when you think how special your children are because it seems you have that much more to lose should tragedy strike. You may feel especially invested if you have only one child after your baby dies.

Overprotectiveness

When he was jaundiced at birth I was sure that he had liver problems; the first cold, I was sure it was pneumonia. Everything that kid did I was sure was going to end his life. I didn't leave that baby with a sitter for over a year. I did not let that child nap without my interrupting the nap for a year. I was terrified he was going to die and I was gonna be sure that I was going to be there when he did. I didn't even want to leave him with my husband because I just knew that if something happened to him and I wasn't there, that would be it for me, if that happened with two kids. I remember thinking, "I will just definitely kill myself then, definitely."

—Sarah

Overprotective feelings naturally arise from firsthand experience with the death of a baby. It is normal to worry and to feel more vigilant about protecting your children from harm. You may feel that tragedy can strike at any time, without warning. You may feel that life is very tenuous, that you can't count on everything turning out all right. Many parents find that these overprotective feelings linger for years, but they are most apparent through the first year or so after a new baby is born. You may also feel overprotective of your older children, even though you felt relatively carefree before your baby died.

If you are raising a surviving child or children from a multiple birth, you may struggle with the opposing feelings of not wanting to bond too much and of being fiercely overprotective. You may be afraid to love a surviving baby because the more you open your heart, the more you will grieve for the other baby or babies. And the more you love, the more you may fear for your survivors, especially if they are tiny, fragile or sick. In addition, you've had no time to come to terms with your feelings of grief and vulnerability before you are faced with an infant to care for. You can benefit from extra support in coping with your fears and in daring to fall in love with your baby. (The following chapter on protective parenting may be particularly helpful to you.)

All parents worry about their children, but I think there's a certain amount of denial that exists that allows you to not really believe in your heart that something is going to happen to them. And then when something *does* happen to one of your children, you know it can happen, you know it's for real.

—Anya

I think about the fact that she could die, probably more than most parents, and that scares me. I don't think most parents think about that or want to, but it's reality. It could happen.

—Cindy

At first I was afraid to love Nicholas, a child full of life, for fear of losing him. For so long, I felt as though I only knew how to love dead children and I was frightened that Nicholas, too, would die.

—Sheila

After the baby died, I would lay in bed worrying about my 2-year-old. I was afraid that something was going to happen to her, and then my other baby would be gone.

—Jane

I was never afraid when Donna was little. Then, after I lost the baby, I was so overprotective—here she was, 10 years old, and I couldn't let go.

—Martina

In particular you may feel vulnerable to:

- fears that you won't be able to keep this baby
- fears that the baby will have a life-threatening illness or accident
- fears about the baby dying during sleep

Parents vary on how vulnerable they feel, but it is normal to have these and other fears. As time passes and your child survives infancy, it may become easier to relax, but you may always feel susceptible to the fact that this child too could die.

Fears That You Can't Keep This Baby

In the months after your new baby's birth, you may feel anxious that this baby isn't yours to keep. You may feel as though the baby belongs to someone else, or you may be convinced that the baby will die or be taken away. Kitty remembers, "I didn't fall instantly in love with her because I felt like someone was going to snatch her away, just like with Melanie." Martina agrees: "Up until she was about a year old, I went through times of feeling like I was taking care of a baby that wasn't mine, that she wasn't really ours and someone was going to come and take her and I wouldn't see her again."

I was prepared for anything, if anything happened. I was amazed that I could have a baby that was healthy. I felt close to her immediately, but it took me a long time to really believe that everything was going to be fine. I didn't want to let her out of my sight. The first year I was totally frightened all the time that something would happen to her.

—Liza

These feelings can provoke a lot of anxiety, especially since they are often accompanied by the feeling that you have little control. Over time, however, you will feel more confident that this is your child to keep.

Fears of Illness or Accident

Even if your baby is robust and healthy, you may worry about a mild illness turning into a life-threatening situation. You may be anxious about rare or undiscovered diseases attacking your infant. You may be on guard against accidents such as choking, falling or car wrecks. Rose sums up her fears: "With Lori, I just never knew. I thought if she didn't have some kind of problem internally, that she would die of SIDS. If she didn't die of SIDS she'd die of something else, get hit by a car, whatever." If your child does have health problems, your overprotective feelings can be intensified. Do be careful that you don't overcompensate for your protective urges by ignoring signs of illness or neglecting hazardous situations. This could actually endanger your child's health and safety.

> I always worried about him choking on something and I always thought I was going to feed him Cream of Wheat until he was 5 so I would never have to worry about him choking. I have had a first-aid class so I know what to do, but that doesn't mean I could do it if I had to. I think of all these off-the-wall things that could happen to him.
>
> —Peg

> I can handle a little sickness, but if they get really sick, I become very uptight and supersensitive to them. Like the time Kim had pneumonia when she was 16 months old and I immediately esca-lated that into something really life-threatening. Unfortunately, when Jared was 8 days old we discovered he had meningitis, which *is* life-threatening. He was admitted to the hospital and was on antibiotics, and we just sort of lived there for a while. It was real scary because I thought, "This baby is going to be taken away from me too."
>
> —Anya

> He got a rash and I didn't want to rush him to the doctor. I didn't want to be one of *those* mothers because I had been to the doctor so much, and I thought, "We're not going to start this." Then it turned out to be a serious staph infection!
>
> —Desi

Fears about Your Baby's Sleep

Many parents feel anxious when the baby is sleeping. A sleeping baby is so still and quiet, you may feel compelled to check the baby's breathing often during naps and at night. You may be afraid to leave your sleeping baby alone, as if by being there you can somehow provide a protective shield to ensure your baby's survival. Watching or checking your baby may help reassure you that your baby is safe and sound.

Lena remembers often waking up in the night and touching her baby's face "to make sure he was still warm." Rose recalls, "I never let her out of my sight. Many times I would lay there and just watch her nap for two hours rather than getting up and doing anything. I thought she was going to die any time I couldn't see her."

Particularly in the first few months, some parents panic when the baby is quietly sleeping. To reassure themselves, they sometimes wake the baby.

> I think it's a fear that stays there after you lose a baby. Every five minutes I was over there, "If you're not breathing, kid, or I can't see you move, you're waking up!" It's not as bad now, but I'm constantly watching her to see if she's still breathing.
>
> —Martina

> Every night I would put my hand on her back to make sure I could feel her breathing, and if I couldn't, I'd try and do something that would make sure she'd breathe. She started sleeping through the night very early and that scared me. One time she slept through the night and I was thinking, "I've got to get some rest, so I want to sleep in," but there's another part of me thinking, "What happens if I get up and find out ... ?" So there would be mornings when I was afraid. "Is she just sleeping late or is something wrong?" I couldn't enjoy sleeping in.
>
> —Bryn

If you consider yourself to have a lot of control over what happens or if you hold on to the belief that you can somehow prevent tragedy from occurring, you may feel especially vigilant. You may even worry that such close monitoring is compulsive, but if checking the baby helps you feel less anxious, do it.

Harnessing Your Overprotectiveness

Many parents are concerned about being overprotective. Especially as your children grow older, you may try to hide it, disguise it or control it in order to encourage their natural curiosity and exploration.

> I do worry that I'm too overprotective of him. I tend to try and protect him from things. With my first pregnancy I planned to go right back to work, and now here he is, he's going to be home for two more years. He went to preschool for six weeks and he hated it, and so I said "If the kid hates it, why should he go?" and consequently he hasn't gone back since. I'm not sure he's going to ever go to kindergarten. And I think if all this had never happened to me with my first child, I would have said, "Too bad, you don't

like preschool. You go to preschool—kids your age go to preschool—you go!"

—Sarah

It can be very hard to let go and allow your children to experience any
independence, challenge or difficulty. Leaving your child with a sitter may
be doubly hard at first. You may want to cling to your children, to give of
yourself, so that they will have everything they need from you. There are
times when this is appropriate. Especially during infancy and toddlerhood
there is a lot of protective parenting that is nurturing and not stifling.
However, by holding on too tightly, you give your children the impression
that the world is a dangerous or unmanageable place. By letting go, yet
remaining available, you give your children the security to become independent, the confidence to meet challenges and the courage to overcome
difficulties. It helps to remember that attending to your children's need for
dependence *and* independence is part of being a responsive parent. (Refer
to chapter 16 for more about the positive aspects of protective parenting.)
Remind yourself that

- you can't always have control over things that happen,
- some situations *are* harmless,
- expressing your feelings of anger and hurt over your baby's
  death may reduce some of the anxiety associated with your
  overprotective urges, and
- as you learn to let go, you may feel a sense of triumph over your
  worries.

The loss has made me overprotective of Emily, and they warned me
about that, and I am. The other day we went to a park with one of
my girlfriends, and she has a girl who's three days older than Emily.
Her little girl went over to the slides and just started playing. And I
thought, "I can't let Emily go down the slide by herself; I can't sit
back and let her do it alone! I have to be there and stand there!"
But I can't go in the sand since I have a cast on my foot, so I had to
decide—let her go or she won't be able to play. And I let her go and
it was really hard. She got up those slides and did like every other
kid, and it was a good feeling to me. I said, "Wow, I let her go and
she did it!" I didn't even realize I could do that ... and it made me
realize I was overprotective. It was hard sitting there watching,
believe me, but the next time it won't be so hard. ... I think it'll get
easier [over time], as I grow more and realize that I have to give her
that space. As she gets older too, I'll trust her balance more.

—Cindy

Fortunately, many parents notice that as their children grow older and
thrive, they can relax a little more. If your baby remains in good health and

develops normally, you can be reassured that there are no hidden problems. As time passes, you can feel more confident and less vulnerable; you can build some trust that this baby will survive. Cindy remembers, "In her first bath she screamed and I cried, so my mom bathed her. Now I dunk her in there and say 'You're OK.' I feel more comfortable now since we lived through the newborn period."

Later, if you decide to have another baby, you may be more relaxed even during infancy. Your overprotective feelings will diminish as you become accustomed to having a healthy child, but even so, you may always worry about tragedy because you know it can happen.

> The doctor kept saying, "She's fine. Don't think about the past." I couldn't help it. I couldn't help but say life is very tenuous, you cannot count on it. I kept waiting for her to get older because I'd say, "When she gets to be 6 months old I'm going to feel a lot more at ease." When she was 6 months old, I was saying, "When she's a year old I'm going to feel so much better." I still don't have a guarantee, but I'm not afraid like I was. I was nervous when she was a little baby, but now that she's getting older I feel more free.
>
> —Bryn

> I had a successful baby. Lori was alive and well, and I knew I could do it. A baby of mine could live past five days. So with Anna, I'm probably raising her a little bit more normally. I've gotten in the routine of having healthy kids and I know that they'll probably be fine. I'm over those paranoid feelings, other than little surges of panic. I don't think Anna is going to die every time I leave her in the bedroom.
>
> —Rose

The Replacement Child

According to psychological and medical literature, the replacement child syndrome occurs when parents idealize their dead child and seek to "replace" that child by having a new baby. When the new baby is born, the parents may have difficulty focusing on this child as an individual separate from the child who died, even imposing expectations for the new baby to be like the dead child. This new baby then grows up in the shadow of the dead sibling.

Naturally, this syndrome is considered unhealthy, especially for the new baby. Thus, parents who have had a baby die may worry about falling into that trap. However, there are a couple of other replacement feelings that are benign and very common among bereaved parents:

- the feeling that you had another baby because you didn't have the one who died, in effect having another baby to fill your empty arms

- comparing your babies, wondering if your dead baby might have been similar to the new baby

Despite your concern about seeing the new baby as a replacement, at some point you will realize that no other baby can replace the one who died. Although this realization can be painful, it is an important step toward recognizing that your subsequent child is an individual, separate from your baby who died. Then you can appreciate and accept your subsequent child for who he or she is, and not expect this child to be a replica of the baby who died.

I had an amnio so I knew it was a girl, and I did that specifically for two reasons. One, I wanted to be able to say there are problems I know this baby won't have, and two, I wanted to know the sex because I had always wanted a girl and I knew that if it was a boy I was going to have that sense of loss to deal with and that if it was a girl I was going to have to work on separating her from Heidi. I remember when I got the results, being excited it was a girl but being really frustrated or sad and crying for a long time. The doctor said, "Well, you have a healthy baby girl." But I was thinking, "Why couldn't it have been Heidi."

—Holly

My neighbor was pregnant the same time I was and she had a boy about a month before I did and she brought him in, and at first I thought, "This is really cruel." But I held her baby and I realized, "This isn't my baby, nobody's baby is going to take the place of my baby. This isn't who I'm aching for. I'm aching for that specific baby, MY baby." I was really relieved that she brought him over and I didn't covet her baby.

—Bryn

Perhaps you would not have had your new baby if your other baby hadn't died. Perhaps you feel as though you are trying to fill that empty slot in your family. Whatever your intent, eventually you will discover that this new baby can never totally erase your emptiness, nor take your other baby's special place in your heart.

Some parents idealize the baby who died and impose those perfect expectations on subsequent children. These parents inevitably feel disappointment in the subsequent children, who cannot possibly live up to the idealized image.

It can help to remember that all babies have fussy periods, need a lot of attention and supervision, wake up during the night and go through challenging stages. The reality of what's involved in parenting can help you let go of your idealizations and be less resentful of your surviving children.

For instance, Bryn was able to finally let go of her fantasies after her subsequent baby was born. She admits, "It helped me to be exhausted in the middle of the night and saying, 'If she cries one more time, how am I going to get up?' That helps to see the reality of it, the good and the bad. It would have been so awful if I had not been allowed to have a baby. It's so healthy to have reality there."

Most parents compare their babies without idealizing. The less time you had with the baby who died, the more curious you may be. It is natural to look at your subsequent children and wonder if the baby who died would have been similar. Would they have had the same curls? Would they have walked at the same age? Would they have both resembled their father? Cindy remarks, "When you look at Emily and see how she acts, you wonder if Nicole would have been like her and looked like her and all that." Kitty agrees: "When Julie was born she looked an awful lot like Melanie, so I kind of feel like I can watch her grow up." It is natural to think about all the experiences you've missed with your baby, and to look at your subsequent children and get an idea of what might have been. Liza observes: "It's a feeling that you'd like to have five or six children so that all the personalities combined, you'd be able to see what the baby who died would be like."

Particularly if you have another baby of the same sex, it is natural to fear you will have trouble separating the two babies. It is natural to mix up their names, for instance, as most parents with more than one child do. Your dead baby is not living with you, but dwells in your heart, and his or her name may come to mind naturally.

> One time I slipped and I said "Nicole" instead of "Emily," and everybody went "GASP! Why did you do that? Are you going crazy? Are you confusing these babies? What's wrong with you?" And I cried and thought, "What's wrong?" And then my mom goes, "Would you people calm down? I mean, if she had two kids, one named Nicole, and Nicole was here and she said 'Nicole' to Emily or 'Emily' to Nicole, nobody would even give it thought, but because Nicole is dead everybody freaks out." She said, "We've talked about Nicole for a year. We go to her grave. Nicole is what we've called your baby all this time. We've talked about your baby Nicole, and now you slipped and said 'Nicole' instead of 'Emily': big deal!" But it scared me. I thought "Oh no, what's wrong with me?" And I've done it a couple times since then.
>
> —Cindy

This curiosity and comparison may not diminish over time because you will never know what that baby would have been like. However, as you get to know your new baby as an individual, rather than confusing the two babies, you may simply wonder how similar they might have been.

Talking about the Baby Who Died

Even if you have just begun to contemplate a subsequent pregnancy, you may already know that you plan on telling your future children about the baby who lived and died before them. Sharing this information gives your baby a rightful place in the family. Indeed, your children may treasure this knowledge as they get older and understand what they have missed.

For many parents, a major concern is "When do I tell them?" Children are naturally inquisitive and imaginative, so the subject can come up in a number of ways. If you have pictures or mementos that are easily accessible, or older children who bring it up, your deceased child may be just another member of the family. Conversations can occur spontaneously as your children ask "Who's that?" or "Can I play with this?" Your child may also bring up the topic inadvertently by saying things like, "I'm pretending I have a big sister" or "I wish I was a twin!" If you haven't talked about it yet but think your children are old enough to hear what you have to say, pick a quiet rainy afternoon to pull out your keepsakes and share them. If they are ready, they will be interested in seeing them. And even if you put it off until the kids are grown, it is never too late to share these things with them.

> I have a picture of him on my refrigerator, so when I look at him I say, "There's Matthew," and I take Alex [age 1] and I say, "That was your brother." He's too young to understand yet, but that's just how I am. And I say things like, "He would've liked you; you would've liked him."
>
> —Kara

> I want to wait until the kids are 8 or 9. I guess I want them to *understand*. I think they'll be sad and I think they'll want to go see the grave, but I don't want Meg going to kindergarten and bragging, "I had a brother" and showing off about it and chatting about it like it meant nothing. So I thought if she was a little older she might understand it. I just don't want it to become trite.
>
> —Bess

What to Say

In general, speak openly and honestly; answer questions directly and simply. If you happen to offer too much information, your children will probably ignore what goes over their heads and ask you to elaborate on whatever they're worried about or trying to grasp. Especially when the children are young, they may have some strange ideas about death, but this might not cause them any anxiety. If you remain available for questions, your children will be more likely to engage your help if they do have concerns.

At one time Gary [age 3] wanted to know if he could dig Jamie up and play with him. I thought I did a really great job of explaining death to him, and then he asks, "Can we go dig him up and play with him?" Then I showed him a picture of Jamie, and you think you're so smart with your kids and you're just not. I thought I did this great discussion, "This is your brother, he died, etc.," and like a week later there's a picture of him at my mother's house—of him when he was a baby—and he said, "Oh look, there's me when I was dead." So I don't know *what* he understands.

—Sarah

Discomfort with death typically has to do with fears of loss, abandonment and the unknown. Speak reassuringly about what happened and about death in general. If your children realize that theoretically you could die tomorrow, tell them about the plans you have for their guardianship. Knowing that they won't have to suddenly fend for themselves, be all alone or go to a dreaded orphanage (like in old movies) can give them peace of mind.

Finally, a big part of death is the grief that survivors feel. Don't hesitate to shed some gentle tears or talk about how it made you feel sad or angry. Tears and feelings are tangible evidence of your love for all your children, not just the departed ones. Your subsequent children can find comfort in your feelings of parental devotion.

The Subsequent Child's Sense of Loss

As your child grows, having a sibling who is dead will acquire new meaning. At first, she or he may think of it simply in terms of the family being smaller than it might have been. Later, as your child learns about the roles different relationships play, she or he may have a better idea of the brotherly or sisterly friendship that is missing.

Just as it is important for you not to idealize your dead child, it may be important to talk to your subsequent child about not idealizing the dead sibling. The missing brother or sister would not have been perfect. There would have been the typical spats over toys and turns, squabbles over who's the best and competitions for your time and attention. To have an older brother or sister as protector and mentor is another fantasy. Remind your youngster that while this might have been the case sometimes, like any relationship, there would have been the good times and the bad.

To have a realistic idea of what has been lost can help your child come to terms with it. On the other hand, holding on to some idealization can be normal, even after your discussion. You needn't be concerned unless your child is obsessed over a period of time or showing other signs of emotional disturbance. (For more information, refer to "Providing the Support and Reassurance Your Children Need" in chapter 11.)

Multiple Birth Survivors

The most striking thing Sophie did as a baby, which led me to
believe she knew something was missing in her life, involved her
bedtime ritual. When she was old enough (at 8 or 9 months) to
manipulate her stuffed animals, she went through a long period
when, after being placed in her crib, she would take an animal
which she was given and very deliberately turn it upside down and
place it with the head at her feet between her legs. I would often find
her sleeping this way. This was poignant as this was the way she and
her brother were positioned *in utero*—she vertex (head down) and he
breech (feet first). It seemed as though she was finding comfort in re-
creating, reexperiencing her twinship at bedtime.

—Lisa

If you are raising a surviving baby or babies from a multiple pregnancy,
talking to them about the siblings who are missing is a tender task. If you
know that a survivor is identical to one who died, she or he may feel a unique
sort of loss. Even with fraternal multiples, they were still wombmates and
the relationship might have been exceptionally close. If you are raising a sole
survivor, she or he may wonder about the special kinship of having a sibling
who's the same age. If there is more than one survivor, they *know* what
they're missing, and that is hard too.

If you are facing the complicated challenge of raising one or more
survivors from a multiple birth, here are some suggestions.

Try to Integrate Your Deceased Baby or Babies into the Family from the Beginning

Surviving multiples can benefit greatly from knowing very early on
about the circumstances surrounding their conception and birth. As your
children grow older, this understanding will naturally grow and change, but
because it's knowledge they've always had, there's no shocking or dramatic
unveiling of a secret. However, if you've put it off, it is never too late to
reveal the truth. Many children are proud of and interested in being part of
a multiple birth. And most survivors who weren't told until adulthood
report that they regret not knowing. While growing up, many felt deeply
that something was missing, and finally learning about their twin (or triplet,
etc.) sibling was a relief—like finding the missing piece to a puzzle.

We never "told" Sophie about her twin. Rather we have let her
learn about him as she learned about the rest of her family. Using a
photo of Teddy, we played a very simple naming game as she began
to babble and talk, which introduced her to our relationships.
"What's Mommy's name; Daddy's name; your sister's name?" I

would ask and then I'd answer "Lisa," "Doug" or "Mia." "What's your brother's name?—Teddy." ... Soon she was able to answer for herself. In this way, Teddy gently and easily became part of her vocabulary.

—Lisa

Answer Questions and Encourage Pretend Play on the Topic

As your child gets older and starts asking questions, you may find it useful to look at the photographs and illustrations in books about pregnancy and birth. Your child may seem preoccupied with the topic and it may be a prevalent theme in pretend play. Imaginary play is a valuable way to master ideas and feelings, and over time, your child's obsession should diminish. Naturally, if you have concerns about feelings or behaviors, it may help to talk with a family counselor or other parents who are raising surviving multiples. The Center for Loss In Multiple Birth (CLIMB) has a lot of literature and suggestions to offer (see appendix C). You can also refer to *The Essential Partnership* by Stanley Greenspan (see "Books on Parenting" in the bibliography).

Help Your Surviving Child Gain a Realistic Idea of What Might Have Been

If your child frets about having lost a "best friend," let her or him grieve. Just as you don't like to be told, "Be thankful for what you have," or "You can always have another," surviving multiples will not benefit from hearing about their other best friends or siblings they might have. No one can take a twin's (or triplet's, etc.) place. On the other hand, you can remind your child that while some multiples are very close, others are as tight or distant as "regular" siblings. Don't go overboard in emphasizing how special the relationship(s) would have been.

Separate Your Grief from Your Child's Feelings of Loss

Recognize that your grief upon the death of your baby or babies is separate and quite different from your surviving child's or children's grief about missing twin, triplet, quad or quint siblings. Don't expect or push them to understand *your* loss. And resist projecting your own feelings of anguish onto them. Let them figure out how they are affected by the information surrounding the pregnancy and birth and the absence of their wombmates.

Reassure Your Children of Their Completeness

In helping them to grasp their own loss, avoid fostering the notion that their lives are hopelessly incomplete. It is paramount that you reassure your survivors that while you miss the other(s) as well as the idea of twins (or triplets, etc.), you are so very glad to have them. Let them know that having them is sufficient and rewarding, and that they are far more than just "part of a broken set."

> Our "approach" (not consciously taken for the most part) to talking to Sophie about her twin brother has been very soft and gentle, letting him always be a part of her consciousness and our family circle and letting her needs and questions lead our responses. And to take care of our own needs in grieving for our son so that our grief was not unduly displaced onto our relationship with her. None of this has been *easy* and many tears and aching moments have come along the way and surely there will be more. [But] I cannot imagine having done things any differently.
>
> —Lisa

For more information and support around talking to your children, see "Integrating Your Baby into the Family" in chapter 17 and "Other Children in the Family" in chapter 11.

Points to Remember

- Most parents feel that their relationship with surviving children, especially those born afterward, is profoundly affected by the death of their baby.
- It is normal to feel a greater appreciation for your surviving children.
- It is normal to feel overprotective, hoping to avoid another tragedy.
- Overprotective feelings diminish over time as you continue to work through your grief. These feelings may also fade as you become accustomed to having a child who can be healthy and survive and as your child grows more independent and competent.
- Harnessing your overprotective feelings can be difficult, but as you feel less vulnerable, letting go frees you from the burden of watching your child's every move.
- It is normal to worry about confusing your new baby with the baby who died.
- It is normal to look at your new baby and wonder if your dead baby might have been similar in appearance, personality or talent.
- It helps to have a realistic view of parenting, so that you do not idealize your baby who died and place those idealized expectations on your new baby.
- If you decide to talk to your subsequent child about the baby who died, speak openly, honestly and reassuringly. Most children treasure their knowledge of a sibling who came before them.
- If you are raising survivors from a multiple pregnancy, it can be particularly beneficial to talk about the dead baby or babies from the beginning, to help your survivors gain a realistic idea of what might have been and to reassure them of their completeness.

16

Protective Parenting

Bereaved mothers and fathers come into parenthood with a special eagerness to dote on their babies and to be excellent parents. But many parents hold back from doting, afraid they'll produce children who are dependent, clingy and spoiled—not marks of effective parenting.

What many parents don't realize is that it is possible to be attentive and responsive without being intrusive and spoiling—to be a protective parent without being *over*protective. "Protective parenting" is a reconciliation of both the desire to be doting and the desire to be excellent. Protective parents follow their hearts and their instincts on nurturing their children, respecting them as individuals and giving them what they *need*.

This chapter encourages bereaved mothers and fathers to dote on their babies, and guides them in their desire to be "protective parents."

Following Your Nurturing Instincts

There is nothing like the death of a baby to shock parents into their most basic, instinctual parenting mode. The mother especially, whose very core cries out for the lost child, may be both bewildered and impressed by the intensity of her mothering urges. Then when a new baby is born healthy and alive, she may be reluctant to close off that part of herself that is consumed and awed by the infant.

> Even before Shelley was born, I knew that sleeping with the baby was the only way to go. It felt so natural and right and made so much sense ... . So instead of buying a crib, Mark and I bought a king-size bed. Mark was skeptical, but I reassured him we could always buy a crib later. Needless to say, he was won over in the first week, and in Shelley's room, our old double bed waits for her.
> —Winnie

Unfortunately, there is a lot of social pressure for mothers to restrain themselves and resist doting on their babies. They are scolded for being "overprotective" of their little ones or "spoiling" them with their devotion and attention. They are warned against losing themselves in motherhood, as if this were a place where brains permanently turn to mush, where personal hobbies and interests are forever cast aside—and heaven forbid they should become sleep deprived! Indeed, you may be afraid to dive into motherhood for fear that you will lose yourself. You may return to school or work or keep up a feverish schedule, trying to juggle your needs for self-actualization with your baby's needs for a mother. You may not get support and encouragement from those who can remind you that mothering a baby is a relatively temporary state of affairs in your life. You may simply be warned that if you give yourself over to your baby, you'll never get yourself back.

There are also many misguided beliefs about child rearing that discourage mothers from doting on their babies. Many of these myths can be traced to religious, philosophical and social contexts, particularly from the last couple of centuries. For instance, certain religious doctrine justified harsh punishment and deprivation as ways to promote moral development and ensure heavenly reward. Theories about child development focused on strict management and training independence from birth. Philosophers and psychologists promoted the idea that humans had risen above nature—that we were products of our environment and children had to be properly molded into possessing good qualities such as an even temperament and regular sleeping habits. The application of science to parenting also gave rise to the belief that there must be one right way to raise a child. Needless to say, many parents were intimidated by these widely held assumptions and opinions. In addition, being a "good parent" meant doubting your nurturing instincts and obeying "expert" advice.

From Dr. Spock in the 1940s to Dr. Mom in the 1990s, there has been a shift away from these stern assumptions and rigid ideals. The trend has been toward

- viewing human nature as inherently good and focusing more on encouragement, guidance and accountability, and less on punishment and shaming
- maintaining general flexibility, like feeding on demand and sleeping with the baby
- accepting babyish behaviors like clinging and sucking
- recognizing that many temperamental traits like shyness, moodiness, distractibility, emotional intensity and irregular eating and sleeping are inborn and *not* a result of faulty mothering
- considering it developmentally appropriate for babies and children to be immature, selfish, impulsive and needy (i.e., how they're supposed to be!)
- respecting the ways nature has equipped mothers and babies to respond to each other
- understanding that parenting is an art, not a science

In the past decade, pediatricians, psychologists and child psychiatrists like William Sears, Marianne Neiffert, Stanley Greenspan, Eda Le Shan and

Stanley Turecki have written parenting books that question many of the old rules about how to raise good children. They point out the disadvantages of rigid schedules, punishment and ignoring a baby's cries. They highlight the advantages of trusting an infant's cues (babies are born knowing what they need), respecting a child's special temperament and development (every child is unique), meeting dependency needs (a need doesn't go away until it's fulfilled) and having realistic expectations (babies aren't bad, they're just *young*).

This nurturing style of parenting now endorsed by the "experts" is nothing new. These ideas are an integral part of ancient mothering wisdom that has a long, rich, cross-cultural history. Some of the best parenting ideas can be observed in gentle tribal cultures around the world whose ways of living have not changed much over the past few centuries.

Traditional Mothering

The typical traditional mother suckles her baby often and the world-wide average weaning age is 4 years. The baby's need for close contact is viewed as legitimate and natural, so by day the mother carries her infant close to her body, and at night they sleep together.

Mother quickly becomes attuned to her newborn's cues and learns when elimination is imminent so she can be prepared. As early as three months, the mother begins to use her familiarity with her baby's patterns and cues and teaches her baby to associate certain sounds, positions or places with elimination. In many primitive cultures around the world, babies are effectively toilet trained well before the age of 2 years.

Interestingly, in the past century, western societies have attached severe psychological consequences to being held a lot, sleeping with mother, demand feeding, late weaning and early toilet training—in spite of the fact that human babies have thrived under these conditions for thousands and thousands of years. Remember, diapers, bottles, strollers, cribs and multi-bedroom houses are modern inventions and still are not accessible to most of the world's parents.

Traditional Mothering for Modern Times

Just because an idea or method is ancient or worldwide doesn't mean you should adopt it. However, researchers and experts are rethinking their bias against the "primitive" or foreign, and finding sound biological, psychological and developmental evidence for embracing much of what mothers have always known. For the most part, the traditional ways of gentle tribal cultures are gaining respect and acceptance in the modern world simply because they are relaxed, efficient and make good sense.

These traditional mothering ways are relaxed and efficient because they don't rely on fancy gadgets or implementing schedules. Instead, they rely on the valid assumption that babies respond to internal cues and can indicate what they need to grow and develop—even newborns give clear signals about what they like and dislike. So, a mother listens to her baby's cues and uses common sense. For instance, one baby may need to nurse to fall asleep and may thrive on sleeping with the mother, while another baby may not fall asleep until she's laid down, or perhaps sleeps better when left alone.

Relaxed, efficient, common-sense approaches also put a lot of stock in the fact that each baby's development is basically determined by her genetic, biological heritage. The idea that biology is largely responsible for development is gaining more credibility with new advances in genetic research. We already take for granted that teeth and the thickness and length of head hair, for example, will come in and grow according to genetic programming. We are starting to accept that motor development, like sitting, crawling, walking and drawing, have inherent timelines that cannot be significantly speeded up by extra coaching.

Even in areas of emotional development, such as with separation anxiety, there appears to be an internal timeline and individual differences—some children are more sensitive to separation than others. While a baby's temperament can be exacerbated by environmental influences, characteristics such as sensitivity, shyness, disposition or activity level are largely inborn and consistent throughout childhood. And so, we are beginning to appreciate the biological origins of personality and emotional development.

Others areas of development, such as sleeping through the night and feeding, remain stubborn strongholds in the "parents should maintain and exercise control" department. Even though these too are biological processes, parents brag if their 4-month-old is sleeping in eight-hour stretches, or if their 10-month-old gobbles down a variety of solid foods. Although they like to take credit for these marvels, they are merely lucky in the crapshoot of genetic inheritance. Just as likely, they could have given birth to an infant who sleeps in two-hour stretches or a baby who declines solid foods for the first year. Although a heavy sleeper and keen eater can make a parent's life easier, alas, these traits are determined far more by biology than by training.

Another traditional idea coming into vogue is that it takes a community to raise a child. Modern mothers who wonder why they are going nuts raising their children in relative isolation can look to the past. Nuclear families throughout history typically lived with extended family in small, closely knit communities. A mother and her children spent their days with other mothers and children, not cordoned off into single-family houses or apartments. The children had intimate and long-standing relationships with other adults and kids. Getting together was spontaneous and easy, just a matter of course in regular daily cooperative living—not meticulously scheduled between commitments and errands. Mothering burnout was warded off with adult conversation throughout the day, and the little ones were supervised regularly by older kids and relatives.

Nowadays, full-time motherhood is spectacularly challenging. In our society, most mothers don't get their needs met for support, adult contact and relief from child care, and then they feel guilty for feeling deprived and resenting their children. It is important that you find ways to meet those legitimate needs for community. When you feel ready and able, try joining play groups, gym classes, mother support groups and going to the playground; these are some of the ways you can hang out with other moms and kids. Don't expect yourself to mother alone!

Reassuring tips for mothering your new baby (remember, dads can be mothering too):

- Take advantage of your primed eagerness to be close to your baby and to be a responsive parent.
- Listen to your mothering urges and listen to your baby. Follow your baby's lead and do what feels most nurturing to you and your baby.
- Don't worry about being "manipulated" by your baby or young child. Assume your child is communicating a genuine need. It is always appropriate to be emotionally generous.
- Babies and young children do not engage in infantile behaviors to control or trouble their parents. Nor do they cling, nurse, cry, explore or chew on things out of bad habits. They do these things out of internal drives and needs. Little children aren't bad, they're just *young*.
- Letting go is an important part of parenting, but it should be a gradual, child-driven process. True independence arises from having dependable and responsive caregivers during infancy and childhood.
- While books and friends offering support and advice can be invaluable, remember that you are the ultimate expert on what feels good for you and your baby.
- Relax, dote and enjoy yourself and your baby. Especially during the first few weeks or months, when your time is consumed by feeding, diaper changing and sleeping, try to have realistic expectations, that is, if you manage to brush your teeth, you're overachieving!

Wanting to Be the Best Parent Possible

I think you better appreciate something that's harder to get. I think he's more special. I would hope that I would treat any baby that I had well and do my best, but I think it just makes me more aware of how much I did want him and how special babies really are and that you're really responsible once you have them for how they grow up.

—Peg

Like many bereaved parents, you may want to be the best parent possible out of a sense of responsibility to do the right thing with your precious children. You may feel extra devoted and take your parenting very seriously.

Wanting to do your best is a positive goal. Your heightened awareness can enable you to be a more conscious parent. You may carefully evaluate your parenting style and work toward becoming a nurturing and firm but flexible parent. You may decide to work on communication skills instead of yelling at, isolating or spanking your children. You may decide to learn how to discipline in ways that teach and encourage your children, rather than using punishment.

> I think I'm more patient or more tolerant of some things than I would have been if I hadn't lost a baby. Not to the extent of not feeling comfortable stopping certain things, but it just makes you stop and think, "Is this really important?" You know, he might not even be here. I'm concerned about doing the right thing, the right parenting things. I want to do things that are basically good for him. I want to provide him with good experiences. I don't believe in Super Baby, but I want to give him the best, be a good parent.
>
> —Hannah

> I think just being there for him and loving him and giving him security so he can grow, to me is the most important thing that I can do for him.
>
> —Sarah

Disciplining Your Precious Children

In striving to be the best, some parents find it hard to set limits with subsequent children. You may find it difficult to allow your children to feel any frustration or disappointment. You may feel they have a special entitlement to everything they want.

> With Lori I think maybe that I've created a lot of bad habits—the fact she won't take a nap because I never let her. I never got those good disciplines started. Life was totally undisciplined. Whatever occurred to me—if I felt like holding her all day, I'd hold her all day. I was never real disciplined with her, so she's not a real disciplined child.
>
> —Rose

Some children do well with spontaneity and flexibility, while others do best with structure and routine. All children benefit from reasonable limits. Some parents hesitate to set limits because they don't want to control their children or enforce rules with punishment. However, setting limits actually refers to *discipline*, which means teaching and encouraging, *not* controlling and punishing. Discipline, which is far more effective than punishment, includes:

- remaining friendly with children, and being firm but flexible
- being an empathic and responsive listener to your children's feelings, needs and ideas
- getting to the root of problems
- negotiating solutions
- letting your children make choices between acceptable alternatives

For example, a child may refuse to wear snow pants. Instead of forcing him to wear them, an effective parent might listen and discover that snow pants make him feel babyish. Then, together, they can negotiate a solution—perhaps long underwear or heavy sweatpants. Or the parent can offer a choice: "If you put them on, you can play in the snow; if not, you can play inside." Parents can give even a toddler choices, such as "Do you want to get dressed by yourself or do you want me to dress you?" Children may also respond to this suggestion: "If you make a *good* decision, I won't have to decide for you." Instead of inviting power struggles, this gentle but firm guidance helps your children learn self-control, responsible behavior and how to make good decisions.

As a bereaved parent, you may be tempted to give in more than you should. Or in your efforts to avoid being permissive, you may overcompensate and become too strict. Finding the right balance between flexible and firm is an art and will be different for each child and each situation. By trial and error, you can figure out what works best. Here are some guidelines that may help:

- As long as you are generally firm, you can make exceptions and stay in charge. This flexibility lets your child know he is important and that life isn't too rigid.
- Respect your child's preferences, likes and dislikes. This shows you value him or her as a unique and separate individual.
- Choose your battles carefully. If you let your child be the boss of some things, she'll willingly let you be the boss of other things.
- Be clear about who owns the problem. Sometimes the solution lies in the parent adjusting expectations, being more flexible or letting go.
- If you are waffling, or if the limit is unreasonable, your child will sense this and test you. To reduce waffling and avoid unreasonable rules, say "Yes" more often and reserve "No" for when you are sure.

- When trying to make a point, the more calmly and sparingly you talk, the more your child will listen. If there is definitely no room for negotiation, say so, and then resist getting into a heated discussion about it.

When people say parenting comes naturally, they are right, but it comes naturally the way you learned it from your parents and caregivers. As such, what comes naturally is sometimes ineffective. This can be especially true in the arena of discipline. At first, trying to do things differently can feel unnatural, even downright scary. And when attempting new skills, there will be a period of adjustment where things may briefly get worse before they get better. Expect this difficulty and see it as a sign that you really are making progress. Then with practice and support, and particularly when you see positive results slowly emerge, effectiveness *can* become natural. For more parenting ideas, information, support and reassurance, recommended reading is listed in "Books on Parenting" in the bibliography.

If you are looking for parenting books and classes, try to find ones that recognize the uniqueness of every child, every parent and every family. Beware of authors and teachers who admonish parents to follow their instructions, spout off absolute rules of parenting or give rigid advice that promises specific results. Wise experts support and respect parents as collaborators, helping them uncover underlying problems and find tailor-made solutions that can work for their special situation. Wise parents see experts as consultants, not bosses. They dare to question. They keep what works for them and their child, and toss what doesn't.

Perfection

In your eagerness to do right for your precious child, you may strive for perfection. While this seems a noble goal, it is unreasonable and ultimately aggravating and self-defeating. Perfectionistic tendencies may arise out of a need to control or a need for approval, and may harken back to your own childhood. It is fine to have high standards, but perfection is not possible—for you or your child. Be generous and treat your mistakes as opportunities for growth. In fact, making mistakes is an integral part of effective parenting—as long as you admit to them and learn from them. Sometimes, it is the only way to figure out what works.

Also remember that children are resilient in the face of parental blunders. Don't consider every microscopic event as potentially traumatic, and don't consider every microscopic behavior as evidence of deeper problems. Expect yourself to be a good enough parent to a good enough child.

I had some idea that there was some kind of perfect parent and I was going to do that, that I would never scold her, and I just let my imagination go wild with me. I felt like I could just be Super Mom because of what had happened. It's been kind of a shock to find out that I'm pretty ordinary. ... I somehow thought I could read all the books and be a perfect mother, and it's been difficult to realize that no one has all the answers and that I really have to go from day to day.

—Liza

Sacrifice

Being the best parent does not mean being a martyr. While some parental sacrifices are inevitable and important, being totally selfless wears you down and reduces your patience, flexibility, warmth and self-respect. Indeed, your children will benefit if you maintain a balance between your needs and their needs. Your needs for sleep, relaxation and order are just as important as their needs for attention, nurturing and spontaneity. The best way to meet your children's needs is by getting some of your own needs met too. You can't make a withdrawal if your account is empty!

Finding a balance *can* be challenging, and depending on the child, the right balance may be meeting one hundred of her needs to one of yours. It is the nature of babies that oftentimes it's in everyone's best interest to make sacrifices for the little one. And occasionally you may find yourself deeply in the red, in order to help your child through rough spots. But do stay aware that your needs count too. The occasional movie, bubble bath, night out or afternoon alone can do wonders toward recharging your spirit. Nurturing yourself in these ways translates into better parenting.

Love and Anger

Being the best parent does not mean banishing angry feelings and vengeful thoughts. Unfortunately, you may not know how to feel angry at your child without associating it with shame, fear, pain or abandonment. You may not know how to express it without lashing out or withdrawing from your child. Because of all you've been through, you may think you are not entitled to be aggravated by your precious child. But anger is an integral part of an intense and loving relationship, a way to learn about deeply felt needs and to claim boundaries and fairness. Just as the measure of a good marriage is not the absence of conflict but how it is resolved, so it is in the parent-child relationship. Being angry with your child is inevitable. The trick is to learn how to deal with it, not how to avoid it.

When I was growing up, the worst feeling one could have was anger. Mad feelings weren't allowed—but of course they were everywhere—and we couldn't talk about it. Now that I have a 3-year-old who can be quite exasperating, I'm trying to unlearn the shame and recognize that being angry doesn't make me this horrible mother. If I lose it and scream at her, we talk about it openly,

instead of pretending it didn't happen, like when I was a kid. I want
Shelley to know that anger is just another powerful emotion that
has its place along with all the others, including love.

—Winnie

First recognize that it is natural to feel exasperated with your children.
Peg comments, "I do sometimes lose my patience and I try not to do that.
I try to deal with things rationally. ... That's hard sometimes with a 2-year-
old." Sarah recalls, "I was holding Gary at like three o'clock in the morning
and I was thinking, 'WHY don't you go to sleep?!' and feeling so guilty for
even getting the least bit angry at this kid." Parenting can be exhausting and
frustrating. Sometimes it is a burden you resent. You are entitled to these
feelings.

Being able to sit down and have a cup of tea ... . With a toddler,
they want you up and around. I get selfish and then I feel guilty
because I wanted this child so bad and now I'm upset because I
can't have thirty minutes to myself. We put him to bed at eight
o'clock, but that's still not enough time.

—Desi

My support group kept telling me not to feel guilty if there are
times when I think, "Why did I do this?" You've got to know that
there will be times when you say, "Why am I a parent?" You know,
you're up at three in the morning, your kid is really sick, you're
afraid for them and all this. I think it was good that they told me
it's OK to have those normal feelings of "What did I do this for?"
because you think you've got to always be sold on motherhood
because you lost a baby and you don't have the right to complain
about your baby.

—Bryn

As a bereaved parent, you may have expected to feel nothing but
devotion or maybe just a tad irritated sometimes. As a result, you may
especially struggle with your feelings of anger. When you resent or feel
aggravated with your children, it doesn't mean you love or deserve them any
less. It probably *does* mean you could use some time for yourself. Here are
a few suggestions for dealing with anger and some of the situations that
provoke it:

- Recognize that everyone in the family is entitled to their
  emotions—joy, fear, sadness *and* anger. Teach your child to
  identify, verbalize and express feelings constructively (e.g., no
  hurting, use words).
- Accept your child's tantrums and fussiness for what they are—

a way to vent emotions or blow off steam. Take them in stride and as a sign that your youngster is stressed out by fatigue, overstimulation, frustration, pain, hunger or new changes in her life. Empathize and remind yourself that this too shall pass.

- When your baby or child is having a meltdown, it is most helpful to remain calm. While this can be supremely challenging, your little one draws on your serenity in order to put herself back together. If you are in a public place, people will admire your serenity and tact.

- Recognize that much of parental overreaction comes from unresolved childhood hurts and current stresses. If you can find appropriate outlets for your anger and ways to heal old wounds, you will feel less inclined to lash out at the kids. In turn, you will feel more competent and better enjoy your children in spite of the noise, mess and demands they make.

- If you are on the verge of having your own meltdown, you can bring yourself back from the brink by taking a deep breath, focusing on your surroundings and, in quick succession, naming ten objects and their colors. This works by breaking the emotional ties to old or outside issues and bringing you back to the present.

- Sometimes you may be enraged because you feel hurt, helpless or ineffective as a parent. You may holler, "I can't stand it anymore!" or "Why can't you listen to me?" Resist blaming yourself for your child's problems or negative feelings. Don't put unrealistic pressure on yourself to have all the answers or to always be in command. Recognize your limits and appreciate your strengths.

- Feelings of rage, however fleeting, are terrifying. Although having these feelings is normal and OK, consider them to be a warning light, indicating that you need to find ways to reduce the stress in your life, before you act on those feelings. Get away and do things for yourself. Confide in a friend about your feelings. Join a parenting class or group (you'll be comforted to hear others talk about feeling pushed to the limit). Counseling can help you unload demons from the past or figure out ways to deal with a challenging child. If you can reduce stress, get more of your needs met and find support, much of your anger will naturally diminish.

Before I had Shelley, no one could have prepared me for how much I could completely love *and* be so angry at a child. I realize that having lost a baby makes me appreciate Shelley so much more but that doesn't make me immune to horrible fantasies of revenge when I'm so aggravated I can't see straight! I do think, though, that I am more motivated to figure out ways to keep from crossing that thin line between "good mother" and "crazy person."

—Winnie

Protective Parenting in Action

More than anything, protective parenting refers to protecting your children's individuality and self-esteem. The necessary skills include responding to needs, using effective discipline, helping your children deal with a wide range of emotions, respecting them as separate individuals, being their advocate and letting them follow their own paths while providing guardrails that shrink over the years. As a protective parent, you may strive to be nurturing, empathic, responsive, respectful, encouraging, balanced, tolerant and patient. It is also imperative that you expect yourself to be *imperfect*.

Protective parenting does *not* mean sheltering your children from life's inevitable complications. This can be tempting, but limits, mistakes, negative feelings and obstacles are the very things that hold valuable life lessons. Instead, give your kids the tools they need to grow and cope with adversity.

- Help your children learn to deal with (and sometimes negotiate) limits and rules. When reasonable and effectively enforced, rules guide children toward independence, responsibility and self-control. Expect them to complain or resist sometimes. After all, children are not known for saying, "You're right Mother, it's OK."

- Help your children face the consequences of their behavior. Your children's best teachers are the natural consequences of their actions. Resist the temptation to bail them out (unless lives are at stake—but remember, children don't starve when they forget to take lunch to school). Resist the temptation to lecture. The less you say, the more they will internalize the lesson. Let the chips fall and trust that your children will want to be more responsible and self-controlled next time.

- Help your children learn to cope with negative emotions. When your children experience an emotion such as anger, sadness, disappointment, frustration, greed or impatience, you may become uncomfortable or irritated. As a result, you may try to fix, shame, distract, force or talk your children out of the emotion. Instead, learn to empathize, acknowledge and validate. Your children will feel comforted by your understanding and the situation will be diffused instead of escalating.

- Take their anger in stride. When you set limits or follow through with consequences, your children (particularly toddlers and adolescents) will be angry with you at times. Remember, they don't love you any less. Flexibility has its place, but when the situation warrants it, stand firm because their anger doesn't necessarily mean you should back off. Anger against limits is a natural part of growing up.

- Be honest about your anger. Children need to learn that their actions affect others. *Do* protect your children from hurtful outbursts. Learn to express your irritation in ways that motivate your children to genuinely care about where you draw the line.
- Be honest about your faults. You won't always be kind and patient. You won't always know the right thing to do. Admit your mistakes and apologize. Your children will respect your honesty and decency and you'll make a fine role model.
- Help your children face obstacles and cope with hardship. Life is supposed to be a deep experience, sometimes complicated, even difficult and painful. Therein lies its richness. Don't try to confine your children to shallow, clear, smooth waters. Indeed, you won't always be *able* to prevent your children from being unhappy or hurt. Whenever your children are having difficulty, you can't, nor should you always fix it. Sometimes the best thing a parent can do is offer a shoulder to cry on.

Balancing Career and Motherhood

After experiencing the death of a baby, you may feel especially invested in parenthood. You may be surprised by how deeply connected you feel to your babies. And from that investment and connectedness comes a desire to be with your surviving or subsequent baby most or all of the time. Naturally, you may wonder, "How on earth will I be able to go back to work and hand this beloved bundle to another caregiver?"

You may also feel a shift in your priorities. While before you'd always imagined juggling career and children, now motherhood seems more precious to you. It is common for bereaved mothers to have a change of heart and become full-time moms. (While this is primarily an issue for mothers, fathers too may feel a shift in their priorities and become less concerned with climbing the corporate ladder, working overtime or conforming to popular definitions of success.)

Although scary, it's OK to change your goals and leave the workforce. It's also OK to reconsider after a few months or years and go back. Volunteer work, occasional consulting, temporary, seasonal or part-time work are other ways to keep your foot on the career track. Dust off your brain occasionally and read trade journals or periodicals. Or simply remind yourself that you're on sabbatical. You can feel like you still have a career without having a job.

Many mothers work outside the home because it feeds their soul. But if you work primarily for financial reasons and you are unhappy at work, can't imagine leaving your precious baby, or are stressed to the max by juggling career and parenthood, you may want to examine whether you can afford to quit. When you consider day-care, taxes, transportation, meals, wardrobe and payroll deductions, you might discover that the actual amount of money you bring home isn't worth the emotional toll.

Whether your job is financially worthwhile or not, the bottom line is what helps you feel fulfilled. Find the balance that helps you feel your best, and fine-tune it as you and your baby grow and change. If you decide to work outside the home, remind yourself that this helps you to be a better mother to your precious little one. And if you decide to stay home, remind yourself that this is a legitimate and valuable endeavor. In fact, it could be the greatest career move you ever make!

Reconsidering How Many Children to Raise

The first pregnancy after a loss is hard enough, but deep down, many mothers feel that the odds or the stars or divine blessing is in their favor. They may feel like they've paid their dues and now they will surely have a healthy baby. It is a *second* subsequent pregnancy that may loom overwhelmingly full of anxiety. To tempt fate again seems foolhardy, a prescription for failure and heartache.

The bottom line is, the more vulnerable you feel, the less likely you'll want to risk it. You may try until you have a surviving child and then run for cover and call it quits. Indeed, you may sense that you would be a better parent if you were raising fewer children. If you do pare down your original dreams, you will need to mourn this loss also. Do remember that the blessing of a family is not measured by its size or composition, but by the love it holds.

Like a substantial number of parents whose first baby or babies have died, your subsequent child may be your only surviving child. You may feel that having one healthy child is so gratifying, you don't need or want to push your luck again. In addition, particularly if your surviving child is still young, you may wonder, "Why should I preoccupy my time and emotional energy with reproduction when I could be devoting myself to *this* precious little one?" Indeed, you may sense that with one, it's easier to savor every moment.

If you are planning on one child, don't let the myths about being an only child or the over-romanticized ideas about having siblings get in the way of feeling good about raising a one and only. This may be the family size that is right for you. Or it may be the family size you've been given. It's also true, whether you have one or twenty-one children in your arms, that when you know there will be no more babies, you will grieve. This is normal and it's OK. It is natural to feel sad that your baby days are over.

Points to Remember

- Bereaved mothers and fathers come into parenthood with a special eagerness to dote on their babies and to be the best parents possible.
- Parenting comes naturally—the way you learned it from your own childhood. Learning to be a more effective parent takes an open mind, practice, persistence and extra support. The reward is a more fulfilling and harmonious relationship with your precious children.
- As you discover your own special style of parenting, it can be helpful to examine parenting advice and methods in their cultural and historical contexts.
- In recent years, parents and professionals have been rediscovering the nurturing, relaxed, efficient, common-sense approaches still practiced in gentle, traditional cultures.
- Good parenting books teach you how to think, not what to think. Wise experts support and respect parents as collaborators. You are the ultimate expert on what is right for you and your child.
- Avoid the unrealistic goal of being the perfect, selfless, cheerful parent in order to deserve this child you longed for. Instead, simply strive to do your best and learn from your mistakes. Imperfect people can be excellent parents.
- Even though you may aim toward being a better, more nurturing parent, it is still normal to feel resentment and irritation at times. Instead of trying to avoid anger, learn how to deal with it honestly and constructively.
- Remember to nurture yourself too. Having some time to yourself, to feed your soul, recharges your parenting energy and skills.
- Rather than sheltering your children from hardship, "protective parenting" involves giving them the tools to cope with life's disappointments and difficulties. This includes nurturing them, using effective discipline, acknowledging their feelings and respecting their individuality.
- Try to find the balance between career and motherhood that helps you feel fulfilled and lets you attain your desire to be the best parent you can be.
- Feelings of vulnerability and wanting to be the best parent possible can lead you to reconsider how many children to raise. Whether you raise one or a dozen children, it is natural to grieve when you know your baby days are over.

17

Remembering Your Baby and Moving On

You will always remember your baby. As you grieve and come to terms with your loss, you find that life goes on. Your sadness never completely disappears, but it does subside and acquire new meaning.

For many parents, grieving and surviving the death of a baby teaches them about life and about themselves. You may come through the experience with new coping skills, new friends and new insights. You may surprise yourself with the courage and stamina you have displayed. Liza observes, "I must be a lot stronger than I thought I was. I'm amazed that a person can reinvest in life after going through this."

You may feel more in touch with your feelings and understand the value of expressing them. You may be more sensitive to other bereaved people and better able to offer support. Meryl notes, "I think I found a lot more compassion for myself and for others—consideration, understanding, accepting other people *and* myself."

You may feel a heightened appreciation for the things you have; you may have straightened out your priorities. Holly remarks, "I value life more and my child more. I try not to take things for granted or dwell on picky little things that don't matter." Peg agrees: "It makes me aware of what's really important. I worry about the big things, try and deal with those, and I'm much calmer about the little things." Lena adds, "I treasure life more than I ever did—my own, my children's, even the ants on the driveway."

You may have learned to slow down your pace, appreciate the simple things and live in the moment. Perhaps you're dropping out of the rush to accomplish so much all the time and instead, setting aside more free time. Winnie explains, "I've really simplified my life. I've learned to say 'No.' Now I ask myself whether I'm doing this or that because I want to, or because I *should*. I'm tossing out some of the *should's*."

You may decide to give up trying to control those events that are out of your hands and put your energy into controlling those you can. Meryl comments, "It made me more accepting to life and that these things happen. Sometimes we have all the control in the world and other times, there isn't any control at all."

You may become more assertive. You may feel a sense of entitlement, that you deserve the best because you've been through the worst. You may be more able to stand up for yourself, to take care of yourself, to get what you need, instead of always sacrificing for others. Lena points out, "I have come to value more what I do and realizing I have to do things for me too. I can't be all things to all other people." Kelly agrees: "Now I look out for *me* first and then I do for others, because when Scott died I discovered nobody watches out for me, but me! Since I made this decision, I feel much better about myself and I have more self-respect." Rose elaborates, "I'm my own person now and I don't know if I'd have become that way if I hadn't lost Jessica. I think that forces you to get in touch with yourself, what you need."

You may also feel more self-reliant, that in a crisis you can count on yourself, but not necessarily others. You may feel wiser and older for your age, less naive, more vulnerable to life's twists and turns. Lena observes, "I've acquired the courage to face things I wouldn't have been able to face before as easily." Most parents eventually feel that through adversity, they have grown in some way that prepares them to cope with whatever the future holds.

> I had to come to grips with some pretty intense things about myself and I ended up liking myself and learning things about myself I probably never would have learned had I not lost Jamie. People shouldn't have to learn those things that way, but I learned a lot of strengths that I had. Had someone told me my baby would die, I would've said, "Well, I just couldn't handle anything like that." Well, yes I could, I can, and I will again if I have to!
>
> —Sarah

Remembering

Integrating Your Baby into the Family

For many parents, a meaningful way to integrate the baby into the family is by telling their other children about the baby sibling who died. Particularly for your subsequent children, you may want them to know there was a brother or sister before them. To talk about the baby is another way to acknowledge his or her existence and to validate your love. Jessie comments, "I hold a place for her. She's still our first child and Lynn's older sister."

> Now I think of her more as a sister to my other children than I do the baby that I didn't have. We think of her as a part of our family, and Paul [age 6] talks about her. When Julie [age 1] is old enough to understand, she's going to understand that she did have a sister.
>
> —Kitty

> I know a lot of people who say, "Well, my mom had a stillborn," like that didn't really matter, it wasn't important. But that was your sister or brother! I want Emily to feel, "Yeah, I had a sister that was older than me, but she died and her name was Nicole."
>
> —Cindy

You may think that your subsequent children are too young to understand or appreciate the significance of a baby sibling who isn't around. Liza notes, "I've shown Michelle [age 3] his picture, but she just seems to think it's a little baby." You may decide to wait until your children are older or start asking questions. But if you don't want to wait, you can try telling your children by explaining what happened and showing pictures and other mementos, even though it may be a while before they can grasp the concept of death or of a sibling who isn't visible. If your children misinterpret what you tell them, you needn't be alarmed. Your children are simply fitting the information into their own intellectual framework. As they get older and more sophisticated, you can help them reorganize their ideas. (Also see "Talking about the Baby Who Died" in chapter 15.)

When People Ask, "How Many Kids Do You Have?"

Another way parents integrate the baby who died into the family is to explain about all their children. You may decide to do this with everyone or just certain people. Holly explains, "It depends on who it is and how much of an explanation you want to get into and whether you want to see their jaws fall open and have them feel like they stuck their foot in their mouth." Hannah adds, "I sort of play it by ear. If I don't say that I had her, I feel bad about it. But then I think, 'Well, I didn't want to get into a lengthy discussion, so it's OK.' " Maya feels comfortable with this simple statement: "I have three children; two are with me, and one died." Sherokee Ilse uses an even simpler version: "I have two living children."

Even if you tell people, they may not recognize your baby as a member of your family. Jessie points out, "It upsets me sometimes when they see my 1-year-old and they say, 'Oh, this is your first child' or 'This is your first Mother's Day.' I feel bad that Meghan is being deprived of those things that were rightfully hers."

Moving On

If you decide to have another baby or to adopt a child, being a parent can help you overcome feelings of failure or give you a window into what might have been. Parenthood can also add a sense of fullness to your life. Lena notices, "I feel like a much more caring, loving, nurturing person since having Ryan." Peg adds, "It kind of makes up for what I've been through. I don't feel like I'm waiting for something anymore." For many mothers, having a child to raise helps them to move on and remember, because this child is another link, a sibling to the baby who died.

> With Leslie being born, it really helped me because here was somebody who needed me. I wasn't going to be able to sit around and be depressed because I needed to be there for her. She helped

me. She filled my life, she filled my hours. When she was 2 years old, somehow I could tell I was better.

—Bryn

Whether you have a child to raise or not, it helps to realize that you are more things in this life than a parent. You are yourself first. You can live a full life, finding satisfaction in a wide variety of activities and interests. You can take on many roles among your relationships and work.

Remembering, Moving On

Memories are a way to hold on to what we've loved and lost. Although you move on, you take your memories with you. The memories do fade, but you will never totally forget them. Though your loss becomes less central to your life, you will keep a place in your heart for your baby who died.

I really feel it's important you just don't forget about them. Christopher is a real part of our lives. And I'll never forget him. I don't want to.

—Rayleen

After three years I finally could be who I am without being "a person who had a dead baby." I finally separated myself from that … but I can still picture him when I was holding him. Now I can't remember what his face looked like, but I can remember feeling the weight on my arm.

—Bryn

Instead of being on your mind all the time, it becomes part of your history. You know, you don't meet new people and discuss your dead baby anymore. I actually know people that don't know that I've lost a baby, and it isn't because I'm hiding it, it's just because it isn't part of my conversation. It just happened to me and I'll always be sad and I'll always have one less child.

—Sarah

I came to realize how precious "remembering" really was in the early days of grief. Sleepless nights spent imitating Lindsay's little sighs as she was dying in my arms. … Such painful memories and yet so tender! Even the smallest incident had monumental importance: words said, glances and nuances, her hand clutching mine, her breath in my ear, her silky hair caressing my cheek. I pored over the few photographs we had, enlarging this one, cropping that one just so, to bring her face a little closer. And then while I was remembering one day, I smiled. I almost felt guilty, but, oh, she was just so very precious! The same memories that once brought me such heartache and pain were the very same ones I had come to cherish and cling to with such tenacity. In the beginning, I could not imagine "going on" without her, until I realized she could "go on" with me.

—Dana

Song for an Empty Cradle
For Andrea

Out my bedroom window rests my gaze
Through the mist of emptiness and pain's grey haze
I watch the patterns softly formed and changed,
The hillsides' grasses gently rearranged
By the winds' caressing touch.

From my womb she fell; my breath was stilled
By fear and pain and yet my heart was filled
By the overwhelming wonder of what was Andrea
That now lay white and quiet in my hand.
My baby, my prayers, the life that I had planned

Were gone. And in their place was left
A desert. Hot and empty so bereft
of hope, save for the splintered dreams I'd planned
That shined like broken bottles in the sand.

And soon the minutes into long months turn,
And even with time's comfort still I yearn
To hold her once in warm embrace
And say goodbye, and yet, there is a place
I carry her still, within my heart, steadfast;
For even the briefest of memories last.

Out my bedroom window rests my gaze
Through the mist of emptiness and pain's grey haze
I watch the patterns softly rearranged
And know my life, my dreams have all been changed.
My daughter's life was brief yet such
That in my emptiness I have so much.

—Clara Wilbrandt-Koenig

A Note to Caregivers*

Whether you are a health care provider or a concerned friend or relative, you can offer invaluable support to bereaved parents. Here are some guidelines to keep in mind.

Face Your Own Feelings about Death

Feelings of disappointment, failure, fear, sadness and anger over the death of a baby are quite natural. By acknowledging your own feelings, you will be better able to approach parents openly and supportively. They appreciate those who share their feelings and are comforted by knowing others grieve with them.

Educate Yourself about Grief

If you understand the impact of a baby's death on a family, you will be in a better position to offer support. Your awareness of the behavior and emotions that accompany grieving will enable you to reassure parents and help them realize their reactions are normal. You will also feel more comfortable around grieving parents.

Affirm the Baby

Personalize the parents' loss by referring to "the baby" and using the given name. Avoid using terms such as "products of conception" or "the stillbirth." Refrain from statements that devalue the baby who died such as, "You're still young, you can have another." The parents loved *this* baby. Don't try to persuade them to forget and move on—parents need to remember and dwell on the baby. By talking about the baby directly and sensitively, you can help parents acknowledge the loss and express their feelings. For those experiencing parenthood for the first time, however briefly, the idea that they are parents should be recognized.

---

*Adapted from the author's article, "Perinatal Loss: Providing Support for Bereaved Parents," published in *Birth* 15:4, December 1988, pp. 242–46, by Blackwell Scientific Publications.

Validate the Parents' Grief

While the urge to ease parents' sorrow is natural, remember, there is nothing you can say or do that will take away their pain. Since the baby is constantly on their minds, avoiding the subject only makes them feel more isolated and invalidated. Refrain from statements that belittle their grief such as, "It's really for the best." They can only find silver linings for themselves at their own pace, and even then, these will not banish their grief. Instead of offering solutions or platitudes, simply tell them how sorry you are and that you are thinking of them. Knowing that you care and understand makes a difference.

Be a Willing Listener

Parents benefit from telling their story over and over. Even if you know the details, you might ask, "Would it help to tell me about your baby?" This is an invitation parents usually welcome. By listening with empathy and acceptance, you give the parent a chance to air thoughts and feelings without fear of judgment or pressure to "feel better by now." If the parent starts to cry, this is OK. They are crying healthy tears and you have given them an opportunity to express themselves.

Continue to Offer Support as Time Passes

While the first year or so is most difficult, many parents feel abandoned or pressured to feel better after just a few weeks or months. Not wanting to burden you with their troubles, they may hesitate to discuss the baby or their feelings. If you pose general questions such as "How are you doing?" parents easily assume you only want to exchange pleasantries. Emotionally vulnerable, they may find it hard to seek out your support, choosing to withdraw instead.

By broaching the subject, you can let them know you are thinking of them and the baby. They will appreciate your initiative. You can demonstrate a willingness to listen by continuing to ask specific questions about their situation. Parents usually are eager to discuss matters such as: "What was the most difficult part about your baby's death?" or "What are some of your favorite memories?" or "What are some helpful and/or not so helpful things people have said to you?" Ask to see photographs or other mementos. If you have the opportunity, express your remembrance on the anniversary of the baby's due date, birth or death, or on special holidays. By inviting parents to share their grief, you will be providing genuine personal support.

If you work with bereaved parents in a clinical setting, consider these guidelines.

Show Cultural Sensitivity

Nowadays, diversity is the norm. Whether you work in a large city or a small village, remain open-minded and become culturally aware.

- Even if the parents look like you, act like you or talk like you, do not assume that they feel or think like you.
- Remember that some people have a basic fear or distrust of authority figures. Whether they hail from foreign countries ruled by corrupt or brutal regimes or from the oppressive inner cities of this country, some parents will not automatically look to you for help and support. You can earn their respect and trust, but it may take extra time and effort.
- Always ask parents about their religious *and* spiritual beliefs. Ask about their rituals for honoring the dead. Seek clarification from other family members or cultural and religious agencies.
- Look beyond the language barrier and relate to the person. When using a translator, keep your words to the most common usages and to a minimum. This reduces the chances of filtering or confusion. Be aware of the importance of nonverbal communication. Touch is more appropriate in some cultures than others.
- Encourage the supportive presence of many family members. Remember that loud displays of weeping are considered normal and appropriate in many cultures.
- Your best credential is your sincerity.

Give Clear Medical Information and Options

Parents need factual, straightforward information on the medical condition of the baby and mother. Withholding information only builds resentment. Parents also benefit from making their own decisions, even the most difficult ones. It gives them a sense of control at a time when they are likely to feel powerless. Outline their options and factors to consider. Respect their decisions. Gather information about baptism, autopsy, disposal of the body and funeral arrangements so they will have access to it and time to consider what they want to do. Giving parents extra time allows them to overcome some of the shock as well as consider their options. The time factor is especially important for decisions that may be irreversible.

Educate the Parents about Grief

Providing information can serve to encourage expression of emotions and reduce feelings of isolation. Prepare parents for the unexpected emotions and reactions that may occur: insomnia, fatigue, despair, anger and even illusions of seeing or hearing the baby—all are experienced by many other parents. When they feel discouraged, reassure them. Grieving takes time. Couples often benefit from reminders about the importance of communicating with each other and accepting their own grieving styles. If the opportunity exists, it is also helpful to educate their friends and relatives about what to expect and offer guidance as to how to be supportive.

Encourage Collecting Memories and Mementos

Medical staff are in a unique position to influence what can become vivid memories. If the situation is applicable, encourage parents to hold their dying baby. It may seem dramatic, but it gives them a special opportunity to nurture and comfort their child. Equally important, after death, offer them the chance to see and hold their baby—regardless of the age or developmental stage. Offering this opportunity more than once gives parents a chance to say their goodbyes and demonstrate their love in physical ways. Tell parents where, how and for how long the baby's body will be kept and who to ask if they want to see the baby again (make sure babies are readily accessible). Gently suggest that they might bathe, dress, kiss, cuddle and examine their baby's body. Parents need to spend ample time with the baby, particularly after medication and the initial shock have worn off. With a multiple birth, parents find it most affirming to see all their babies together, even if some are living and some are dead. Arrange this whenever possible.

Save locks of hair, footprints and handprints, records of weight and length, hospital identification bracelets and clothing that the baby wore. Offer photographs of the baby or encourage parents to take their own. When parents have access to a camera, remind them to take a variety of shots and poses, including pictures of the full body, facial close-ups, dressed or naked, unwrapped and cuddled by the parents. Photographs can most vividly preserve treasured memories of their baby.

Make Special Arrangements

Bereaved parents should be offered the choice of having a private room away from the maternity ward. To avoid implying banishment, be sure to offer this in a way that lets parents know that they are welcome to stay in maternity. Unlimited visiting allows the opportunity for additional support from family members and friends. Flagging the chart or door can help prevent staff from making inappropriate remarks about breast-feeding or infant care.

Be Available to Listen

Let parents know you are available upon request. In their vulnerable state they may hesitate to ask for you—parents often feel unworthy of attention or do not want to impose. So, visit regularly and ask specific questions about their feelings and experience. Even if they are not responsive, they can benefit from your caring presence and your touch.

Listening can be difficult. Parents may direct their anger and feeling of helplessness toward medical staff members. They may blame you for the death of their baby. Don't take such outbursts personally. Instead, acknowledge their anger and empathize. This usually diffuses hostility. Remember that, in the long run, this kind of rage is healthier than self-blame, which can lead to self-destructive behavior and chronic depression.

Limit Sedative Use

While an occasional sedative can be useful for getting much-needed sleep, they should not be routinely prescribed since they tend to dull the grief response. Parents who hide in a fog of sedatives will have more trouble working through their grief than those who can experience the intensity of their emotions. It is especially important for parents to be alert when making decisions or spending time with their baby.

Make Follow-Up Contacts and Referrals

Parents need reassurance that their thoughts and feelings are reasonable and that they aren't losing their minds. Follow-up contacts by medical staff or parent groups can be helpful in reminding parents that shock, denial and overwhelming despair are necessary, but temporary, parts of the grieving process.

Many parents find counseling helpful, either as individuals or as a couple. Some parents are relieved that someone recognizes their need for counseling. Others may be in such a state of shock or denial that they do not respond to your support. In this case, a referral to a mental health professional can ensure they receive proper follow-up care. Make sure you refer parents to those counselors who understand the significance of the death of a baby.

Provide Information about Additional Resources

Offer or recommend books, articles or pamphlets that discuss causes, feelings and experiences surrounding pregnancy loss or infant death. These can provide parents with extra reassurance that their grief is normal and shared by others. Written materials also allow parents to absorb information at their own pace and to read over and over the passages that offer special comfort.

Pregnancy and infant loss support groups can be another valuable source of comfort. Sharing stories with other bereaved parents can validate feelings, reduce isolation and improve a couple's communication. Attending a support group can also offer hope for the future as parents observe how others have learned to cope. (See appendix C, "Resources for Bereaved Parents.")

Organize Staff Support

Encountering death can be disheartening, particularly for those dedicated to delivering healthy babies. You may find it difficult to handle the variety of parents' needs or be sensitive to every parent's individual preferences. Having regular perinatal mortality rounds is one way for staff to gather ideas and insight into supporting parents. By talking openly, you can also understand and alleviate some of the stress of dealing with death and grief. Finally, some health care providers can work with bereaved parents more easily than others, and they should be considered important resources.

Journal Writing: A Tool for Grieving, Healing and Growth

- A journal can be a diary, scrapbook, sketch pad, lined or unlined, leather bound or a spiral notebook ... a place where you can unload your deepest feelings, your most private self. It provides structure and a place where you can express your grief.
- Keeping a journal can be very healing. By putting your thoughts, feelings and observations on paper, you move the pain from inside you to outside. In this way, a journal frees you from the burden of holding in your feelings.
- A journal can help you to formulate and clarify what you are going through. When you get in touch with your feelings, you can deal with them constructively.
- Writing can help you zero in on your grief, put feelings into perspective and help you discover solutions. Just by making the effort to write something down, you've come more than halfway toward feeling better and finding answers.
- Writing down your thoughts can clarify your sense of values, as well as uncover those issues most meaningful, challenging or troubling to you.
- In the process of clarifying thoughts and feelings, you may discover areas in which you hold contradictory views. By confronting these contradictions, you can become more honest and clear about where you stand.
- Reading your journal can be a way to affirm what you've been through and provide reassuring evidence of your healing.

How to Keep a Journal

- Keep it simple.
- Do not try to make it perfect.
- Keep your journal absolutely confidential. Otherwise, you start writing for others. Write for YOU!
- Do not censor yourself. Write in your journal without passing judgment on whether thoughts or feelings are acceptable, worthy or good.
- Date your entries. Time frames are important and revealing, particularly with regard to anniversaries.

How to Get Started

- Set aside a regular time each day or so. This will help you make and reserve opportunities for writing. Choose a time when you will be alone. This will free you to express any emotions that come to the surface.
- Start by writing down the first thing that comes to mind. Remember, it's your journal and you are the only author, editor, artist and reader. Rely on your stream of consciousness to get you started and keep you going.
- Tell the story of your pregnancy. How did you find out you were pregnant? What was it like physically and emotionally? Write about labor and delivery. Remember details like sights, sounds, smells, emotions. Write about your child. Even if you could not see or hold the baby, you can describe your heartfelt observations or insights into this child's essence. Describe your relationship to this child. How did you select the baby's name?
- Look at photographs and go over any mementos you have. Describe what memories they spark. How are you feeling right now? What goes through your mind during the day? During the night? What do you find yourself dwelling on? What are you avoiding? What do you feel especially angry, guilty, sad or hurt about? How are other people helping or not helping you?
- Describe how your baby's death has changed you. Do you see or think about things differently? Are you more concerned or less concerned about certain things? Has the pace or focus of your life changed? Where do you find meaning? Where do you find strength? Where do you find hope?
- Besides thoughts, feelings and observations, you can also include:
  - poetry (rhyming is not necessary!)
  - "what if's" and "if only's"
  - quotations or poems you may have read or heard
  - goals and hopes for the future
  - letters—to anyone, including your deceased grandma, God, fate, your higher power, your guardian angel
  - letters to your child—include any unfinished business; ask for reassurance and forgiveness
  - angry letters to whomever or whatever
  - letters to yourself, from the nurturing part of you

- If you remember your dreams, you may want to include at least the most significant ones. Sometimes the act of writing down an especially harrowing or touching or exhilarating dream can give you special insights.
- Besides writing, you can include drawings and other visual material. Write or draw with pens, pencils, markers, charcoal, paint, crayon—whatever feels right. Enclose photos, clippings, stickers, ribbons, fabric, pressed flowers or leaves. Create images of dreams or fantasies. Compose abstract pictures of your positive and negative feelings and wishes.

Trust the process,
learn by doing,
cry with it,
feel empowered by it.

Your journal can become a treasured keepsake—a testament of your anguish and love for your child ... and for yourself.

Resources for Bereaved Parents

There is a strong and vital network of bereaved parents and sensitive caregivers that spans the globe. By contacting any one of the following publishers or national organizations, you will plug into a lifeline of resources to support you as you heal.

Publishers

Call or write for information and catalogs:

A Place to Remember
de Ruyter-Nelson Publications, Inc.
1885 University Avenue, Suite 110
St. Paul, MN 55104
(612) 645-7045 Phone
(800) 631-0973 Toll-free
(612) 645-4780 Fax
www.aplacetoremember.com

Publisher and distributor of books, booklets, certificates of birth and baptism, birth/death announcement cards, sympathy and anniversary cards, memory boxes and baby books.

Centering Corporation, "Your Grief Resource Center"
1531 N. Saddle Creek Road
Omaha, NE 68104
(402) 553-1200 Phone
(402) 553-0507 Fax
www.centering.org

Publishes many titles and distributes books from other publishers. Their catalog lists and describes dozens of books and booklets for parents whose baby has died. Excellent resource.

National Maternal and Child Health Resource Center
2070 Chain Bridge Road
Vienna, VA 22182
(703) 821-8995

Offers free single copies of *A Guide to Resources in Perinatal Bereavement*, published by the National Center for Education in Maternal and Child Health and the U.S. Department of Health and Human Services. This is an annotated list of resources including books, booklets, brochures, magazine and journal articles, audiovisuals and organizations providing information and support to bereaved parents. This is also the umbrella agency for the National SIDS Resource Center.

Perinatal Loss Program
2116 NE 18th Avenue
Portland, OR 97212-2621
(503) 281-3697
www.griefwatch.com

Publisher of *When Hello Means Goodbye*. They offer books for bereaved parents plus certificates of life, announcements and other mementos to commemorate the death of a baby during pregnancy or after delivery.

Pineapple Press
P.O. Box 312
St. Johns, MI 48879

(517) 224-1881

This publisher specializes in books and materials for parents faced with difficult decisions after prenatal diagnosis. Publishes quarterly newsletter

Wintergreen Press
3630 Eileen Street
Maple Plain, MN 55359
(612) 476-1303

Publisher of the classic *Empty Arms* by Sherokee Ilse and other books and resources by this acclaimed author and consultant.

National and International Nonprofit Organizations

Abiding Hearts
P.O. Box 904
Libby, MT 59923
(406) 293-4416
e-mail: hearts@lclink.com

Offers support and information to parents continuing their pregnancies after prenatal diagnosis of fatal (or nonfatal) birth defects. Provides a network that connects parents who are continuing their pregnancies with parents who have already survived this experience, supplies literature to help parents and health care providers prepare for the baby's birth and offers support to friends and relatives of the family.

An Ache in Their Hearts
The University of Queensland,
Department of Child Health
Clarence Court, Mater Children's

Hospital
South Brisbane, QLD 4101 Australia
(07) 840-8154 Phone
(07) 844-9069 Fax
www.sph.uq.edu.au/LossGrief/package

A complete and comprehensive intervention program developed for communities to adopt in order to support families affected by miscarriage, stillbirth, or infant death. The package provides resources for use by families and also *excellent* detailed training programs for health care providers, emergency health workers and volunteer grief companions. An instruction manual discusses the means of implementing the program and modifying it to suit the needs of your community.

Bereavement Services
1910 South Avenue
LaCrosse, WI 54601

(608) 791-4747 Phone
(800) 362-9567 Toll-free
www.Gundluth.org\bereave
e-mail: Berservs@Gundluth.org

Can provide information on local and national parent support groups; provides training for professionals on counseling and follow-up with families who've experienced miscarriage, stillbirth, or newborn death. Offers literature for parents, health care providers and clergy.

CLIMB—Center for Loss in Multiple Birth, Inc.
P.O. Box 91377
Anchorage, AK 99509
(907) 222-5321
www.climb-support.org
e-mail: climb@pobox.alaska.net

By and for parents who have experienced the death of one or more or all of their babies from a multiple pregnancy. Provides a quarterly newsletter, parent contact list, packet of published information, supplemental bibliography, special issues of the newsletter that focus on a particular type of loss or theme, plus other resources.

The Compassionate Friends
National Office
P.O. Box 3696
Oak Brook, IL 60522-3696
(630) 990-0010 Phone
(630) 990-0246 Fax
www.compassionatefriends.org

National nondenominational self-help organization offering support to bereaved parents and siblings. Offers brochures on coping with the death of a baby. English and Spanish.

Pregnancy Loss and Infant Death Alliance
P.O. Box 658
Parker, CO 80134
www.plida.org
www.perinatalbereavementconference.org

An alliance of parents and health care professionals who work together to promote the provision of emotional support for bereaved families who've experienced the death of a baby during pregnancy or infancy. Through PLIDA's sponsorship of the biennial National Perinatal Bereavement Conference, its Web site (www.plida.org) and the PLIDA Awareness Pin, this nonprofit organization promotes education and awareness around the emotional experiences and needs of bereaved families, recommends and endorses standards of care for these families, informs public policy and provides a clearinghouse for supportive resources.

SHARE (A Source of Help in Airing and Resolving Experiences)
St. Joseph Health Center
300 First Capitol Drive
St. Charles, MO 63301
(314) 947-6164 Phone
(800) 821-6819 Toll-free
(314) 947-7486 Fax
www.nationalshareoffice.com

National nondenominational organization offering support to parents at the time of and/or following the death of a baby. Support encompasses emotional, physical, spiritual and social healing and sustaining the family unit. Also provides information, education and resources on the needs and rights of bereaved parents and siblings, to aid those in the community in their supportive roles. Publishes a bimonthly newsletter written by parents and professionals; provides information on nationwide and international parent support groups.

National SIDS Resource Center
2070 Chain Bridge Road, Suite 450
Vienna, VA 22182
(703) 821-8955 Phone
(866) 866-7437 Toll-free
www.sidscenter.org

Sponsored by the U.S. Government Department of Health and Human Services, the resource center offers a variety of free publications on SIDS as well as a resource list and abstracts of periodicals and books published on the topic. The center also keeps a database of all English-language publications on SIDS and where to find them.

First Candle/SIDS Alliance
1314 Bedford Avenue, Suite 210
Baltimore, MD 21208
(800) 221-SIDS (7437)
www.firstcandle.org

First Candle is a research/advocacy group that is extending the SIDS Alliance mission by advocating for increased federal funding of research on stillbirth and miscarriage in addition to SIDS. Provides community education, information, counseling and referrals to families whose babies die.

The following organizations provide educational materials and can refer you to other organizations or resources for your specific situation, concerns and needs:

Genetic Alliance
4301 Connecticut Avenue NW,
Suite 404
Washington, DC 20008-2369
(202) 966-5557 Main office
Hours: 9:00 A.M.—6:00 P.M. EST
e-mail:information@
geneticalliance.org

Group B Strep Association
P.O. Box 16515
Chapel Hill, NC 27516
(919) 932-5344
www.groupbstrep.org

March of Dimes Birth Defects
Foundation
1275 Mamaroneck Avenue
White Plains, NY 10605
(914) 428-7100
www.modimes.org

NORD (National Organization for
Rare Disorders)
55 Kenosia Avenue
P.O. Box 1968
Danbury, CT 06813-1968
(203) 744-0100 Phone
(800) 999-6673 Toll-free (voicemail)
www.rarediseases.org

RESOLVE The National Infertility
Organization
1310 Broadway
Somerville, MA 02144-1731
(617) 623-1156 Phone
(888) 623-0744 Toll-free help line
www.resolve.org

Sidelines National Support Network
(high-risk pregnancy)
P.O. Box 1808
Laguna Beach, CA 92652
(888) 447-4754 (HI-RISK4)
www.sidelines.org

Neonatal Guidelines for Parents and Health Care Professionals

The Colorado Collective for Medical Decisions

The Colorado Collective for Medical Decisions (CCMD) was a group of concerned health care professionals, parents and community members across Colorado who worked together over the course of about five years (1994 to 1999) in order to create community-based guidelines that addressed medical care and end-of-life decision making. To address the medical care of critically ill newborns, CCMD created the Neonatal Guidelines and Neonatal Video *Parents on the Threshold: You Are Not Alone.* Our goal in developing community-based guidelines was to serve the following purposes:

To promote open community discussion around difficult NICU medical/ ethical issues in the hope that these medical resources and technology will be used wisely and humanely

To encourage and enhance the dialogue between the parents and health care professionals during this difficult, heart-wrenching time

To empower physicians to be decision leaders when a baby's prognosis is clear, whether poor or favorable

To facilitate collaborative decision making between health care providers and the parents of critically ill newborns for whom the prognosis is unclear

To support parents emotionally, whatever decision they make for their babies

To remind outsiders that they must be fully informed about the specific medical realities before voicing an opinion about treatment choices or attempting to represent the best interests of any infant

CCMD Neonatal Guidelines

Modern medical technology achieves many good and important goals. A primary goal of neonatal intensive care is to help sick infants become healthy children.

To use technology wisely, we must acknowledge its limitations. For some infants, the burdens of treatment outweigh the benefits.

Parents must be fully informed about the risks, benefits, outcomes and uncertainties of aggressive medical intervention for their individual baby. Whether an infant lives or dies, it is the parents who ultimately live with the result.

When the prognosis is clear, health care providers should be decision leaders.

When the prognosis is unclear (or becomes unclear), health care providers should work collaboratively with parents as decisions are made about an infant's care.

When aggressive intervention is withheld or withdrawn, comfort care should be provided.

When aggressive intervention is pursued for an infant whose outcome is uncertain, physicians should discuss with parents the specific burdens of treatment and how benefits and outcomes remain speculative.

For all NICU infants, regular and timely care conferences between parents and health care teams are an integral part of providing appropriate treatment.

Follow-up care should be provided to all families.

Please copy and distribute CCMD guidelines.

CCMD Neonatal Videotape

Parents on the Threshold: You Are Not Alone was designed to support parents and enhance parent-professional communication when a newborn infant has a poor or uncertain prognosis.

CCMD Guidelines featured as written text in the video:

Infants who are likely to survive should be given appropriate medical care even if they have mental or physical limitations.

Infants who are extremely unlikely to survive infancy due to extreme prematurity should receive comfort care instead of aggressive life-sustaining interventions.

Infants who are extremely unlikely to survive infancy due to a lethal birth defect should receive comfort care instead of aggressive life-sustaining interventions.

Infants for whom survival offers only a short lifetime filled with significant suffering should receive comfort care instead of life-sustaining interventions.

When the outcome of aggressive medical care for an infant is uncertain, the family should be provided with comprehensive information about outcomes.

When the outcome of aggressive medical care for an infant is uncertain, decisions about life-sustaining interventions should be made jointly by the family and medical team.

To obtain copies of the CCMD neonatal videotape, please contact Nickel's Worth Productions, NickelTV@aol.com, (303) 825-5555; dmkdavis@ aol.com for questions and feedback. Each video includes written materials that describe the video's intended uses, offer guidance for providing support to parents and involving them in decision making, plus the CCMD Neonatal Guidelines for medical decision making in the NICU.

Bibliography

Pregnancy and Parenting Web Sites

Storknet

Founded and managed by a bereaved mom, Maribeth Doerr, Storknet is a comprehensive pregnancy and parenting site that also covers pregnancy loss and infant death.
Look on the site map under "Pregnancy & Birth" or go directly to
www.storknet.com/cubbies/pil/
www.storknet.com/cubbies/pailsofhope/
www.erichad.com

Books for Bereaved Parents

Allen, M. and S. Marks. *Miscarriage: Women Sharing from the Heart.* New York: John Wiley and Sons, 1993.

Bernstein, J. R. *When the Bough Breaks: Forever After the Death of a Son or Daughter.* Kansas City: Andrews and McMeel, 1997.

Chethik, N. *FatherLoss: How Sons of All Ages Come to Terms with the Deaths of Their Dads.* New York: Hyperion, 2001.

Davis, D. *Loving and Letting Go: For Parents Who Decided to Turn Away from Aggressive Medical Intervention for Their Critically Ill Newborns.* Omaha, Neb.: Centering Corporation, 2002.

Davis, D. L. *Stillbirth Yet Still Born.* Wayzata, Minn.: Pregnancy & Infant Loss Center, 2000.

DeFrain, J., et al. *Stillborn—The Invisible Death.* Lexington, Mass.: D.C. Heath/Lexington Books, 1986.

DeFrain, J., J. Taylor, and L. Ernst. *Coping with Sudden Infant Death.* Lexington, Mass.: D.C. Heath/Lexington Books, 1982.

Faldet, R. and K. Fitten. *Our Stories of Miscarriage: Healing with Words.* Minneapolis: Fairview Press, 1997.

Jeffers, S. *Embracing Uncertainty: Breakthrough Methods for Achieving Peace of Mind When Facing the Unknown.* New York: St. Martin's Press, 2003.

Horchler, J. N. and R. R. Morris. *The SIDS Survival Guide: Information and Comfort for Grieving Family and Friends and Professionals Who Seek to Help Them.* Hyattsville, Md.: SIDS Education Services, 1997.

Ilse, S. *Empty Arms: Coping with Miscarriage, Stillbirth and Infant Death*, rev. ed. Maple Plain, Minn.: Wintergreen Press, 2000.

―――. *Precious Lives, Painful Choices—A Prenatal Decision-Making Guide.* Maple Plain, Minn.: Wintergreen Press, 1993.

Ilse, S. and L. H. Burns. *Miscarriage: A Shattered Dream.* Long Lake, Minn.: Wintergreen Press, 1992.

Kohn, I., P. Moffitt, and I. Wilkins. *A Silent Sorrow—Pregnancy Loss: Guidance and Support for You and Your Family,* 2nd ed. New York: Brunner Routeledge, 2000.

Kohner, N. and A. Henley. *When a Baby Dies: The Experience of Late Miscarriage, Stillbirth and Neonatal Death,* rev. ed. London: Taylor & Francis Group, 2001.

Luebbermann, M. *Coping with Miscarriage: A Simple, Reassuring Guide to Emotional and Physical Healing.* New York: Prima Publishing, 1996.

McCracken, A. and M. Semel. *A Broken Heart Still Beats: After Your Child Dies.* Center City, Minn.: Hazelden Publishing and Educational Services, 1998.

Mehren, E. *After the Darkest Hour, the Sun Will Shine Again: A Parent's Guide to Coping with the Loss of a Child.* New York: Fireside, 1997.

Miller, S. *Finding Hope When a Child Dies: What Other Cultures Can Teach Us.* New York: Simon & Schuster, 1999.

Minnick, M., K. J. Delp, and M. C. Ciotti. *A Time to Decide, a Time to Heal: For Parents Making Difficult Decisions about Babies They Love,* 4th ed. St. Johns, Mich.: Pineapple Press, 1994.

Panuthos, C. and C. Romeo, *Ended Beginnings: Healing Childbearing Losses.* South Hadley, Mass.: Bergin and Garvey, 1984.

Peppers, L. G. and R. Knapp. *How to Go on Living after the Death of a Baby.* Atlanta: Peachtree Publishers, 1985.

Rando, T. A. *Grieving: How to Go on Living When Someone You Love Dies.* New York: Bantam Books, 1991.

Rosof, B. D. *The Worst Loss: How Families Heal from the Death of a Child.* New York: Owl Books, 1995.

Staudacher, C. *Men and Grief: A Guide for Men Surviving the Death of a Loved One.* Oakland, Calif.: New Harbinger Publications, 1991.

Personal Accounts

Alecson, D. *Lost Lullaby.* Berkeley, Calif.: University of California Press, 1995.

Barney, A. *Stolen Joy: Healing after Infertility and Infant Loss.* Baltimore, Md.: Icarus Books, 1993.

Berg, B. *Nothing to Cry About.* New York: Harper and Row, 1981.

Brunner, S. H. *Perfect Vision: A Mother's Experience with Childhood Cancer.* Fuquay-Varina, N.C.: Research Triangle Publishing, 1996.

Cohen, M. *She Was Born, She Died.* Omaha, Neb.: Centering Corporation, 1983.

DeFord, F. *Alex: The Life of a Child.* Nashville, Tenn.: Rutledge Press, 1997.

Housden, M. *Hannah's Gift: Lessons from a Life Fully Lived.* New York: Bantam, 2002.

Kuebelbeck, A. *Waiting with Gabriel: A Story of Cherishing a Baby's Brief Life.* Chicago: Loyola Press, 2003.

Loizeaux, W. *Anna: A Daughter's Life.* New York: Arcade Publishing, 1993.

Lyon, W. *A Mother's Dilemma: A Spiritual Search for Meaning Following Pregnancy Interruption after Prenatal Diagnosis.* St. Johns, Mich.: Pineapple Press, 1993.

Mehren, E. *Born Too Soon: The Story of Emily, Our Premature Baby.* New York: Doubleday, 1991.

Reid J. *Life Line: A Journal for Parents Grieving a Miscarriage, Stillbirth or Early Infant Death*. St. Johns, Mich.: Pineapple Press, 1993.

Woodwell, W. H. *Coming to Term: A Father's Story of Birth, Loss, and Survival*. Jackson, Miss.: University of Mississippi Press, 2001.

Books on Medical Ethics

All of these books provide philosophical, spiritual, and ethical support for parents' rights to make decisions for their babies.

Anspach, R. R. *Deciding Who Lives: Fateful Choices in the Intensive Care Nursery*. Berkeley, Calif.: University of California Press, 1993.

Belkin, L. *First Do No Harm*. New York: Simon and Schuster, 1993.

Culver, C. M. *Ethics at the Bedside*. Hanover, N.H.: University Press of New England, 1990.

Davis, D. L. *Loving and Letting Go: For Bereaved Parents Who Decided to Turn Away from Aggressive Medical Intervention*. Omaha, Neb.: Centering, 2002.

Dubler, N. and D. Nimmons. *Ethics on Call: Taking Charge of Life-and-Death Choices in Today's Health Care System*. New York: Vintage Books, 1993.

Ellenchild Pinch, W. J. *When the Bough Breaks: Parental Perceptions of Ethical Decision-Making in NICU*. Lanham, Md.: University Press of America, 2002.

Frohock, F. M. *Special Care: Medical Decisions at the Beginning of Life*. Chicago: University of Chicago Press, 1986.

Guillemin, J. H. and L. L. Holmstrom. *Mixed Blessings: Intensive Care for Newborns*. New York: Oxford University Press, 1986.

Gustaitis, R. and E. W. D. Young. *A Time to Be Born, A Time to Die*. New York: Addison-Wesley, 1986.

Kuebelbeck, A. *Waiting with Gabriel: A Story of Cherishing a Baby's Brief Life*. Chicago: Loyola Press, 2003.

Lantos, J. D. *The Lazarus Case: Life-and-Death Issues in Neonatal Intensive Care*. Baltimore: Johns Hopkins University Press, 2001.

Lyon, J. *Playing God in the Nursery*. New York: W. W. Norton, 1986.

Video on Medical Ethics

Parents on the Threshold: You Are Not Alone, produced by the Colorado Collective for Medical Decisions (CCMD) and Nickel's Worth Productions in 1999, is a thirty-minute videotape that supports parents who face life-and-death decisions in the NICU. To obtain an order form, contact Nickel's Worth Productions at NickelTV@aol.com. See Appendix D for more on the video and CCMD's Neonatal Guidelines.

Books for Couples

Bilicki, B. Y. and M. Goetz. *Getting Back Together: How to Create a New, Loving Relationship with Your Old Partner and Make It Last!* Avon, Mass.: Adams Media, 1995.

Doerr, M. W. *For Better or Worse: For Couples Whose Child Has Died.* Omaha, Neb.: Centering Corporation, 1992.

Ford, D. *Spiritual Divorce: Divorce as a Catalyst for an Extraordinary Life.* San Francisco: HarperSanFrancisco, 2001.

Gottman, J. M. and N. Silver. *The Seven Principles for Making Marriage Work: A Practical Guide from the Country's Foremost Relationship Expert.* New York: Crown Publishers, 1999.

Heitler, S. *The Power of Two: Secrets to a Strong and Loving Marriage.* Oakland, Calif.: New Harbinger Publications, 1997.

Hendricks, G. and K. Hendricks. *Conscious Loving: The Journey to Co-Commitment.* New York: Bantam Books, 1992.

Krasnow, I. *Surrendering to Marriage: Husbands, Wives, and Other Imperfections.* New York: Hyperion, 2001.

Tannen, D. *You Just Don't Understand: Women and Men in Conversation.* New York: Quill, 2001.

Viorst, J. *Grown-Up Marriage: What We Know, Wish We Had Known, and Still Need to Know about Being Married.* New York: The Free Press, 2003.

Books for Parents and Children

Ellis, S. *The Baby Project.* Groundwood Books, 1999. (older children and teens)

Erling, J. and S. Erling. *Our Baby Died. Why?* Wayzata, Minn.: Pregnancy Infant Loss Center, 1986. (young children)

Grollman, E. A. *Talking about Death: A Dialogue between Parent and Child.* Boston: Beacon Press, 1976. (parents)

Gryte, M. *No New Baby: For Boys and Girls Whose Expected Sibling Dies.* Omaha, Neb.: Centering Corporation, 1988. (young children)

Heegaard, M. E. *Coping with Death and Grief.* Minneapolis: Lerner Publications, 1990. (older children and teens)

Jewett, C. L. *Helping Children Cope with Separation and Loss,* rev. ed. Cambridge, Mass.: The Harvard Common Press, 1994. (parents)

Johnson, J. and M. Johnson. *Where's Jess?* Omaha, Neb.: Centering Corporation, 1992. (young children)

Mellonie, B. and R. Ingpen. *Lifetimes: The Beautiful Way to Explain Death to Children.* New York: Bantam Books, 1983. (all ages)

Schaefer, D. and C. Lyons. *How Do We Tell the Children?: A Parent's Guide to Helping Children Understand and Cope When Someone Dies.* New York: Newmarket Press, 1985. (parents)

Sims, A. M. *Am I Still a Sister?* Albuquerque: Big A and Company, 1992. (older children and teens)

Books on Infertility, Pregnancy and Health

Chism, D. M. *The High-Risk Pregnancy Sourcebook: Everything You Need to Know.* Los Angeles: Lowell House, 1997.

Cooper, S. L. and E. S. Glazer. *Choosing Assisted Reproduction: Social, Emotional and Ethical Considerations.* Indianapolis: Perspectives Press, 1999.

De Crespigny, L. *Which Tests for My Unborn Baby?: A Guide to Prenatal Diagnosis.* Oxford, England: Oxford University Press, 1992.

Diamond, K. *Motherhood after Miscarriage.* Holbrook, Mass.: Bob Adams, 1993.

Douglas, A. and J. R. Sussman, *Trying Again: A Guide to Pregnancy after Miscarriage, Stillbirth, and Infant Loss.* Dallas: Taylor Trade Publishing, 2000.

Douglas, A. and J. R. Sussman. *The Unofficial Guide to Having a Baby.* New York: MacMillan, 1999.

Dunwold, A. and D. G. Sanford. *Postpartum Survival Guide.* Oakland, Calif.: New Harbinger, 1994.

Falker, E. S. *The Infertility Survival Handbook: Everything You Never Thought You'd Need to Know.* New York: Riverhead Books, 2004

Kleiman, K. R. and V. D. Raskin. *This Isn't What I Expected: Overcoming Postpartum Depression.* New York: Bantam Books, 1994.

Lanham, C. C. *Pregnancy after a Loss: A Guide to Pregnancy after a Miscarriage, Stillbirth or Infant Death.* New York: Berkley Publishing Group, 1999.

Lasker, J. and S. Borg. *In Search of Parenthood: Coping with Infertility and High-Tech Conception.* Boston: Beacon Press, 1987.

Lerner, H. M. *Miscarriage: Why It Happens and How Best to Reduce Your Risks— A Doctor's Guide to the Facts.* New York: Perseus Publishing, 2003.

Luke, B. *Every Pregnant Woman's Guide to Preventing Premature Birth: A Program for Reducing the Sixty Proven Risks That Can Lead to Prematurity.* New York: Times Books, 1995.

McIntyre, A. *The Complete Woman's Herbal: A Manual of Healing Herbs and Nutrition for Personal Well-Being and Family Care.* New York: Henry Holt, 1995.

Moran, V. *Fit from Within: 101 Simple Secrets to Change Your Body and Your Life—Starting Today and Lasting Forever.* Chicago: Contemporary Books, 2002.

Peoples, D. and H. R. Ferguson. *Experiencing Infertility: An Essential Resource.* New York: W. W. Norton, 1998.

Remen, R. N. *Kitchen Table Wisdom: Stories That Heal.* New York: Riverhead Books, 1996.

Reuben, C. *The Healthy Baby Book: A Parent's Guide to Preventing Birth Defects and Other Long-Term Medical Problems Before, During, and After Pregnancy.* Los Angeles: Jeremy P. Tarcher, 1992.

Rich, L. A. *When Pregnancy Isn't Perfect: A Layperson's Guide to Complications in Pregnancy.* New York: Larata Press, 1996.

Roth, G. *Breaking Free from Compulsive Eating.* Indianapolis: Bobbs-Merrill, 1984.

Rothman, B. K. *The Tentative Pregnancy: How Amniocentesis Changes the Experience of Motherhood.* New York: W.W. Norton, 1993.

Salzer, L. P. *Surviving Infertility: A Compassionate Guide through the Emotional Crisis of Infertility,* rev. ed. New York: HarperPerennial, 1991.

Sears, W. and M. Sears. *The Pregnancy Book: Month by Month, Everything You Need to Know from America's Baby Experts.* Boston: Little, Brown and Company, 1997.

Semchyshyn, S. and C. Colman. *How to Prevent Miscarriages and Other Crises of Pregnancy.* New York: Macmillan, 1990.

Simkin, P., J. Whalley, and A. Keddler. *Pregnancy, Childbirth and the Newborn: The Complete Guide*, rev. ed. New York: Meadowbrook Press, 2001.

The Staff of RESOLVE with Diane Aronson, Executive Director. *Resolving Infertility: Understanding the Options and Choosing Solutions When You Want to Have a Baby.* New York: HarperCollins, 1999.

Tracy, A. E. and R. H. Schwarz. *The Pregnancy Bed Rest Book: A Survival Guide for Expectant Mothers and Their Families.* New York: Berkley Publishing Group, 2001.

Books Written for Health Care Providers

Bowlby, J. *Attachment and Loss*, vol. 3, *Loss.* New York: Basic Books, 1980.

Caplan, A. L., R. H. Blank, and J. C. Merrick, eds. *Compelled Compassion: Government Intervention in the Treatment of Critically Ill Newborns.* Totowa, N.J.: Humana Press, 1992.

Edelstein, L. *Maternal Bereavement: Coping with the Unexpected Death of a Child.* New York: Praeger, 1984.

Hollingsworth, C. E. and R. O. Pasnau, eds. *The Family in Mourning: A Guide for Health Professionals.* New York: Grune and Stratton, 1977.

Isle, S. *Giving Care, Taking Care: Support for the Helpers.* Maple Plain, Minn.: Wintergreen Press, 1996.

Jackson, E. N. *Understanding Grief.* Nashville, Tenn.: Abingdon Press, 1957.

Jonsen, A. R., and M. J. Garland, eds. *Ethics of Newborn Intensive Care.* The Regents of the University of California: Health Policy Program and Institute of Governmental Studies, 1976.

Kennell, M. H., and J. H. Klaus. "Caring for Parents of a Stillborn or an Infant Who Dies," in *Maternal–Infant Bonding.* Edited by J. H. Klaus and M. H. Kennell. St. Louis: The C. V. Mosby Company, 1982.

Kluger-Bell, K. *Unspeakable Losses: Understanding the Experience of Pregnancy Loss, Miscarriage and Abortion.* New York: W.W. Norton, 1998.

Limbo, R. K. and S. R. Wheeler. *When a Baby Dies: A Handbook for Healing and Helping.* LaCrosse, Wis.: Resolve Through Sharing, 1986.

Parkes, C. M. *Bereavement: Studies of Grief in Adult Life.* New York: International Universities Press, 1972.

Parkes, C. M. and R. S. Weiss. *Recovery from Bereavement.* New York: Basic Books, 1983.

Peppers, L. G. and R. Knapp. *Motherhood and Mourning: Perinatal Death.* New York: Praeger, 1980.

Rando, T. A., ed. *Parental Loss of a Child.* Champaign, Ill.: Research Press, 1986.

Woods, J. R. and J. L. Esposito, eds. *Pregnancy Loss: Medical Therapeutics and Practical Considerations.* Baltimore, Md.: Williams and Wilkins, 1987.

Books on Parenting

Preemies, Infants, and Toddlers

Bumgarner, N. J. *Mothering Your Nursing Toddler*. Franklin Park, Ill.: La Leche League International, 1980.

Davis, D. L. and M. T. Stein. *Parenting Your Premature Baby and Child: The Emotional Journey*. Golden, Colo.: Fulcrum Publishing, 2004.

Kitzinger, S. *The Year after Childbirth: Surviving and Enjoying the First Year of Motherhood*. New York: Charles Scribner's Sons, 1994.

Klaus, M. H., J. H. Kennell, and P. H. Klaus. *Bonding: Building the Foundations of Secure Attachment and Independence*. Reading, Mass.: Addison-Wesley, 1995.

Luddinton-Hoe, S. M. and S. K. Golant. *Kangaroo Care: The Best You Can Do to Help Your Preterm Infant*. New York: Bantam Doubleday Dell, 1993.

Madden, S. L. *The Preemie Parents' Companion: The Essential Guide to Caring for Your Premature Baby in the Hospital, at Home, and through the First Years*. Cambridge, Mass: Harvard Common Press, 2000.

Newman, J. and T. Pitman. *The Ultimate Breastfeeding Book of Answers: The Most Comprehensive Problem-Solution Guide to Breastfeeding from the Foremost Breastfeeding Expert in North America*. Roseville, Calif.: Prima Publishing, 2000.

Sears, W. and M. Sears. *The Attachment Parenting Book: A Commonsense Guide to Understanding and Nurturing Your Baby*. Boston: Little, Brown and Company, 2001.

Tracy, A. E. and D. I. Maroney. *Your Premature Baby and Child: Helpful Answers and Advice for Parents*. New York: Berkley Books, 1999.

General Approach to Parenting

Davis, L. and J. Keyser. *Becoming the Parent You Want to Be: A Sourcebook of Strategies for the First Five Years*. New York: Broadway Books, 1997.

DeBecker, G. *Protecting the Gift: Keeping Children and Teenagers Safe (and Parents Sane)*. New York: Random House, 1999.

Douglas, A. *The Mother of All Baby Books: The Ultimate Guide to Your Baby's First Year*. Indianapolis, Ind.: Hungry Minds, 2002.

Gottman, J. *The Heart of Parenting: Raising an Emotionally Intelligent Child*. New York: Simon and Schuster, 1997.

McClure, V. *The Path of Parenting: Twelve Principles to Guide Your Journey*. Novato, Calif.: New World Library, 1999.

Small, M. F. *Our Babies, Ourselves: How Biology and Culture Shape the Way We Parent*. New York: Anchor Books, 1998.

Meeting the Challenges

Calderone, M. S. and J. W. Ramey. *Talking with Your Child about Sex*. New York: Ballantine Books, 1983.

Faber, A. and E. Mazlish. *How to Talk So Kids Will Listen and Listen So Kids Will Talk*. New York: Rawson-Wade, 1999.

————. *Siblings without Rivalry: How to Help Your Children Live Together So You Can Live Too.* New York: Avon Books, 1998.

Greene, R. W. *The Explosive Child: A New Approach for Understanding and Parenting Easily Frustrated, "Chronically Inflexible" Children.* New York: HarperCollins, 1998.

Greenspan, S. I. *The Challenging Child: Understanding, Raising, and Enjoying the Five "Difficult" Types of Children.* New York: Addison-Wesley, 1995.

Koplewicz, H. S. *It's Nobody's Fault: A New Hope and Help for Difficult Children and Their Parents.* New York: Times Books, 1996.

Kurcinka, M. S. *Raising Your Spirited Child: A Guide for Parents Whose Child Is More Intense, Sensitive, Perceptive, Persistent, Energetic.* New York: Harper-Perennial, 1992.

Le Shan, E. *When Your Child Drives You Crazy.* New York: St. Martin's Press, 1985.

McKay, M., ed., et al. *When Anger Hurts Your Kids: A Parent's Guide.* New York: MJF Books, 1996.

Miller, N. B. *Nobody's Perfect: Living and Growing with Children Who Have Special Needs.* Baltimore: Paul H. Brookes Publishing Company, 1994.

Nelson, J. *Positive Discipline: The Classic Guide for Parents and Teachers to Help Children to Develop Self-Discipline, Responsibility, Cooperation, and Problem-Solving Skills,* rev. ed. New York: Ballantine Books, 1996.

Paris, T. and E. Paris. *I'll Never Do to My Kids What My Parents Did to Me: A Guide to Conscious Parenting.* New York: Warner Books, 1994.

Samalin, N. *Love and Anger: The Parental Dilemma.* New York: Viking Penguin, 1991.

————. *Loving Your Child Is Not Enough: Positive Discipline That Works.* New York: Viking Penguin, 1987.

Sears, W. *The Fussy Baby: How to Bring Out the Best in Your High-Need Child.* Franklin Park, Ill.: La Leche League International, 2002.

————. *Nighttime Parenting: How to Get Your Baby and Child to Sleep.* New York: Plume Books, 1999.

Sears, W. and M. Sears. *Parenting the Fussy Baby and High-Need Child: Everything You Need to Know from Birth to Age Five.* Boston: Little, Brown and Company, 1996.

Taubman, B. *Why Is My Baby Crying?* New York: Fireside/Simon and Schuster, 1990.

Thevenin, T. *The Family Bed: An Age Old Concept in Child Rearing.* Wayne, N.J.: Avery Publishing Group, 1987.

Turecki, S. *The Emotional Problems of Normal Children: How Parents Can Understand and Help.* New York: Bantam Books, 1994.

Index

SHARING THE GIFT OF COMFORT

A special note from the publisher

Empty Cradle, Broken Heart focuses on providing emotional support to grieving parents after the death of their baby during pregnancy, delivery, or in infancy. This book shows the wide range of emotions and reactions that parents can experience, and it suggests strategies for coping. With factual information and the words and insights of other bereaved parents, you can establish realistic expectations for your grief and know that *you are not alone*. This book is meant to walk with you as you grieve, guiding you along your emotional journey and encouraging you to do what *you* need to survive your baby's death.

Many grieving parents have found support and comfort in this book:

"I can't tell you enough how much I have loved Empty Cradle. *You really get all the issues involved in grieving for a beloved baby so right. I still reread sections of it I find comforting."* —K. Banigan-White, Massachusetts

"Nothing will bring back my baby, but this book has helped me throughout my grieving and healing process. I was hesitant about which book(s) to read, but now I know that I won't need to read anything else." —A mother, Illinois

Many bereaved parents have contacted us, wishing to donate copies of this book to their health care providers, hospitals, or parent support organizations so that other grieving parents might benefit. If this book has helped you too, and you want to share it with other parents, Fulcrum Publishing is happy to offer you a discount for multiple copies that will be donated.

For details, please contact Fulcrum at 800-992-2908 or via e-mail at info@fulcrumbooks.com and ask about making an *Empty Cradle* donation.

"Empty Cradle, Broken Heart not only sits by your side, it reaches out and touches your heart." —Joy Johnson, codirector of Centering Corporation, Omaha, Nebraska